A STRANGE LIBERTY

A STRANGE LIBERTY

POLITICS DROPS ITS PRETENSES

JEFF DEIST

**FOREWORD BY
PAUL GOTTFRIED**

**INTRODUCTION BY
THOMAS J. DILORENZO**

MISESINSTITUTE

AUBURN, ALABAMA

THE MISES INSTITUTE, founded in 1982, is an education and research center for the study of Austrian economics. In support of the school of thought represented by Ludwig von Mises, Murray N. Rothbard, Henry Hazlitt, and F.A. Hayek, we publish books and journals, sponsor student and professional conferences, and provide online education. Mises.org is a vast resource of free material for anyone in the world interested in these ideas. We advocate a radical shift in the intellectual climate, away from statism and toward a private property order.

For more information, see mises.org, write us at info@mises.org, or phone us at 1.800.OF.MISES.

Th e Mises Institute
518 West Magnolia Avenue
Auburn, Alabama 36832
mises.org

ISBN: 978-1-61016-764-2

To my late father,
who understood liberty better than Thoreau.

Contents

Foreword

Paul Gottfried

In my more than fifty years in academia and as a writer, I have found there are few people who see things as I do. Jeff Deist may be one of them. Along with many of his colleagues at the Mises Institute, Jeff carries on the traditions of the Old Right: opposed to leviathan state, antiwar and thus deeply suspicious of foreign interventionism, and traditional in cultural outlook.

Jeff is a student and an admirer of the late Ludwig von Mises and F. A. Hayek, two giants in the world of Austrian economics, but given modern realities he does not share their faith in democracy. Both men identified democracy with a political system that would allow peaceful transfers of political power according to prescribed procedures. In the twenty-first century, Deist is not so sure.

In *A Strange Liberty*, Jeff, who is a legal scholar, political thinker, and social critic, argues persuasively that the faith in democracy as a force for internal peace and dependable constitutional restraints has not worked as its defenders Mises and Hayek predicted. Instead, we are left with centralized tyrannies, highly disputable election results, ideologically driven media, and state educational systems that have made war on "traditional" gender identities and whiteness. The question, then, is not "How do we preserve our democracy?" but "How do we escape from a totalitarian administrative state, its surveillance operations, and the lies told by its public relations allies?" Jeff does not believe these problems will simply resolve themselves. It will take action.

A Strange Liberty calls for the relentless pursuit of decentralization in whatever manner this course is still open to decent, freedom-loving citizens. Quoting from, among others, the late Angelo Codevilla, a bold scholar of government and an unabashed critic of our democratic decadence, Jeff proposes that states that oppose federal overreach and woke indoctrination react against these evils through noncompliance. He shows again and again that the federal government's behavior has been blatantly unconstitutional for a very long time. As the book chronicles, the Department of Justice, the IRS, and other federal agencies have all been repeatedly unleashed on those whom the one-party state wishes to target. In light of this situation, state governments should not be obliged to serve slavishly a federal administration that is making war on some of its citizens. Up until Joe Biden's election, it was in fact the Left, with media incitement, which was calling for resistance to the federal government, on behalf of marijuana use, sanctuary for illegals, and gay marriage before that. Why shouldn't the Right or the non-Left have the same right to disobey federal directives which are coming from a regime that is openly hostile? Jeff here has given outraged citizens a voice and heartens them to pursue this practice of resistance through state or local governments where they can. Although he knows it's not clear this strategy will be sufficient to work against federal overreach, he encourages us to get out of our chairs and be proactive in finding ways to push back.

In *A Strange Liberty*, there is more of the mood and wit of H.L. Mencken's *American Mercury* than the spirit of *National Review*. This anthology does not just duplicate the positions of a previous generation. It is a creative return to truths that were never lost and should be given an active voice again.

Introduction

Thomas J. DiLorenzo

Jeff Deist's *A Strange Liberty: Politics Drops Its Pretenses* is a collection of more than forty essays that apply Austrian economics and libertarian theory, especially the writings of Murray Rothbard, Hans-Hermann Hoppe, and Ron Paul, to many of the big issues of the day: failure of democracy; the attacks on civil society; fake pandemics and the never-ending national emergency state; immigration; strategies for freedom.

"Politics without Pretense" is a perfect description of the first section of essays. Here Deist discusses the inherently conflicting nature of politics—compared to the inherently *cooperative* nature of economic freedom and mutually advantageous exchange in the marketplace. Following in Rothbard's footsteps, Deist notes the prescience of the ideas from John C. Calhoun's 1850 *Disquisition on Government* where Calhoun wrote of how a written constitution would never be sufficient to stop the "net tax consumers" (those who benefit more from government spending than they pay in taxes) from politically overwhelming the net taxpayers, leading to virtually unlimited government. This of course came to pass long ago.

Deist states the obvious fact that is nevertheless shocking to the typical American, who has been indoctrinated all of his or her life about the supposed necessity of a gigantic nation-state and the "god" of democracy. But democracy, Deist points out, is *futile* in a nation with more than 330 million people, a veritable political "tower of babble" on steroids.

The best hope, he says, is federalism—the one uniquely American contribution to political philosophy. Several of the essays explain the theory behind decentralization, or federalism, and offer practical advice on how to achieve it. Unlike "left libertarians" who are scared to death of being criticized by the far left Southern Poverty Law Center (or, God forbid, the *Washington Post!*), Deist doesn't shy away from the S word, arguing that secession is the very essence of self-determination. "[S]ecession movements represent the last best hope for reclaiming our birthright," he writes. Thomas Jefferson would heartily agree, as did Ludwig von Mises and Murray Rothbard. And as would almost all of the American Founding Fathers, who fought a long and bloody war in order to secede from the British Empire. "Separation," or secession, was "the" principle of the American Revolution, said Massachusetts Senator Timothy Pickering, who was George Washington's adjutant general during the Revolution and later his secretary of war and secretary of state.

There are several wonderful essays on secession, decentralization, subsidiarity, localism, and nullification as the means by which we can regain our liberties. They all share Deist's theme that all crises are ultimately local and that "the" question of the twenty-first century is about centralization versus decentralization of state powers. "Our task is to end the charade of one nation," he writes. The regime is illusionary, after all—based on mountains of lies, myths, and propaganda. It is one big, phony Wizard of Oz charade that will collapse if enough Americans come to understand that they greatly outnumber the relatively small cabal of political connivers, liars, and manipulators who run it. That's how the "mighty" Soviet Union fell apart. As the late Yuri Maltsev, who was born and raised in the Soviet Union and who once worked for Mikhail Gorbachev said, for decades no one there believed *anything* the Soviet government said. They only pretended to. Not even the largest totalitarian dictatorship in modern history could survive that. The Soviets were forced to allow their "satellite states" to walk away peacefully (with minimal last-ditch thuggery).

Deist describes the state as sort of a blob that eventually swallows everything in its path. It's hard to argue with this since, as he writes, for much of the population the state has replaced family, religion, civil society, and even respect for the elderly. It has also toiled mightily to replace plain English and logic with its "state-linguistic complex," which seeks to impose new words and new meanings for old words in pursuit of totalitarian political power.

Languages evolved over centuries in civil societies; the current American state wants to command that we speak only in ways that enhance its powers, says Deist. It's all part of the nefarious plan of "destructionism," or the literal destruction of existing society— the primary goal of socialists everywhere, as Mises explained in his 1922 book, *Socialism*.

A particularly intriguing essay is "Secession Begins at Home." It is based on Hoppe's theory of "bottom-up revolution," whereby persuasion and democratic institutions are used to effectively secede from the central state at the individual, family, community, and local levels. Ignore the central state and turn your back to it rather than attempting to reform it, in other words. Don't lift a finger to help in the enforcement of unjust and unconstitutional federal laws at the local level, for "without local enforcement by compliant local authorities, the will of the central government is not much more than hot air," wrote Hoppe. This would suggest that elections for local sheriffs may be far more important to freedom than presidential elections. The essay "How to Secede Right Now" contains a list of action points to be implemented now as strategy to start the bottom-up response.

There are essays on money and banking that very clearly explain why the Fed is no longer a central bank but "a lawless economic government unto itself." The essay "MMT: Not Modern, Not Monetary, Not a Theory" eviscerates the latest hoary, mercantilist propaganda in support of a governmental monetary monopoly— "modern monetary theory," or MMT. After reading it, you are bound to agree that it would be more accurately named "Zimbabwean Monetary Theory."

Jeff Deist is no fan of the current Democratic Party propagandist and *New York Times* columnist Paul Krugman. You will find that Deist has the man perfectly pegged as an "intellectual lightweight" who makes no attempt to appear nonpartisan for the sake of academic integrity; incessantly cites opinions as facts; accuses his critics of being, well, liars; and feels that he doesn't need to win over anyone who disagrees with him. He is a museum-quality specimen of a typical *New York Times/Washington Post* government establishment mouthpiece.

Ludwig von Mises was the greatest economic thinker of the twentieth century (arguably of any century). Another particularly fascinating chapter in *A Strange Liberty* speculates on what Mises would think about the West today in terms of the health of Austrian economics, central banking, academia, immigration, and nationalism. Spoiler: Mises would be "amazed by the sheer force of central bank money creation" today.

Having been a university economics professor for forty-one years, I agree completely with Deist's description of the academic economics profession. In fact, I have believed this characterization to be true ever since I was in graduate school in the late 1970s. As Deist writes: "Most economists don't concern themselves much at all with finding truth or helping us better understand the world, or serving humanity by working to increase our wealth and happiness. From my perspective, economics exists mostly to provide sinecures for people whose chief concern is whether a tiny group of their peers think they're smart."

Paul Samuelson, whose introductory economics textbook dominated the textbook market from 1948 to the 1980s and who had a tremendous influence on the economics profession, admitted as much in a 1970s essay in the *Journal of Political Economy*. What motivates academic economists like himself, he said, is the prospect of procuring "the applause of our peers." It was precisely this kind of egomania that immediately drew me away from "mainstream" economists like Samuelson and his ilk and to the Austrian school. It was blatantly obvious that the Austrians were of the exact opposite mindset. Their writings all struck me as being the products of economists who were deeply determined to better understand how the world works and to spread this knowledge for the good of society, the applause of "peers" be damned. And they did not restrict themselves to very narrow specialties within economics like the mainstream did; instead, they applied history, mathematics, statistics, philosophy, and sociology in their writings—not to acquire the applause of three or four peers but to better understand reality.

Unlike open-borders libertarians, who behave like little ayatollahs in denouncing or defaming anyone who disagrees with them, Deist presents a scholarly discussion in a roundtable format of immigration featuring pro and con ideas taken from the writings of Ludwig von Mises, Murray Rothbard, Walter Block, and Hans-Hermann Hoppe. He proves that the issue is not as simple (or simplistic) as the open-borders libertarians say it is. After all, Americans have been *debating* immigration policy since the Louisiana Purchase.

The section on strategy contains six essays and is worth the price of admission itself. You will learn that Deist thinks that we live in "post-persuasion America," where most people are beyond persuasion; that libertarians are yet to really face the sober reality of what has happened to American freedom; and that they are essentially "politically vanquished." Nevertheless, in "The Case for Optimism" he says optimistically, the state is financially unsustainable, just as the Soviet Union was. "The New Rules of Engagement" is a battle cry for how to proceed—individually and on the local level—against leviathan policies that are strangling us.

More importantly, the kind of libertarianism described in *A Strange Liberty*, of a world organized around civil society and markets (*not* crony capitalism) is bound to appeal to the traditional American penchant for pragmatism. What is truly *unrealistic*, Deist points out by quoting Rothbard, is that: "The man who puts all the guns and all the decision-making power into the hands of the central government and then says, 'Limit yourself,'" is approached with adulation for guidance and wisdom. History has proven "limited constitutional government" to be one of the biggest oxymorons of all time.

A Strange Liberty can be thought of as a detailed *road map for freedom*.

Politics

I

Politics Drops Its Pretenses

C an the increasing politicization of life in America be stopped, or even slowed?

To be sure, average Americans do not want this. Most people prefer not to lead overly political lives, beyond perhaps voting once in a while and grumbling about taxes or potholes. Most people prefer to focus on work, family, hobbies, sports, or a million other pursuits instead of politics. We watch the game instead of attending the Tuesday night city council meeting. But increasingly we all feel the pressure, drawing us inexorably into a highly-politicized world which demands we take binary "sides" on Trump, impeachment, abortion, guns, climate change, and far more. This politicization seeps into our jobs, family lives, neighborhoods, places of worship, social interactions, and even our sports and entertainment.

The most salient feature of national politics in 2019 America is its lack of pretenses. The two political Americas, represented by Red and Blue teams, no longer pretend to share a country or any desire to live peaceably together. Much has been made of this cold civil war on both the Left and Right, and much of what has been

***

This article originally appeared October 15, 2019, on mises.org.

made is probably over-hyped. Americans, after all, are materially comfortable, soft, addled, diabetic, and rapidly aging; the over-65 population is set to double in the coming decades. Hot civil wars require lots of young men with nothing to lose who are not busy playing *Fortnite*. But the overall mood of the country is decidedly hostile and suggestive of irreconcilable differences.

So how does our political system address this? By throwing gasoline on the fire, in the form of another national election in 2020. That looming contest already tells a story, it's not about healing or coming together. Today the political class is more open about its desire to hurt and punish opponents; in fact, revenge and punishment feature prominently in the political narratives that fill our media feeds.

Hillary Clinton recently quipped that maybe she should run against Donald Trump in 2020 and "beat him again," openly positioning her personal vendetta as the rationale for seeking the presidency. "The issues," such as they are, take a distant backseat to her more pressing goal of defeating both Trump and his voters in a visceral way. Her 2020 candidacy, should it materialize, will coalesce around revenge: voters failed her not once but twice, in 2008 and 2016. Her campaign, almost by necessity, will be a scorched-earth exercise in revenge against the Deplorables.

Her potential Democratic primary rival Elizabeth Warren, meanwhile, appeared last week at an LGBT equality town hall—organized by CNN for the express purpose of further politicizing sex and sexuality (so much for pre-political rights). In response to a softball question about gay marriage (likely planted), Warren sneered that a hypothetical religious man should marry a woman "if he can get one." Needless to say the audience loved it, which tells us less about Warren's safe, vanilla views than it does about the setting and mood of attendees. Identity politics is required, not optional.

These presidential aspirants, like Trump, no longer care to maintain a facade of representing all Americans or smoothing over divisions when elections are over. Nobody runs for president to represent all Americans, and of course, nobody *could* in a far-flung country of 330 million people. Candidates who give lip service to the idea, as Tulsi Gabbard and Andrew Yang have, gain little traction in the media-driven bloodsport. The presidency is about winning either Red or Blue America, not both, and presidential candidates will be far more open about this in 2020—and with their hostility for the Electoral College. They are in the business of winning at all costs, not persuading. Fifty-one percent of the electorate will do, and the rest *deserve* to suffer for not going along with the program.

The standard explanations and justifications for politics are breaking down. Democratic consensus and needful compromise and good governance were always empty bromides, but today our political overlords understand and pander to an altogether different mood. The Trump presidency, like the Brexit vote, was never accepted by the same elites who spent the early twenty-first century gushing about the sanctity of democracy.

The entire pretense for democratic politics, ostensibly the peaceful transfer of political power and the consensual organization of human affairs, now gives way to new and uncomfortable questions. What if we cannot vote our way out of this? What if the structural problems of debt and entitlements and central banking and foreign policy cannot be solved politically? What if the culture wars are unwinnable? What if we have reached the end of politics as an instrument for keeping American society together?

Democracy and politics will not alleviate our problems; only committed individuals working in the intermediary institutions of civil society can. Democratic elections can work locally, and in small countries or communities; Switzerland's system of express subsidiarity comes to mind. And clearly the best hope for America's survival will come through an aggressive form of federalism or subsidiarity, one that dramatically reduces the winner-take-all stakes of national elections. But mass democracy, in a country as large as America, is a recipe for strife, bitterness, endless division, and much worse.

Murray Rothbard said in *Power and Market* that "ballots are hailed as substitutes for bullets." But in modern America, politics leads us closer to war, not closer to peace and justice and comity. Why should we accept weaponized mass politics when we have civil society, markets, and non-state institutions?

We need an anti-politics movement just as surely as we need an antiwar movement.

2

What We Lost on September 11

The cliché is true: September 11, 2001, represents a defining American moment. Generation X and Millennials suddenly had their own day of infamy, just as their parents and grandparents had Pearl Harbor and the Kennedy assassination. 9/11 marked the end of a relatively untroubled time in the US following the 1980 and 90s, and the beginning of a dark turn that continues to this day. Optimism, an enduring feature of the American psyche (rightly or wrongly identified as buncombe by Mencken) suddenly was in short supply.

Lives were lost, along with innocence. But the innocence lost that day had less to do with terrorism or even the threat of terrorism than it did with what we all knew was coming: an exponential

---

This article originally appeared September 11, 2017, on mises.org.

rise in the size and scope of the American state. The specter of growing state power frightened even those eager to endorse it, as most Americans were in the days following.

For libertarians, 9/11 was especially troubling precisely because of the intense public demand for Congress and the Bush administration to *do something*. Whether that something was rational, just, or even served American interests was almost beside the point. The people wanted blood, and after the images of bodies jumping from the twin towers who can blame the politicians in DC for obliging them? If there are no atheists in foxholes, there are very few libertarians after terrorist attacks. Our uneasy job was to counsel reason and restraint, even if that meant shouting into a wind tunnel.

The entire US national security apparatus, a trillion-dollar enterprise extending far beyond the Pentagon and alphabet soup intelligence agencies like the CIA and NSA, had failed utterly in its ostensible mission. All the airport security, nuclear missiles, air defense command centers, bombers, fighter jets, aircraft carriers, destroyers, spooks, spies, analysts, and supercomputers could not protect a single American from a small group of middle-class Saudi kids with box-cutters and a few hours of Cessna training.

So what should have been a profoundly embarrassing and soul-searching moment for the US national security state became an exercise in chest thumping. War room sessions at the White House made for good TV optics, but humility rather that hubris was in order. The question of what to do could not be answered without understanding what went wrong and what motivated the perpetrators. But not a single federal employee was fired because of 9/11, at least not so far as Senator Rand Paul can tell.

Instead, both Congress and the Bush 43 administration reacted predictably to 9/11 and poured it on: we will spend whatever it takes, do whatever it takes, and go wherever it takes to get the people who did this.

Sixteen years later, the War on Terror has yielded hundreds of thousands of dead and injured Americans, Iraqis, and Afghans, ongoing and intractable wars disguised as nation building, the Patriot Act, illegal executive actions, trillions in new federal debt, vastly increased federal surveillance powers, rubber stamped FISA court warrants, TSA at the airports, a useless Department of Homeland Security, overflowing VA hospitals, and increasingly militarized police here at home. More importantly, it has yielded a distressing complacency toward grotesque federal power.

It has not yielded peace, or liberty, or security. But liberty vs. security was never the choice.

A Personal Aside

I vividly remember the morning of September 11 in Washington, DC. It was sunny and beautiful, with no trace of August's oppressive humidity. Ron Paul's staff arrived at his office in the Cannon building around 8:00, ready for a typical Tuesday schedule of rote "suspension" bills (e.g., bills naming post offices) and gearing up for the week ahead.

The office had a TV to monitor C-SPAN and activity on the House floor. Although both the House and Senate were in session that day, as customary, debates and votes would not begin until sometime in the afternoon. So we had CNN playing in the background when sometime after 9:00 they began to show footage of smoke billowing from one tower in the World Trade Center. CNN's announcer wondered whether a small plane somehow had blundered into the building.

When word filtered down that the cause was not a small plane, things became more tense both on CNN and in our office: was this terrorism? We began to flip channels to find more information, and that's when we realized it would be no ordinary Tuesday.

Around 9:45 the Capitol Police came through the building barking at us to evacuate. It became clear there was no "plan," just a bunch of people shouting, running around, and pounding on doors. If anything, the underground tunnels beneath the House office building were safer than the streets outside—especially if gunmen or bombs were lurking.

Instead, police herded us outside, to go nowhere. The lawns surrounding the buildings were full of incredulous staffers milling about, making calls on their flip phones. The streets around the Capitol were impossibly jammed with cars attempting to get out. Some pedestrians headed to the Metro stations, but the subway was overwhelmed too. Nobody would get home easily or quickly. The corner liquor store, Subway, and nearby Taco Bell wisely stayed open and did brisk business.

About this time rumors began to swirl about the Pentagon being targeted, but of course we didn't know what to believe. Urban legends grew and just as quickly were debunked: a car bomb went off in front of the State Department! Foggy Bottom is on fire! More planes are headed for the Capitol Dome! One can only imagine how social media would react today.

Keep in mind the entire Capitol complex, consisting of the Capitol building itself, the House and Senate office buildings, the Library of Congress, and the Supreme Court, is one or two square kilometers at most. Its daytime population, mostly staff, is about 25,000 people. Note also that the Supreme Court and Library of Congress have their own police.

A typical town of 25,000 might have a force of 20 or 30 law enforcement officers. The US Capitol Police force, by contrast, has more than *2,000 officers.* Its budget is larger than the Atlanta police department! And while the DC Metro police have plenty of real crime to deal with, the Capitol complex is quite safe. Capitol police really serve as the personal security force for members of Congress more than anything else. So, some animals really are more equal than others.

3

PC Is About Control, Not Etiquette

I'd like to speak today about what political correctness is, at least in its modern version, what it is not, and what we might do to fight against it.

To begin, we need to understand that political correctness is not about being nice. It's not simply a social issue, or a subset of the culture wars.

It's not about politeness, or inclusiveness, or good manners. It's not about being respectful toward your fellow humans, and it's not about being sensitive or caring or avoiding hurt feelings and unpleasant slurs.

But you've heard this argument, I'm sure. PC is about simple respect and inclusiveness, they tell us. As though we need progressives, the cultural enforcers, to help us understand that we shouldn't call someone retarded, or use the "N" word, make hurtful comments about someone's appearance, or tolerate bullies.

If PC truly was about kindness and respect, it wouldn't need to be imposed on us. After all, we already have a mechanism for the social cohesion PC is said to represent: it's called manners. And we already have specific individuals charged with insuring that good manners are instilled and upheld: they're called parents.

This article is adapted from a speech given at the Mises Circle in Dallas–Ft. Worth on October 3, 2015.

Political Correctness Defined

But what exactly is PC? Let me take a stab at defining it: Political correctness is the conscious, designed manipulation of language intended to change the way people speak, write, think, feel, and act, in furtherance of an agenda.

PC is best understood as propaganda, which is how I suggest we approach it. But unlike propaganda, which historically has been used by governments to win favor for a particular campaign or effort, PC is all-encompassing. It seeks nothing less than to mold us into modern versions of Marx's un-alienated society man, freed of all his bourgeois pretensions and humdrum social conventions.

Like all propaganda, PC fundamentally is a lie. It is about refusing to deal with the underlying nature of reality, in fact attempting to alter that reality by legislative and social fiat. A is no longer A.

To quote Hans-Hermann Hoppe:

> [T]he masters . . . stipulate that aggression, invasion, murder and war are actually self-defense, whereas self-defense is aggression, invasion, murder and war. Freedom is coercion, and coercion is freedom. . . . Taxes are voluntary payments, and voluntarily paid prices are exploitative taxes. In a PC world, metaphysics is diverted and rerouted. Truth becomes malleable, to serve a bigger purpose determined by our superiors.

But where did all this come from? Surely PC, in all its various forms, is nothing new under the sun. I think we can safely assume that feudal chiefs, kings, emperors, and politicians have ever and always attempted to control the language, thoughts, and thus the actions of their subjects. Thought police have always existed.

To understand the origins of political correctness, we might look to the aforementioned Marx, and later the Frankfurt school. We might consider the work of Leo Strauss for its impact on the war-hungry think tank world. We might study the deceptive sloganeering of Saul Alinsky. We might mention the French philosopher Michael Foucault, who used the term "political correctness" in the 1960s as a criticism of unscientific dogma.

But if you really want to understand the black art of PC propaganda, let me suggest reading one of its foremost practitioners, Edward Bernays.

Bernays was a remarkable man, someone who literally wrote the book on propaganda and its softer guise of public relations. He is little discussed in the West today, despite being the godfather of modern spin.

He was the nephew of Sigmund Freud, and like Mises was born in Austria in the late nineteenth century. Unlike Mises, however, he fortuitously came to New York City as an infant and then proceeded to live an astonishing 103 years.

One of his first jobs was as a press agent for President Woodrow Wilson's Committee on Public Information, an agency designed to gin up popular support for US entry into WWI (German Americans and Irish Americans especially were opposed). It was Bernays who coined the infamous phrase "Make the World Safe for Democracy" used by the committee.

After the war, he asked himself whether one could "apply a similar technique to the problems of peace." And by "problems," Bernays meant selling stuff. He directed very successful campaigns promoting Ivory Soap, for bacon and eggs as a healthy breakfast, and ballet. He directed several very successful advertising campaigns, most notably for Lucky Strike in its efforts to make smoking socially acceptable for women.

The Role of "Herd Psychology"

Bernays was quite open and even proud of engaging in the "manufacturing of consent," a term used by British surgeon and psychologist Wilfred Trotter in his seminal *Instincts of the Herd in Peace and War* published in 1919.

Bernays took the concept of herd psychology to heart. The herd instinct entails the deep seated psychological need to win approval of one's social group. The herd overwhelms any other influence; as social humans, our need to fit in is paramount.

But however ingrained, in Bernays's view the herd instinct cannot be trusted. The herd is irrational and dangerous, and must be steered by wiser men in a thousand imperceptible ways—and this is key. They must not know they are being steered.

The techniques Bernays employed are still very much being used to shape political correctness today.

First, he understood how all-powerful the herd mind and herd instinct really is. We are not the special snowflakes we imagine, according to Bernays. Instead we are timorous and malleable creatures who desperately want to fit in and win the acceptance of the group.

Second, he understood the critical importance of using third party authorities to promote causes or products. Celebrities, athletes, models, politicians, and wealthy elites are the people from whom the herd takes its cues, whether they're endorsing transgender awareness or selling luxury cars. So when George Clooney or Kim Kardashian endorses Hillary Clinton, it resonates with the herd.

Third, he understood the role that emotions play in our tastes and preferences. It's not a particular candidate or cigarette or a watch or a handbag we really want, it's the emotional component of the ad that affects us, however subconsciously.

What We Can Do About It

So the question we might ask ourselves is this: how do we fight back against PC? What can we do, as individuals with finite amounts of time and resources, with serious obligations to our families, loved ones, and careers, to reverse the growing tide of darkness?

First, we must understand that we're in a fight. PC represents a war for our very hearts, minds, and souls. The other side understands this, and so should you. The fight is taking place on multiple fronts: the state-linguistic complex operates not only within government, but also academia, media, the business world, churches and synagogues, nonprofits, and NGOs. So understand the forces aligned against you.

Understand that the PC enforcers are not asking you, they're not debating you, and they don't care about your vote. They don't care whether they can win at the ballot box, or whether they use extralegal means. There are millions of progressives in the US who absolutely would criminalize speech that does not comport with their sense of social justice.

One poll suggests 51 percent of Democrats and one-third of all Americans would do just that.

The other side is fighting deliberately and tactically. So realize you're in a fight, and fight back. Culturally, this really is a matter of life and death.

We Still Have Freedom to Act

As bad as PC contamination may be at this point, we are not like Mises, fleeing a few days ahead of the Nazis. We have tremendous resources at our disposal in a digital age. We can still communicate globally and create communities of outspoken, anti-PC voices. We can still read and share anti-state books and articles. We can still read real history and the great un-PC literary classics. We can still homeschool our kids. We can still hold events like this one today.

This is not to say that bucking PC can't hurt you: the possible loss of one's job, reputation, friends, and even family is very serious. But defeatism is never called for, and it makes us unworthy of our ancestors.

Use humor to ridicule PC. PC is absurd, and most people sense it. And its practitioners suffer from a comical lack of self-awareness and irony. Use every tool at your disposal to mock, ridicule, and expose PC for what it is.

Never forget that society can change very rapidly in the wake of certain precipitating events. We certainly all hope that no great calamity strikes America, in the form of an economic collapse, a currency collapse, an inability to provide entitlements and welfare, energy shortages, food and water shortages, natural disasters, or civil unrest. But we can't discount the possibility of these things happening.

And if they do, I suggest that PC language and PC thinking will be the first ornament of the state to go. Only rich, modern, societies can afford the luxury of a mindset that does not comport with reality, and that mindset will be swiftly swept aside as the "rich" part of America frays.

Men and women might start to rediscover that they need and complement each other if the welfare state breaks down. Endless hours spent on social media might give way to rebuilding social connections that really matter when the chips are down.

More traditional family structures might suddenly seem less oppressive in the face of great economic uncertainty. Schools and universities might rediscover the value of teaching practical skills, instead of whitewashed history and grievance studies. One's sexual preferences might not loom as large in the scheme of things, certainly not as a source of rights. The rule of law might become something more than an abstraction to be discarded in order to further social justice and deny privilege.

Play the Long Game

I'm afraid it might not be popular to say so, but we have to be prepared for a long and hard campaign. Let's leave the empty promises of quick fixes to the politicians. Progressives play the long game masterfully. They've taken one hundred years to ransack our institutions inch by inch. I'm not suggesting incrementalism to reclaim those foregone institutions, which are by all account too far gone—but to create our own.

PC enforcers seek to divide and atomize us, by class, race, sex, and sexuality. So let's take them up on it. Let's bypass the institutions controlled by them in favor of our own. Who says we can't create our own schools, our own churches, our own media, our own literature, and our own civic and social organizations? Starting from scratch certainly is less daunting than fighting PC on its own turf.

Conclusion

PC is a virus that puts us—liberty loving people—on our heels. When we allow progressives to frame the debate and control the narrative, we lose power over our lives. If we don't address what the state and its agents are doing to control us, we might honestly wonder how much longer organizations like the Mises Institute are going to be free to hold events like this one today.

Is it really that unimaginable that you might wake up one day and find sites with anti-state and anti-egalitarian content blocked—sites like mises.org and lewrockwell.com?

Or that social media outlets like Facebook might simply eliminate opinions not deemed acceptable in the new America?

In fact, head Facebook creep Mark Zuckerberg recently was overheard at a UN summit telling Angela Merkel that he would get to work on suppressing Facebook comments by Germans who have the audacity to object to the government's handling of migrants.

Here's the Facebook statement:

> We are committed to working closely with the German government on this important issue. We think the best solutions to dealing with people who make racist and xenophobic comments can be found when service providers, government, and civil society all work together to address this common challenge.

Chilling, isn't it? And coming soon to a server near you, unless we all get busy.

4

Intergenerational Conflict Will Get Worse

The excellent British online magazine *Spiked* recently published "Caring for the elderly in an ageist society," by Dave Clements, warning about deteriorating attitudes toward elderly people in the UK. As the article points out, there is more to the problem than logistical and financial concerns about providing socialist medical care to an aging population. Nor do increasing lifespans in the West, with attendant increases in loneliness and age-related morbidity, account for this unhappy state of affairs. No, the root of the problem is simply a lack of caring and empathy, made worse by fewer intact multi-generational families and alienation between taxpayers and pensioners:

> These are not just technical questions for the social-care sector to grapple with. They are far bigger than that, touching upon the issue of what kind of society we want to live in, and what we expect of each other. At root, there is the issue of what we regard as individual and collective responsibilities; and what the duties of the young are to the old; and the question of how elderly people come to decide for themselves how they should be cared for later in life.
>
> More than that, the problems facing the social-care system need to be understood in the context of a wider

This article originally appeared November 28, 2018, on mises.org.

generational hostility that is compounding, if not driving, a longstanding official neglect of older people's care.

Sad, yes, but entirely predictable. Britain, perhaps faster and more vigorously than most Western countries, has fallen prey to the doctrine of "presentism": an ahistorical narrative in which the past is always bad and repressive, feelings and "lived experiences" (generally quite lacking among the young, yes?) prevail over facts, and group identity dictates ideology. If the past is all wrong, the people who *lived in it* and even prospered during it surely are not to be admired or cared for:

> "Negativity about ageing and older people is pervasive in our society," says Caroline Abrahams at Age UK. Whether it's the nasty sentiment that Brexit voters are a bunch of selfish old bigots whose demise can't come too soon, or that Baby Boomers have been piling up problems for moaning millennials, or that old people are just getting in the way with their "bed-blocking" and their unreasonable expectation that younger folk should subsidise their state pensions, free bus passes, TV licences and winter fuel allowances—again and again, we see generational disdain for older people.

Democracy, as usual, doesn't help. Brexit voters in the Leave camp skew older, more rural, and more "English." Remainers skew younger, urban, and more "European." In their 2014 independence referendum, younger Scottish voters overwhelmingly chose to leave Britain and fully embrace the European Union; older Scots chose the perceived safety of London pensions over counting on Holyrood and Brussels state pensions and state-provided healthcare, even more sacrosanct in the UK than Social Security and Medicare are here, will never be reduced or addressed by voting. Yet just as the American entitlement system faces a $200 trillion shortfall—the likely cost of future promised benefits minus likely future tax receipts—Britain's younger taxpayers will struggle mightily in coming decades to pay ever-expanding old-age pensions.

America is in the same boat, with the population above age 65 set to double over the next thirty years. Republicans and Trump voters are older, whiter, more rural or suburban, and more likely to see America in far rosier terms than the average Ocasio-Cortez supporter. Social Security, which in 1940 boasted more than 100 paying workers to one beneficiary, today struggles with a ratio of less than 3 to 1. And those three workers in many cases are decidedly younger, more Left-liberal, less white, and less affluent than the one beneficiary. Unskilled workers, recent immigrants, and teenagers often work at low-wage hourly jobs, but still pay full Social Security taxes on their meager earnings.

All of this is a recipe for intergenerational strife.

The baby boomer mantra—never trust anyone over 30—is now bequeathed to millennials, but for very different reasons. In many senses millennials are more conservative than their grandparents were at the same age, particularly when it comes to sex, recreational drugs, education, and a carefree live-for-today attitude toward life. There is no millennial version of *Easy Rider* or *American Graffiti*; slacker paeans like *Superbad* show teenagers with low aspirations and no interest in eclipsing boomer nonconformity. But millennial distrust for older Americans is based on the strong perception that today's economic and social horizons are far less robust for them than previous generations, generations that are happy to ride out the clock until entitlements run out.

It will get worse. Cultural, economic, fiscal, and political fault lines in America today all bode ill for harmony between younger and older generations. But what should we expect in a country where politics and government dominate? Where transfer payments dominate old age and government schools dominate youthhood?

Family, religion, and civil society don't play nearly the same role for young people today as for Baby Boomers, who rebelled against all three. What we're left with, in the view of many Americans, is a society where government is the only thing we all belong to. Many scoff at the notion of any natural order, without recognizing that government simply substitutes an unnatural political order run by those in power.

Sensible societies harness the energy, optimism, and beauty of youth in productive ways: their talents are unleashed in art, athletics, business, and technology (not war). But apart from standout exceptions young people are not the leaders of sensible societies, because we recognize that what one believes at 16 or 20 or 25 will change, and often change radically. So sensible societies venerate the wisdom of older people, wisdom that is separate and distinct from mere information. Unlike data on a smartphone, this wisdom passes down naturally—albeit not without friction—because everyone recognizes the healthy and mutually beneficial connection between generations. Over time bad ideas, traditions, and modes fall away, replaced by new and better ones.

Decaying, dysfunctional societies, by contrast, pit generations against each other at the ballot box and otherwise. Politics and government become powerful weapons in an intergenerational cold war. Aging Western populations skew the demographic political balance in favor of older people, especially active older voters. Brexit, Trump, and the Scottish independence referendum have now exposed this growing reality.

5

The Wrong Elites

To mount an effective response to the reigning egalitarianism of our age, therefore, it is necessary but scarcely sufficient to demonstrate the absurdity, the anti-scientific nature, the self-contradictory nature, of the egalitarian doctrine, as well as the disastrous consequences of the egalitarian program. All this is well and good. But it misses the essential nature of, as well as the most effective rebuttal to, the egalitarian program: to expose it as a mask for the drive to power of the now ruling left-liberal intellectual and media elites. Since these elites are also the hitherto unchallenged opinion-molding class in society, their rule cannot be dislodged until the oppressed public, instinctively but inchoately opposed to these elites, are shown the true nature of the increasingly hated forces who are ruling over them. To use the phrases of the New Left of the late 1960s, the ruling elite must be "demystified," "delegitimated," and "desanctified." Nothing can advance their desanctification more than the public realization of the true nature of their egalitarian slogans.

—Murray N. Rothbard, "Egalitarianism and the Elites"

This article originally appeared April 6, 2022, on mises.org.

During a panel discussion at a recent Mises Institute event, one presenter described her son's Ivy League university as "elite," even as she lamented the perverse and harmful covid mandates imposed by its administration. Those mandates, by the way, were overwhelmingly supported both by students at this particular college and their parents.

Another panelist responded with "We need new elites!" to applause from the audience.

This is painfully true. We desperately need new and better elites, because the politically connected class in America spent the last hundred-plus years ruining education, medicine, diplomacy (peace), money, banking, big business, literature, art, and entertainment, just for starters. And yet they have the temerity to attack the inevitable populist reactions to their own dismal failures!

The first step in this process is withdrawing our sanction of existing elites whenever and wherever we can. This can be as easy as turning off CNN or as difficult as not sending a child off to seek the fading prestige of an Ivy League degree. But we have to turn our backs on them. We have to upend the incentives and institutions that make their undeserved elite status possible.

Undeserved in this context means state connected. This feature more than any other marks today's "unnatural" elites, by which we mean elites who owe their status largely to government connections rather than merit. It can be hard to identify in some cases: some elites, such as Jeff Bezos, performed brilliantly in the marketplace yet also maintain deep ties to the worst of the American superstate. Amazon sells cloud services to a host of criminal federal agencies, and Bezos himself solely owns the CIA organ the *Washington Post*.

Russian oligarchs, much in the news these days, are said to fall in this category of unnatural and undeserving elites. While the dictionary definition of "oligarch" is straightforward—a member of a controlling elite with nearly absolute political power—the current usage is broader. It has come to mean "foreign billionaire who made money in unholy ways," and as such presumably applies to Vladimir

Putin and his purported billions in assets amassed on a modest salary. But many Russians obtained power and wealth through close connections to the former Soviet Union, buying up state assets on the cheap during the cronyist early 1990s. Are they all to have their property seized now, like Roman Abramovich and his shares of the Chelsea Football Club in London? What law justifies this, what tribunal issues such an order, and what police agency enforces the seizure? These trifling questions about the "rule of law" go unasked and unanswered; we're at war with Putin!

But aren't US elites oligarchs too? When we consider the nexus of state and corporate power, we find plenty of American examples beyond the aforementioned Bezos. New York University professor Michael Rectenwald coined the term "governmentalities" to describe publicly traded companies like Google and Amazon that are so intimately connected with the federal state as to become deputized to act as state agents. When we consider how far-reaching this nexus really is, how many American elites truly deserve their status?

Consider Elon Musk, who recently sold part of his Tesla stock and purchased a 9 percent interest in Twitter, gaining a board seat in the process. His wealth derives in part from his clearly meritorious efforts building and selling PayPal; his business acumen in investing the PayPal proceeds; and his visionary, indefatigable efforts building both Tesla and the private SpaceX. Surely a man of his intelligence and entrepreneurial drive is a natural, worthy elite?

Well, maybe. At least some of his Tesla stock wealth is due to government subsidies helping to create a market for his EVs, and SpaceX contracts directly with NASA. Perhaps Mr. Musk didn't ask for these subsidies and would be quite wealthy and successful without them—but they cloud the issue.

Are the Obamas oligarchs? After all, their reported $70 million net worth derives *entirely* from trading on their time in the White House. How about George W. Bush and his $40 million, given how he inherited money and then sold his oil and gas concern to a company owned by George Soros? Consider Joe Biden, whose net worth soared from less than $30,000(!) in 2009 to nearly $10 million today. He literally has not had a proper job since 1970! Surely he is an oligarch, in the sense of unearned wealth and power?

What about Stacey Abrams, the onetime Georgia gubernatorial candidate who claimed a net worth of $109,000 in 2018 but now discloses a net worth of $3.17 million? What has she built or created? Is she an oligarch, with unearned wealth and status due solely to politics? How about CNN's Anderson Cooper, born into the bosom of Vanderbilt wealth and elite schools (not to mention the obligatory intern stint at the CIA) and then given a prominent platform on a major cable station? Is he in any way deserving of his status?

Russian oligarchs, American pols, and state-connected billionaires are all cut from the same cloth: they didn't earn, or fully earn, their wealth and position in society. But we must expect this. Rule by elites, at least to an extent, is indeed inevitable. Every society, across time and across place, manifests this. Democracy doesn't solve or change it, but merely transfers status away from merit and toward politics. Democracy simply creates different—worse—elites in the form of a permanent managerial, bureaucratic class that no more reflects the consent of the governed than Putin represents the will of all Russians.

Political and economic liberty is about the freedom and prosperity average people enjoy in any society. It is the measure of whether elites are natural or unnatural, deserving or undeserving. In the poorest and most corrupt countries, elites fatten their own Swiss bank accounts while parasitically draining citizens of their meager resources. In the wealthiest and least corrupt countries, elites act far more benevolently (e.g., Prince Hans-Adam II in Liechtenstein). Most countries across the West today lie somewhere in the middle. But the covid crisis showed us that once again the situation is getting worse.

What we need is not to eliminate elites, but to create better ones.

In his essay "Natural Elites, Intellectuals, and the State," Hans-Hermann Hoppe describes how modern states usurp the role of worthy individuals in society who possess natural authority:

Such a theory has been presented by Bertrand de Jouvenel. According to his view, states are the outgrowth of natural elites: the natural outcome of voluntary transactions between private property owners is non-egalitarian, hierarchical, and elitist. In every society, a few individuals acquire the status of an elite through talent. Due to superior achievements of wealth, wisdom, and bravery, these individuals come to possess natural authority, and their opinions and judgments enjoy wide-spread respect. Moreover, because of selective mating, marriage, and the laws of civil and genetic inheritance, positions of natural authority are likely to be passed on within a few noble families. It is to the heads of these families with long-established records of superior achievement, farsightedness, and exemplary personal conduct that men turn with their conflicts and complaints against each other. These leaders of the natural elite act as judges and peacemakers, often free of charge out of a sense of duty expected of a person of authority or out of concern for civil justice as a privately produced "public good."

The small but decisive step in the transition to a state consists precisely of the monopolization of the function of judge and peacemaker. This occurred once a single member of the voluntarily acknowledged natural elite was able to insist, despite the opposition of other members of the elite, that all conflicts within a specified territory be brought before him. Conflicting parties could no longer choose any other judge or peacemaker.

How do we identify "good" elites, wise leaders who will act and guide the world in benevolent ways? Leaders who care about civilization, property, prosperity, peace, justice, fairness, conservation, and charity? We start by turning our backs on politics, media, academia, and popular culture and looking to the real world examples around us. In our family, work, social circles, and local communities are the men and women who can replace our very unnatural overlords. Men and women who understand *inequality and human differences* as the inescapable starting point of human society, which in Ludwig von Mises's view allows for "collaboration of the more talented, more able, and more industrious with the less talented, less able, and less industrious," which "results in benefits for both."

This, then, is the egalitarian rub. Progressives of all political stripes oppose the idea of natural elites not because of their claimed egalitarianism or dislike of hierarchies: *they oppose the idea because it contemplates a hierarchy not established by them.* A natural elite also means that intelligence, ability, attractiveness, charisma, wisdom, discretion, and quiet confidence—all very unequally distributed in nature—become the characteristics of those holding greater influence in society.

Government is mostly beyond hope or redemption. And we don't need elites for governance; markets perform that function far better and far more democratically. Our focus should be on the intermediary institutions of civil society, saving those that can be saved and building new ones where the damage is too great. We begin this process with real elites, the actual "adults in the room." We desperately need to desanctify the current crop and replace them with much better and nobler people.

6

We Don't Believe You

David French, maybe *National Review*'s most reliably wrong scribe, issued this gem in response to the FBI raid on Donald Trump's residence in Florida:

 David French ✓
@DavidAFrench   ...

Given that we still haven't seen the warrant, much less the warrant application, the immediate frenzied anger at the FBI is completely unjustified. There is no constitutional, statutory, or moral foundation for the belief a former president is above the law. So, wait. /1

9:57 AM · Aug 9, 2022 · Twitter Web App

896 Retweets   **178** Quote Tweets   **6,904** Likes

 Tweet your reply   Reply

 David French ✓ @DavidAFrench · Aug 9
Replying to @DavidAFrench
If the DOJ's actions turn out to be unjustified, then responsible officials should be held accountable. But it's wrong to "presume" an abuse of power. And talk of "civil war" is horrific, frivolous Twitter LARPing, right until a deranged man picks up a rifle. Take a breath. /end

593   467   3,471

This article originally appeared April 11, 2022, on mises.org.

Imagine thinking federal police agents and lawyers will be "held accountable," or that presidents are not above the law! Is this an afterschool special? "Let's wait and see, folks, before we judge the situation. It might be perfectly on the up and up! Have faith in the rule of law and trust the process!"

French, in keeping with the listless residue of Conservative Inc., either can't or won't face the reality of postgoodwill America. This starts and ends with politics. If politics is war by other means, subterfuge is part and parcel of every battle and skirmish in that war. We are not required to take a combatant's claims at face value, blundering ahead like Lucan and Cardigan at Balaclava. The contrary, in fact. Any political statement made today, by any politician or candidate or public official, can be answered thus: "We don't believe you." And with this comes a corollary: "We don't trust you."

When the Left talks about banning assault rifles, for example, we all know the true ambition of the gun controllers—many of whom are open and honest about their desire to completely eliminate private ownership of firearms in America. Progressives apply the same lens to bans on late-term abortion. But the Trump era, enhanced by the perverse dopamine incentives of social media, took this disbelief and distrust to a new rhetorical level. Witness today's poisonous political lexicon, one that makes clear any presumption of *good intentions* is gone: insurrection, treason, racist, Nazi, fascist, domestic terrorist, MAGAt. These terms are not used to persuade, but to dehumanize and banish. Which of course is nothing new in politics. But it's worth pointing out the Frenchist folly of claiming that democratic norms are poised to reassert themselves and bring us together once Orange Man is gone.

The FBI raid on Mar-a-Lago is an obvious example of America watching two politicized movies. We are not required to judge it apart from the broader political context, like children examining a single rock. The entire event is bound up with the larger war against Trump, one which began almost immediately after he was elected, with the Russiagate campaign. The goal of that ongoing war is to ruin both Trump and his family, salting the earth with their populist movement of Deplorables. Trump and his supporters must be destroyed politically (at the very least), ensuring Trump cannot run for president again but also that *no candidate* outside the uniparty's acceptable parameters can ever run again. So one of the most important campaigns in America's political war effectively seeks to criminalize a whole category of dissent—or at least place dissenters outside the bounds of acceptable society. If you doubt any or all of the 2020 presidential election results, you are an election denier. If you protested at the Capitol, you are an insurrectionist. If you question Russian collusion, you are a Putin supporter. And so forth.

We have not seen the FBI's warrant or the supporting evidence presented to the magistrate. Was the raid an actual step toward a criminal prosecution? What were the actual crimes contemplated and the specific evidence sought? We don't know, but at this point, *it doesn't matter*. Merrick Garland surely knew Republican partisans would view the raid as pure political harassment, a warning to Trump, his family, and close associates. He also surely knew that many Democratic partisans hope to gin up legal arguments to disqualify the former president from running again (either under the Fourteenth Amendment or, more dubiously, under this federal statute). And of course he knew a media brouhaha would ensue. So there are two broad but conflicting interpretations of Garland's actions. First, he is a brave defender of the rule of law who doggedly follows the evidence wherever it goes, with no consideration for politics, appearances, or timing whatsoever. Second, he knew exactly how ardent Trump fans would react to the warrant and seizures, *and actively intended this effect*. In other words, he intended to send a threatening message and quell political enthusiasm for Trump 2024.

Decent people can and should resist a world organized around politics, and deplore the politicized state of America. Ordinary Americans don't want to live political lives and have their personal and professional relationships defined by this terrible environment. But politics is interested in us, as the saying goes. So we arm ourselves with a clear-eyed worldview, put away childish things, and never accept political pronouncements at face value. "We don't believe you" is always the default position.

7

The Privilege of Politics

Actor Chris Pratt finds himself a target of left Hollywood and various social media enforcers for his apparent lack of support for Joe Biden, a sin in his industry. Pratt has endorsed neither Biden nor Trump, which seems eminently sensible for a boy-next-door type who plays superheroes and adventurers in big blockbusters. But staying quiet is never enough for the political jackals, who insist silence is violence and a form of privilege. Trump is a Nazi; his electorate is full of hateful fascist enablers and this is no time for quietude. To make matters worse, the reticent Pratt also belongs to a Christian church which is "anti-LGBT"—which is to say not anti-LGBT at all, but simply not in full conformity with the language and demands of its accusers.

When his actor friend and sometime costar Mark Ruffalo rushed to defend Pratt's character, the Twitterati reacted angrily but predictably:

This article originally appeared October 22, 2020, on mises.org.

Kat Kinsman ✔ @kittenwithawhip · 20h
Replying to @MarkRuffalo and @prattprattpratt
His church is anti-LGBTQ. That is extremely political at a time when people's rights and freedoms and very lives are at stake. That's how I see him living his life.

💬 276   🔁 573   ♡ 15.4K   ↥

Kat Kinsman ✔ @kittenwithawhip · 20h
You, Mark, are in a position where you can talk to your friend about how his actions—and inaction—are harmful to people without the societal protections, platform, and wealth that you two are lucky to have. I hope you will.

💬 58   🔁 269   ♡ 9K   ↥

Lucy 🏳️ @LucyRebel20 · 22h
Replying to @MarkRuffalo and @prattprattpratt
He goes to a church that harms LGBTQ+ people and defends that.
This isn't it Mark.
Maybe stand up for your fans and be an ally while supporting your friend by helping him evolve.
Telling hurt people they are wrong isn't helpful.

💬 200   🔁 122   ♡ 4.5K   ↥

Yolanda Machado ✔ @SassyMamainLA · 21h
Replying to @MarkRuffalo and @prattprattpratt
Mark, while you have the privilege of his political choice not affecting you, the vote he casts for any GOP in this era is HARMING marginalized and vulnerable communities.

& If he is OK casting a vote for someone who separated families & put kids in cages, he's not "solid."

💬 395   🔁 173   ♡ 3.2K   ↥

iced coffee dream ✦ @clay_risingsun · 22h
Replying to @MarkRuffalo and @prattprattpratt
Must be nice to be able to not be overtly political ☹️☹️☹️☹️☹️

💬 19   🔁 112   ♡ 6.9K   ↥

Roxane @Roxi_MW · 22h
Political apathy is a luxury of the privileged.

💬 39   🔁 532   ♡ 6.7K   ↥

This is a classic case of the Imposers positioning themselves as the Imposed Upon: LGBT advocates weaponize and contort simple words—hurt, harm, apathy, privilege, marginalized, vulnerable—in ways reminiscent of Orwell's "Politics and the English Language." They use words in consciously dishonest ways. They shift the parameters of what it means to "support" or "oppose" LGBT causes into a stark binary: you are for us or against us. Simply living one's life peaceably is not an option in this bizarre worldview.

And the Imposer's unconditional terms change constantly, seemingly overnight. One cannot avoid conflict by being "not overtly political," as Ruffalo termed Pratt. The accusations against his church, for example, amount to nothing more than a demand for unconditional surrender of any theology or doctrine which does not comport with today's instant (though far from universal) view of transgenderism. Unless and until that happens, his church is *per se* transphobic and evil: indifference, or even kind and loving disagreement, cannot satisfy the Imposers.

It does not matter whether Pratt's church welcomes everyone, even those individuals it considers engaged in sin (which presumably includes just about every person on earth). It does not matter whether Pratt is a good person or friend to his fellow actors. His church must affirmatively endorse the views of LGBT activists; Pratt must actively endorse Biden. Anything else is weaponized privilege.

Of course this is nonsense, but the Imposers always claim to be the Imposed Upon. Media and politicians play along, and then social media voices join the chorus until the original reality becomes completely obscured: both Chris Pratt and his church were minding their own business and not hurting anyone. The Biden and LGBT activists came looking for them, not the other way around.

What incredible arrogance and hubris! *This* is real privilege: the privilege of demanding others not only share your political views but also see the world in starkly political terms. This is real hate, actual hate, not the phony kind imagined on Hate Has No Home Here yard signs.

When taken to an extreme, a positive rights worldview requires not only conformity and acquiescence with the political project of the day, but your affirmative participation. Not keeping up with the latest outrage, political machinations, or campaign—*not leading a wholly political life*—becomes a dereliction of duty.

Political liberty is quite simple, but not easy. We all owe our fellow citizens a duty not to aggress against them or their property, and not to commit fraud against them. In the broader societal sense, we all should strive to be kind, open, and generous with everyone we meet, unless and until they give us a reason to be otherwise. But that is all we owe. Being apolitical or even antipolitical is your absolute right. At best, politics is an uneasy and imperfect mechanism for peacefully transferring political power; at worst, it is barely a substitute for war. More commonly, politics is a turf battle waged by rival gangs to control the state apparatus (the turf is us and our money). Politics is not noble, virtuous, or even necessary. The people attacking Chris Pratt, and even hoping to harm his career, reputation, and finances, hold no moral high ground.

My great aunt, now departed, once told me about a decision she and her husband made as newlyweds just after World War II. Starting life together in a very modest house, they wanted to build lasting memories with family and friends. So they made a pact: they would never discuss politics in their home or allow guests to discuss politics. In her view politics was like sex and religion, a private matter. They wanted to avoid the disharmony and rancor they had witnessed among their own parents and families a decade earlier over the Roosevelt administration's New Deal programs. They determined their hearth and home would be devoted to happiness, an apolitical refuge where every visitor would be welcome.

The goal is a less political world, not a world which bends to our political will. We are not Imposers. So participate in politics and voting if you like, or refrain if you like. Voting is optional and anonymous for a reason. But never let anyone force you into taking a political stance, or even to hold a political stance. In 2020, privilege manifests as political extortion. Push back against these bullies.

Secession and Decentralization

8

Self-determination, Not Universalism, Is the Goal

Conservatives and progressives alike spent the twentieth century arguing for universal political principles. But the world is not so malleable; even in a hyper-connected digital age elites struggle to maintain support for globalism against a tide of nationalist, populist, and breakaway movements. Libertarians should embrace this reality and reject universalism for the morally and tactically superior vision of radical self-determination.

For decades we've been conditioned to believe the world is getting smaller, and thus that globalism in all its forms is inevitable. Instant communication, inexpensive access to digital information, global trade, and cheap fast travel will combine to demonstrate once and for all that nationality, geography, culture, language, ethnicity—and even history—matter far less than a shared humanity.

Given this inevitable reality, old modes of living will be tossed aside by a world hungry for modernity. Universal suffrage, an article of faith in a post-monarchical world, will yield social democracies

---

This article originally appeared May 29, 2017, on mises.org.

with robust safety nets, regulated capitalism, legal protections for women and minorities, and widely agreed-upon norms regarding social issues. Western conceptions of civil rights will spread far and wide, with technology bridging the old boundaries of nation states. Both progressives and conservatives share this vision, although the former emphasizes a supra-national administrative state ("one world government") while the latter focus on globally managed trade schemes under the auspices of international law.

Universalism provides the philosophical underpinnings for globalism. But it does not provide a roadmap for freedom. Libertarians, who want a non-political world organized around civil society and markets rather than the state, have a responsibility to call foul on this inescapably statist narrative. Globalism is not liberty; instead it threatens to create an entirely new level of government. And universalism is not natural law; in fact it is often directly at odds with human nature and (true) human diversity.

Yet many libertarians have taken up the universalism mantra. Calls for the global recognition of rights based on liberal individualism and the promotion of an ill-defined "libertarian cosmopolitanism" suggest the same kind of universalist hubris that imagines an inescapable arc to human history. A form of libertarian universalism is behind the creation of international organizations like the Atlas Network, just as it is behind the impulse to argue for Western "tolerance" and constitutionalism before the nascent Iraqi National Assembly. It's behind the charge that Ron Paul's support for secession and states' rights is illibertarian.

Certainly there are universal normative principles found in libertarianism, especially natural law libertarianism. All humans have a right to sovereignty over their physical bodies and minds, a right to own justly acquired property, and to freely associate (or disassociate) with others. Self-ownership and property rights are central tenets of libertarianism.

But many parts of the world disagree with those tenets, whether we admit this or not. Universal social norms, cultural attitudes, or policy prescriptions are a very tough sell beyond the West. While libertarians can universally condemn slavery, or authoritarian collectivism, it's quite another thing to suggest how other societies ought to organize themselves politically. Yet consistent universalism requires this. Gay rights in America mean gay rights for Saudi Arabia, open borders for Germany means Monaco also must open its doors to refugees, and Texas-style open carry is the prescription France needs to prevent another Bataclan. If US military intervention is justified in Rwanda, it must be justified in Syria. How can a universalist libertarian argue otherwise?

The fundamental problem with universalism is that so few things really are widely agreed upon. Universalists exhibit a special kind of hubris, one that smacks of neo-colonialism: the insistence that others must believe as we do, if only we show them the obvious superiority of our thinking.

But humans not only often fail to believe as we want them to, they also fail to act as hoped. Actions, in fact, tend to be reliably singular. Thus universalism, whether political, economic, or cultural, poses a problem Ludwig von Mises identified decades ago— it is collectivist and unworkable within a praxeological framework:

> The philosophy of universalism has from time immemorial blocked access to a satisfactory grasp of praxeological problems, and contemporary universalists are utterly incapable of finding an approach to them. Universalism, collectivism, and conceptual realism see only wholes and universals. They speculate about mankind, nations, states, classes, about virtue and vice, right and wrong, about entire classes of wants and of commodities.

Not only does universalism fail to fully account for individual human action, it also presupposes some form of overarching arbiter, whether deity or state:

> The essential problem of all varieties of universalistic, collectivistic, and holistic social philosophy is: By what

mark do I recognize the true law, the authentic apostle of God's word, and the legitimate authority. For many claim that Providence has sent them, and each of these prophets preaches another gospel. For the faithful believer there cannot be any doubt; he is fully confident that he has espoused the only true doctrine. But it is precisely the firmness of such beliefs that renders the antagonisms irreconcilable.

As Joe Salerno discussed, in rejecting universalism Mises instead saw self-determination as the highest political end. The smaller and more localized the political unit, the more apt the individual was to live under political terms acceptable to him. For Mises, this was not only a matter of civic comity but necessary to avoid outright civil war and bloodshed:

> The right of self-determination in regard to the question of membership in a state thus means: whenever the inhabitants of a particular territory, whether it be a single village, a whole district, or a series of adjacent districts, make it known, by a freely conducted plebiscite, that they no longer wish to remain united to the state to which they belong at the time, but wish either to form an independent state or to attach themselves to some other state, their wishes are to be respected and complied with. This is the only feasible and effective way of preventing revolutions and civil and international wars.
>
> The right of self-determination of which we speak is not the right of self-determination of nations, but rather the right of self-determination of the inhabitants of every territory large enough to form an independent administrative unit. If it were in any way possible to grant this right of self-determination to every individual person, it would have to be done. This is impracticable only because of compelling technical considerations, which make it necessary that a region be governed as a single administrative unit and that the right of self-determination be restricted to the will of the majority

of the inhabitants of areas large enough to count as territorial units in the administration of the country.

In other words, self-determination is the ultimate political goal. It is the path to liberty, however imperfect. A world of seven billion self-governing individuals is the ideal, but short of that we should prefer the Liechtensteins to the Germanys and the Luxembourgs to the Englands. We should prefer states' rights to federalization in the US, and cheer for the breakup of EU. We should support breakaway movements in places like Catalonia and Scotland (provided they are organic and not engineered by states and their spy agencies). We should admire the Swiss federalist system, where localism is a governing principle. We should favor local control over faraway legislatures and administrative bodies, and thus reject multilateral trade deals. We should, in sum, prefer small to large when it comes to government.

Can a small local state be equally or more illiberal than a large distant one? Of course, although history often demonstrates otherwise. But the Misesian principle remains: the best chance for liberty occurs under rules made by the smallest and closest possible administrative unit to the individual. Each higher level of government attenuates the individual's ability to effect (or affect) such rules.

Decentralization, secession, subsidiarity, localism, and nullification are the tools for greater self-determination, and thus greater liberty. These tools, not universalist platitudes, should be the stock in trade of libertarians trying to make the case for a freer world.

Libertarians aside, there are hopeful signs that both the political Left and Right see the decentralized writing on the wall.

Progressives saw their world profoundly shaken with the successful Brexit campaign and the election of Trump over uber-globalist Hillary Clinton. They reacted predictably: centralized power in DC suddenly was something to be feared and resisted at all costs. Silicon Valley scions began seriously talking about Calexit, mayors from New York to San Francisco called for sanctuary cities and flouting of federal edicts, and the chairman of the Democratic Party declared 2017 the Summer of Resistance. These do not sound like people who believe in the sanctity of elections, or who accept the powers of the unitary executive when the wrong guy wins.

But as libertarians we should applaud this. We can call progressive hypocrites, and they are, but they are correct that voting confers no legitimacy on government. If it takes Trump to make the Left realize there is more opposition among the rubes to social democracy and identity politics than they imagined, so be it. For the first time since the Progressive Era, liberals are contemplating the diminution of federal power. This is a happy turn of events, and one we should encourage. Political decentralization, something the Left resisted mightily throughout the twentieth century, offers them an opportunity to enjoy progressive policies here and now:

> Libertarianism has nothing to say about private communities except this: force and fraud are not permitted. So thousands or even millions of people could come together in areas like San Francisco and voluntarily create single-payer health schemes, gun control zones, income and wealth redistribution, radically progressive taxation, enforced diversity, limits on carbon emissions, free schools, collective child-raising, etc.—the whole panoply of progressive programs.

Conservatives too are starting to recognize that any sense of national identity or unity has been lost. Angelo Codevilla, a Senior Fellow at the Claremont Institute, recently wrote a remarkable essay titled "The Cold Civil War" that is very much worth reading. Codevilla, a serious scholar not prone to hyperbole, sees Trumpist America as nothing short of "in the throes of revolution":

> American society has divided along unreconcilable visions of the good, held by countrymen who increasingly regard each other as enemies. Any attempt by either side to coerce the other into submission augurs only the fate that has befallen other peoples who let

themselves slide into revolution. It follows that the path to peace must lie in each side's contentment to have its own way—but only among those who consent to it. This implies limiting the US government's reach to what it can grasp without wrecking what remains of our national cohesion.

Codevilla continues to use familiar conservative language like "statecraft" and "federalism," but the message of the article clearly shows him in the unfamiliar territory of proposing a radically decentralized America. He is a conservative who finally understands that conservatives simply cannot win under the current political arrangement. They've lost the culture wars, lost the budget wars, lost the mantle of limited government, and lost the Constitution. They exist only to slightly impede the progressive agenda, but even that slight opposition has earned them nothing but hatred and scorn. For a red-blooded, America-loving immigrant like Codevilla, this is unacceptable.

So like progressives he calls for some good old-fashioned Irish Democracy—widespread but passive resistance to central government edicts that impose progressive policies on red states that do not want such policies. Since administrative force can never overcome "waning consensus," what if Texas shut down abortion clinics or North Dakota instituted prayer in schools? What would, or could, the federal government do if dozens of states simply shrugged and decided to reject certain federal regulations or court decisions in matters of "health, education, welfare, and police"?

The answer, as libertarians have long argued, is not much. Three or four million federal employees are in no position to carry out federal rules once any national consensus has fallen apart. In fact, what Codevilla proposes sounds an awful lot like a . . . loose confederation of states. This is a refreshing development from the Claremont Institute, which has a history of lionizing the Great Centralizer Abraham Lincoln.

Claremont may not be the Heritage Foundation or *National Review*, but it is squarely within the boundaries of Conservatism, Inc. So when a publication like the *Claremont Review of Books* features an article calling for radical decentralization to avoid a hot civil war, we should take notice.

Political subsidiarity offers conservatives and progressives a way to coexist, maybe the only way. Hyperbole aside, is a shooting war really unthinkable at this point in America?

Now is the time for libertarians to seize the day and make the case for decentralization. There's never been a better time to sell it. It is time to rebrand libertarianism as a robust, pragmatic, and workable alternative to the phony universalism currently being peddled. Trump showed us the cracks in the globalist narrative. So rather than doubling down on that narrative, we should promote a libertarian vision that actually comports with human nature and reality.

The overarching libertarian political value is self-determination. Decentralization, secession, subsidiarity, and nullification are the mechanisms that move us closer to that value. Insisting on universal values, political or otherwise, is both a strategic and ethical mistake. The future is decentralized; why are so many libertarians arguing for the opposite?

Unless you're a Saudi or a Frenchman, the status of gay marriage or gun rights or any number of things in those countries ultimately is none of your business. This may seem unsatisfactory to libertarians, but only if we imagine that universalism trumps self-determination.

9

Democracy,
the God That's Failing

When Professor Hans-Hermann Hoppe made his famous argument against democracy back in 2001, the notion that voting was a lousy way to organize society was still radical even among many libertarians. Virtually everyone raised in a Western country over the past century grew up hearing "democracy" used as a synonym for wonderful, good, just, and valid. It takes a great deal of unlearning to overcome this as an adult, and to question the wisdom of representative government installed via democratic mechanisms.

Fast forward to 2017, however, and the case against democracy is being made right in front of our eyes. Witness Hillary Clinton, who not long ago gushed about our "sacred" right to vote—that is until her stupendous loss to Trump. Today she clings to the specious nonsense that the Russians somehow influenced our election by planting stories and using social media, which if true would be an excellent argument against voting rights. If the natives are so easily duped by a few silly posts in their Facebook feeds, why on earth is their vote meaningful or sacred?

Other progressives like Michael Moore demand that Trump be arrested, presumably for treason. Left-leaning cable news pundits openly call for Trump to resign or be impeached. Mainstream newspapers wonder whether he'll even finish his four-year term.

This article originally appeared February 17, 2017, on mises.org.

The overwhelming message from the media is that Trump is a disaster, an existential threat that must be stopped.

But it's not just progressives questioning democratic outcomes. Neoconservative Bill Kristol tweets that he'd rather be governed by an unaccountable deep state than Trump. Mild-mannered conservative moralist Dennis Prager, a reasonable and likeable Right winger in my view, argues quite seriously that we are in the midst of a second civil war with those who simply reject their electoral defeat. And the libertarianish jurist Richard Epstein, writing for the somnambulant Hoover Institution, unloads a litany of grievances against Trump that would make Bill Maher blush.

We should recall that as democratic elections go, Trump's victory was perfectly legitimate. Nobody seriously challenges his margins in the key states of Ohio, Pennsylvania, Wisconsin, and Florida. Lamentations about Clinton winning the so-called popular vote are irrelevant and blatantly partisan—the Electoral College is as much a part of the "rules" as having two senators per state.

Meanwhile in the UK, former Prime Minister Tony Blair employs the language of revolution in urging Remain forces to "rise up" against Brexit and overturn the referendum in Parliament. Never mind that Blair is no longer an elected official and holds no government office, never mind that both the referendum process and the Brexit vote were perfectly valid: he just doesn't like the results. His argument that Leave voters had "imperfect knowledge" is both hilarious and disingenuous: voters always have imperfect knowledge about candidates and policies prior to elections; pertinent new information always comes to light after elections. If Blair thinks we can start overturning elections based on any degree of voter ignorance, then I must suggest he begin with the vote in the House of Commons that made him PM. And why does he, a democrat, imagine some right to overturn election results at all?

It's time to call a spade a spade. All of this angst hardly comports with our supposed reverence for democracy. Again, Trump handily and fairly won a democratic election just three months ago.

If he's the devil, a wrecking ball that cannot be stopped by the other branches of government, then our entire constitutional system and its democratic mechanisms are defective. Why doesn't the #never-Trump movement take its arguments to their logical conclusion, and insist an electorate that would install Donald Trump never be allowed to vote again or have any say in organizing society?

The reality is becoming clear, even as it remains uncomfortable for many: democracy is a sham that should be opposed by all liberty-loving people. Voting and elections confer no legitimacy whatsoever on any government, and to the extent a democratic political process replaces outright war it should be seen as only slightly less horrific.

As I stated before the election last year:

> ... no matter who wins, millions of people—maybe 40 percent of the country—are going to view the winner as illegitimate and irredeemable.
>
> In fact, a recent Gallup poll cites that fully one-third of Americans won't trust the election results anyway—which is to say they don't trust government to hold an honest election.
>
> Trump vs. Hillary represents something much bigger: what we might call the end of politics, or at least the limits of politics. Americans, and Europeans too, are witnessing the end of the myth of democratic consensus. Democratic voting, so called, doesn't yield some noble compromise between Left and Right, but only an entrenched political class and its system of patronage.

Great libertarians like Thomas Jefferson have long warned against democracy, even as they uneasily accepted it as a necessary evil. Both Ludwig von Mises and Friedrich Hayek were democrats, men who championed both the virtues of an intellectual elite and the necessity of having that elite gain legitimacy for its ideas through public acceptance. Mises termed democracy a "method for the peaceful adjustment of government to the will of the majority."

Hayek viewed democracy as potentially wise if tempered by built-in safeguards to protect individual liberty.

But these men lived in very different times, coming as they did from pre-war Old Europe. We can't know what they would think of modern social democratic welfare states, or Trump, or Brexit. I suspect they would find democracy quite wanting, in terms of producing what either would consider a liberal society. Both were utilitarians (of a sort) in their economic thinking, and it's not hard to imagine they would take a consequentialist view of a society gone awry via democracy.

Things are getting strange in America when Michael Moore and Dennis Prager start to sound the same, and that's arguably a very good development. We are close to a time when the democracy illusion will be shattered, for good and all. Democracy was always a bad idea, one that encourages mindless majoritarianism, political pandering, theft, redistribution, war, and an entitlement mentality among supposedly noble voters. It's an idea whose time has passed, both on a national and international scale. The future of liberty is decentralized, and will be led by smaller breakaway nations and regions where real self-determination and real consensus is not an illusion. Jefferson and Hoppe were right about democracy, but it took Trump and Brexit to show the world how quickly elites abandon it when they don't prevail.

10

The Subsidiarity Principle

Leftwing vox.com has published a welcome and thoughtful piece on the virtues of devolving political and legal power away from the federal government toward states and localities. This is exactly the kind of conversation honest Americans need to have if we are serious about preventing the kind of political violence witnessed recently in Charlottesville and Berkeley. One overriding feature of the culture wars is that each side justifiably fears the other will impose its way of living through a winner takes all political system. Violence is a natural and predictable response to this, a means of circumventing the ballot box.

The political class makes its living from centralized power and the attendant division it causes. But why should ordinary Americans accept the false choice between one brand of centralized government and another, when the obvious solution is staring us in the face? Breaking up politically is far more practical, and far more humane.

Written by a conservative who apparently supported Evan McMullin in the 2016 election, the *Vox* article raises two pressing questions: whether centralized governance is desirable in a vast country of 330 million people, and more importantly whether it's even *possible*. Are overarching political solutions workable, or does politics simply enrich Washington, DC, while feeding the rapidly deteriorating culture war?

This article originally appeared August 28, 2017, on mises.org.

The author makes his central argument for subsidiarity as a peaceful approach for a large, diverse country:

> . . . decentralization of power requires more than just devolution of a few powers here or there, but a society-wide commitment to transferring power, authority, and responsibility back down the totem pole. A diverse society can sustain itself peacefully when its members are committed to solving problems as locally as possible, involving higher levels of government only when absolutely necessary.

He also uses the seemingly intractable issue of abortion to make his point:

> Where things get much trickier is where a more fundamental issue like abortion is concerned. On this issue in particular, many progressives and conservatives alike hope to achieve a victory that is far more total—more sweeping and national—than I think likely or desirable. That is, conservatives and progressives both seem to think that we need a federal rule about abortion. But we don't, and indeed such a rule poisons the well of national politics. The reason is blindingly obvious: There is no federal agreement about abortion.
>
> Ideologues on both sides will assert that, where highly charged moral issues are concerned, federalism is terrible: If abortion is wrong, it's wrong everywhere. If same-sex marriage is right, it's right everywhere. This is true in abstract moral terms, but it is not true in political terms, and the two are not the same, because it is immoral to compel a people to accept a set of laws with which they do not agree and which they cannot readily change.

Devolving political power is the first step toward making government smaller and less powerful in our lives. National and even supra-national governments are the biggest threats to human liberty and flourishing because they control the weapons of mass destruction: armies, nuclear missiles, central banks, economic sanctions, and trade tariffs. These are the elements of systemic contagion that should terrify us.

Your local city council may be dumb as a box of rocks or even evil, but at the very least it is far more accessible to you. Its damage is likely to be contained, and your ability to flee its jurisdiction may require nothing more than a cross-town U-Haul rental.

Subsidiarity is the most realistic and pragmatic approach to creating more freedom in our lifetimes. Winning 51 percent support for supposedly universalist political principles is a daunting challenge, especially for minority libertarians. We would do well instead to consider the Swiss federal model, which champions the subsidiarity principle:

> Powers are allocated to the Confederation, the cantons and the communes in accordance with the principle of subsidiarity.
>
> The Confederation only undertakes tasks that the cantons are unable to perform or which require uniform regulation by the Confederation.
>
> Under the principle of subsidiarity, nothing that can be done at a lower political level should be done at a higher level.

Imagine Hillary Clinton or Donald Trump campaigning on this idea in 2016: "I can't claim to know what's best for Des Moines or Bangor or Anchorage or Phoenix in every situation. I'm not omnipotent, and neither are 500-odd members of Congress. We should leave most things up to the people who actually live in those towns. Vote for me if you agree."

Subsidiarity is not perfect, just better. Freedom, in the political sense of the word, means the ability to live without government coercion (anarchists and minarchists debate whether all government is inherently coercive). It does not mean the ability to live under broadly agreed-upon liberal norms, simply because truly universalist political norms are so elusive. Free societies don't attempt to impose themselves politically on electoral minorities any more than they attempt to impose themselves militarily on neighboring countries. Politically unyoking different constituencies in America makes far more sense than attempting to contain the hatred and division created by mass majority outcomes.

The world is moving toward decentralization, flattening itself and replacing hierarchies with networks. Libertarians should work to move politics and government in the same direction. Subsidiary is real diversity in practice.

11

All Crises Are Local

"South Dakota is not New York City."

A seemingly innocuous statement, made by Governor Kristi Noem in response to calls for her to issue a coronavirus shutdown across a state with the motto "Under God the People Rule."

South Dakota, after all, is one of the least densely populated states in the vast American West. Surely local circumstances should inform local responses to a communicable disease?

Not so, according to Noem's scolds at change.org. They want the same "theory" applied in Brooklyn and in prairie towns with eleven residents per square mile.

To her tremendous credit, Governor Noem has held firm against the tide of state officials ordering lockdowns and shelter-

---

This article originally appeared April 6, 2020, on mises.org.

in-place directives. As of today, five US states do not have state-wide shutdown orders in place, and some sheriffs too have stood bravely against impositions of soft martial law.

Here are some of Governor Noem's excellent recent statements regarding South Dakota's response to the pandemic:

> The calls to apply for a one-size-fits-all approach to this problem is herd mentality.
>
> The people are primarily responsible for their safety.
>
> Our constitution ensures that the citizen's right is protected. I agree with the role of our government as set forth in our state and in our national constitution.
>
> [I oppose] draconian measures much like the Chinese government has done [and] actions we've seen European governments take that limit [the] citizen's rights.

Refreshing, and also a needed reminder that all crises are local. No matter how rich you are or where you live, you are enormously dependent on localized medical care, food, water, electricity, gas, and general lawful behavior. Every calorie, kilowatt, and drop of water must make its way to your location no matter how complex the underlying economy is today. Doctors, nurses, and drugs must be available within a reasonable distance of your location. None of the physical substances necessary for your survival can be sourced from a global supply chain unless "last mile" delivery remains intact. If faraway production facilities, farms, warehouses, trains, trucks, and power plants break down, eventually Governor Noem's constituents will feel it. People seem to intuit the local impact of a global crisis, and the reality that the greater world is not coming to save them. South Dakotans are entitled to think locally, out of self-preservation, in this crisis.

So are Japanese, Singaporeans, South Koreans, and Swedes, for that matter. There is no UN agreement or statement at work concerning the pandemic, nor any universally agreed-upon supra-national guidelines. International bodies such as the World Health Organization have been unable to project authority during the crisis, much less gain international compliance with their shifting recommendations. Countries around the world have implemented a hodgepodge of policies, and they've done so unilaterally. China brutally locked down its Hubei Province, while Sweden chose to keep public life largely unaffected, with virtually no quarantines or business shutdowns. Many countries chose an intermediate path.

In Europe, the 1985 Schengen Area Agreement allowing open travel between twenty-six European countries has broken down due to the virus, with Germany, France, Spain, Austria, Switzerland, and others closing off borders with armed guards. In a crisis, it turns out a German or French passport really is not a "European" passport after all. Nationalities and citizenship, the bane of political globalists, exist. Whether this fact of life is inherently illiberal depends both on one's perspective and how various nations act internally under duress. Is Germany too trenchant in its response to the virus and Sweden too liberal? Who's to say?

The calculation becomes more and more difficult at scale, moving from the local to regional to national to international to global level. Crises remind us exactly why local matters.

This is exactly what we should expect, and want, in a pandemic: competing visions as to the severity and scope of the problem, differing localized approaches, experimental treatments, and nimble entrepreneurial provision of resources and supplies.

To an extent, there will be a scoreboard. Some countries and some US states will fare better than others. But questions about top-down control from Washington, DC, or beyond, will not go away. Federal agencies such as the Centers for Disease Control and Prevention have looked foolish and impotent throughout this crisis, as has the Trump administration's infectious disease expert Dr. Anthony Fauci. If in hindsight cheap antimalarial drugs and antibiotics prove to be effective treatments, the entire narrative of ventilators and lockdowns will appear foolish and destructive.

Yes, there will be accusations, recriminations, and calls for more bureaucracy and more regulations. The political class will gain; the American people will lose. But there is a silver lining as our already dangerously polarized country begins to understand more deeply how South Dakota really isn't New York City at all—and question why that same political class wants one set of rules for 330 million people. After all, if Brooklyn and Sioux Falls don't need the same policy on coronavirus, what about taxes, guns, abortion, climate change, and everything else?

12

What Will It Take for Americans to Consider Breaking Up?

It's one thing for mass democracy to produce bad results, in the form of elected politicians or enacted policies. It's another when the democratic *process* itself breaks down because nobody trusts the vote or the people who count it. But that's precisely where we are.

As things stand at this writing, last night's presidential election remains undecided and looking ugly. At least six states are still uncalled, and both the Trump and Biden camps have their legal teams claiming victory. We may be in for days, weeks, or even months of legal skirmishes, all of which can only add to our intense political (or more accurately cultural) breakdown.

This article originally appeared November 4, 2020, on mises.org.

Today, perhaps 140 million American voters are in purgatory, fearfully wondering what will happen to them if the other guy wins. This is nothing short of a national psychosis, absurd yet deadly real. And it gets worse every four years, despite the narrowing of any "policy" differences between the two parties over recent decades. If anything, presidential votes are overwhelmingly about tribal affiliations with *our kind of person*, not substantive ideology.

Yes, this is unhealthy. And yes, the psychosis manifests because the stakes are so high. It manifests because government is far too big and rapacious; lawmaking and jurisprudence too centralized in DC; the unitary executive presidency too powerful; and society too politicized. But these are unhelpful truisms. Plenty of Americans abjectly support more government, more centralized political power, an omnipotent president and Supreme Court, and the sharp politicization of every facet of life.

In *Nation, State, and Economy* Mises talks about a "liberal nationalism" and explains what a confident nation requires:

> A nation that believes in itself and its future, a nation that means to stress the sure feeling that its members are bound to one another not merely by accident of birth but also by the common possession of a culture that is valuable above all to each of them.

What, then, is the common culture Americans possess? What binds us together as a unifying principle? Is it language? Religion? Constitutionalism? Love of country? (What country?) Markets? It certainly is not obvious, and few of us feel optimistic about America's future. Worse still, covid lockdowns have attenuated the ostensibly nonpolitical spheres of life—from family and work to sports, dining, movies, and travel. When we stare at ourselves in the mirror all day, and read everyone's innermost thoughts on social media, we find familiarity breeds contempt.

Regardless of how the election turns out, it's obvious America is not much of a country anymore, much less a nation. The sooner we accept this, the sooner we can get to work asserting the principles of federalism, subsidiarity, nullification, and even secession. None of the current frictions will get better over time, but they can get much worse—and our most important task must be to avoid any movement toward outright civil war.

There are workable baby steps toward this. Law professor Frank Buckley writes about "secession lite" in his sober and reasoned book on the subject of a national breakup. Buckley sees a third-way approach between our current dysfunction and an outright breakup into new political entities, primarily through aggressive federalism and state nullification. This echoes sentiments from Professor Angelo Codevilla, who similarly argues that the feds simply lack the manpower to enforce federal laws and edicts on recalcitrant states. Just as blue states declared sanctuary cities as havens from Trump's immigration policies, red states could restrict all manner of federal dictates (abortion and gun control come to mind) while simply daring the feds to interfere. At the end of the day, Codevilla reminds us, there are only a few million of them and many millions of us. And progressives too share this sentiment; even if Biden prevails, they remain shaken by the degree of Trump support. In fact the 2016 election saw *the New Republic* advocate nothing short of a renunciation of the hated red states.

Things don't have to be this way. Americans are lovely people—generous, open. But politics divides them in the worst and most unnecessary ways. It's time to break up, and millions of us sense this instinctively. So what's stopping us?

For one, secession remains bound up with the Civil War and Confederate slavery in the American psyche, distant in time as they are. Manifest Destiny and the westward expansion resulted in a nice, round number of fifty states, a nice, big American number. Throw in a few specious Supreme Court decisions like *Texas v. White*, and it's no surprise many Americans still have concrete between their ears on the subject.

But Trump may have changed all that. And if you want political liberty to retain a foothold in the US, if you want Misesian liberalism to show a heartbeat in the West, you should cheer this.

Americans by and large are lovely people—open, generous, friendly, and quick to forgive. A hyper-politicized environment, where everything is existential and rooted in race, sex, and sexuality, is deeply at odds with our character and well-being. We deserve to live peaceably as neighbors, even if that means breaking up and creating new political entities. Addressing the reality of our dysfunction is not divisive; *the divide already exists*. Our task is to apprehend this and end the charade of one nation.

Civil Society and Culture

13

The Language Vandals

L anguage is a critical tool for communication among humans; we cry "watch out" when a speeding car hurtles toward a pedestrian. We also think of language as a cognitive tool for society at large, since all human learning is closely tied to how we learn and process language.

Yet sometimes we forget language is also an important social and cultural institution. And like all institutions, it is subject to corruption, in the form of capture by elites with agendas quite contrary to those of average people. Since language shapes our understanding of all human interactions, academics from all disciplines—but particularly social scientists—ought to pay more attention to linguistic corruption. When language becomes politicized, managed, and policed, we ought to notice, and we ought to fight back.

I make this very point in an upcoming article titled "Evolution or Corruption: The Imposition of Political Language in the West Today," which will be published this fall in the Italian journal *Etica & Politica* (put out by the University of Trieste Department of

This article originally appeared in Etica & Politica/Ethics & Politics 24, no. 2 (2022): 55–74.

Philosophy). The article argues that top-down impositions, rather than natural evolution, often drive changes in language. It analogizes the linguistic "marketplace" with the market for goods and services. Impositions are akin to central planning, while evolution is akin to spontaneous order in the marketplace. The former occurs when elites in politics, media, journalism, and academia attempt to influence both the words we use and the meaning of those words. This is invariably in service of a statist agenda, just as economic interventions serve preferred interests at the expense of overall wealth and efficiency. The constant use and repetition of the word "gender" (a term relating to grammar) when we should use "sex" is one obvious example of imposed, corrupted language in service of a political agenda (trans). By contrast, the Middle English "whilst" sounds odd to our ear today—having naturally evolved into "while" without obvious or heavy-handed direction.

The great Spanish Austro-libertarian economist Jesús Huerta de Soto applies Carl Menger's theory on the evolution of money to language:

> Thus there is an unconscious social process of learning by imitation which explains how the pioneering behavior of these most successful and creative individuals catches on and eventually extends to the rest of society. Also, due to this evolutionary process, those societies which first adopt successful principles and institutions tend to spread and prevail over other social groups. Although Menger developed his theory in relation to the origin and evolution of money, he also mentions that the same essential theoretical framework can be easily applied to the study of the origins and development of language, as well as to our present topic, juridical institutions. Hence the paradoxical fact that the moral, juridical, economic, and linguistic institutions which are most important and essential to man's life in society are not of his own creation, because he lacks the necessary intellectual might to assimilate the vast body of random information that these institutions generate.

On the contrary, these institutions inevitably and spontaneously emanate from the social process of human interaction which Menger believes should be the main research in economics.[1]

Today, it appears linguistic interventionism is alive and well in the West. Language is a subset of culture, albeit a very important subset, and we can hardly expect progressives to leave it alone. Like culture, language is not property, and it cannot be "owned." But it can be influenced and steered by linguistic vandals seeking to topple old understandings and leave us all overwhelmed and demoralized by the ever-shifting new terminology.

In the quaint, innocent days of 2015, we still called this progressive impulse "political correctness." I attempted to define it then:

> Political correctness is the conscious, designed manipulation of language intended to change the way people speak, write, think, feel, and act, in furtherance of an agenda.
>
> PC is best understood as propaganda, which is how I suggest we approach it. But unlike propaganda, which historically has been used by governments to win favor for a particular campaign or effort, PC is all-encompassing. It seeks nothing less than to mold us into modern versions of Marx's un-alienated society man, freed of all his bourgeois pretensions and humdrum social conventions.
>
> Like all propaganda, PC fundamentally is a lie. It is about refusing to deal with the underlying nature of reality, in fact attempting to alter that reality by legislative and social fiat. A is no longer A.

---

[1] Jesús Huerta de Soto, "The Emergence of Traditional Legal Principles According to Menger, Hayek, and Leoni," in *Money, Bank Credit, and Economic Cycles*, translated by Melinda A. Stroup (Auburn, AL: Ludwig von Mises Institute, 2006), pp. 21–22.

Today, of course, PC is obsolete—replaced entirely by the far broader concept of "woke," which goes well beyond language. And to be sure, "woke" is so vague and so overused as to be a poignant example of George Orwell's meaningless words, which I discuss at length in the article. Meaningless words, Orwell explained, are used in consciously dishonest ways in furtherance of an agenda. They become disembodied from any real meaning or definition, serving as empty slogans for things we like ("democracy") or things we don't like ("fascism").

Here is an example of a progressive using "woke" as code for "the correct left progressive attitudes":

> "Woke" is defined as being aware of injustice in society, especially, but not limited to, racism. Which doesn't seem anything that most people would be opposed to, especially superhero comics, which would seem to be all about fighting injustice but, I guess, welcome to the internet.

Well, no, that is distinctly not what "woke" means. It is self-serving claptrap: "All good people (Us) are woke, which is really just left-wing code for caring and empathetic! Who could deny injustice and racism! I'd hate to think what unwoke people (Them) really believe, ho ho ho!" But these language imposers are not good people at all, or even well-intentioned people. Quite the opposite; they are lying, dissembling, projecting ideologues who want to commandeer the English language. Woke is the animating force behind today's relentless progressive attempts to impose and corrupt language to advance a host of wholly politicized movements.

From my paper:

> Even five years ago, the top-down or centralized force operating to corrupt the language of politics and economics could have been broadly termed "political correctness" (PC). Today the term is obsolete, another example of the rapid (unnatural) evolution of usage in Western society. PC referred more narrowly to acceptable speech, whereas

today's linguistic enforcers seek to impose a whole new mindset, attitude, and way of thinking. Thus, PC has been replaced by an even broader and more amorphous term, "woke." Woke, whether a slur or not, may be used very broadly to represent strident left progressive beliefs regarding race, sex, sexuality, equality, climate change, and the like. Woke demands ever-changing language, and constantly creates new words while eliminating old ones. As a result, "cancellation," de-platforming, and loss of employment or standing all loom large, giving pause to speakers and writers who must consider a new woke orthodoxy.

Ultimately, imposed language attempts to control our *actions*. When we broadly consider politically correct or woke worldviews—i.e. an activist mindset concerned with promoting amorphous social justice—the linguistic element is straightforward.

I'm afraid the paper is embargoed until publication, so I can't provide the actual text yet. Both Orwell and F.A. Hayek figure prominently in it, and it is full of examples of imposed, contorted language issued by politicians, CEOs, central bankers, media figures, advertisers, academics, and elites of every stripe. It argues that language is worth defending from the linguistic vandals at every turn. In fact, language is the one institution we can defend every day through our own thoughts, words, and writing. It is guerrilla warfare, fought every day in the trenches.

14

Notre Dame and What Was Lost

Yesterday's terrible fire at the Notre-Dame Cathedral reminds us how quickly centuries of accumulated "cultural capital" can be destroyed. Oak timbers dating from the 1200s in the roof and spire were lost forever; some priceless stained glass windows appear to have suffered damage. As the saying goes, France is the heart of the West, Paris is the heart of France, and Notre Dame is the heart of Paris—and as such the sight of the iconic church ablaze makes an uneasy if simplistic metaphor for the decline of the West.

"Cultural capital" here of course means something far broader than economic definitions of capital as financial wealth or factors of production. Even the broader Austrian view of capital as heterogeneous production goods, what Rothbard termed an "intricate, delicate, interweaving *structure* of capital goods," can't capture the sum of wealth in a society. Capital ultimately is measurable, reducible to units, while the value of Notre Dame to Catholics around the world cannot be measured. We cannot quantify the cost of its damage or destruction in purely economic terms. But we can recognize a loss. Hundreds of years of wealth bound up in the beauty of Notre Dame's roof and spire are now lost to us forever.

The blogger Bionic Mosquito reminds us that civilizational wealth compounds over time, and thus wealth can be material, cultural, spiritual, even civilizational:

This article originally appeared April 16, 2019, on mises.org.

. . . Think of wealth not just on a balance sheet, but wealth in terms of culture, accumulated wisdom and knowledge, the captured savings of time.

Accumulation and time are key. Healthy societies build and preserve wealth, which is to say they are made up of individuals who strive to create more than they consume. The people who built Notre Dame over two centuries ago, using rudimentary pulleys and scaffolding, certainly did not expect to see the end results of their work. In fact no single Pope, architect, financier, mason, artist, laborer, or French monarch saw the project through from start to completion. But they built something lasting, something of incalculable benefit to future generations. They created wealth lasting far beyond their lifetimes.

All healthy societies do this. The notion of being concerned with things beyond one's lifetime is innately human. Humans are hardwired to build societies, and the most ambitious humans have always sought to build lasting monuments and modes of living. That's not possible unless people work toward a future they will not enjoy themselves. This was especially true for our ancient primitive ancestors, who lived very short and difficult lives. We can imagine how much they wanted to have lasting forms of sustenance: food, water, clothing, shelter—instead of having to produce that sustenance day after day.

In fact, this trait perhaps more than any other is the hallmark of civilization. We can call it many things, but we might just say healthy societies create capital. They consume less than they produce. This capital accumulation creates an upward spiral that increases investment and productivity, making the future richer and brighter. Capital accumulation made it possible for human populations to develop beyond subsistence misery. It made the agricultural, industrial, and digital revolutions possible.

Technical know-how, artistry, and craftsmanship also represent forms of wealth which can be lost over time, and apparently have been. Kiona N. Smith, writing in *Ars Technica*, "Notre Dame Cathedral will never be the same, but it can be rebuilt," questions whether Notre Dame really can be rebuilt in quite the same way:

> While architects have enough detailed information about the cathedral to pull off a technically very precise reconstruction, the craftsmanship is unlikely to be the same. Today, the stone that makes up the cathedral would be cut using machinery, not by hand by small armies of stonemasons as in the 12th century. "Nineteenth-century and 20th-century Gothic buildings always look a little dead, because the stone doesn't bear the same marks of the mason's hand," [Columbia University art historian Stephen] Murray told *Ars Technica*.

Civilization is far more than just economics, but it needs economics. Mises cautions us that it "will and must perish if the nations continue to pursue the course which they entered upon under the spell of doctrines rejecting economic thinking." So when we consider the sad spectacle of Notre Dame burning, we should ask ourselves whether the politics and economics of our age encourage or discourage building wealth for future generations. Even if one reduces the inheritance of Western countries today to material well-being, the threat of losing what makes us rich certainly concerns us all. Short-term political thinking, coupled with demand-driven mania in fiscal and monetary policy, can consume our future just as fire consumed the roof of Notre Dame.

15

Getting Liberalism Wrong

Yoram Hazony, author of *The Virtue of Nationalism* and one leader of a new "national conservatism" project, recently wrote an important and compelling article for *Quillette* titled "The Challenge of Marxism." Hazony says out loud what few Western intellectuals will admit, namely that liberalism is not holding and has not triumphed in 2020 America and Europe. We have not reached the end of history.

Our criticism lies not with Hazony's thesis, but with his particular conception of what liberalism is, what it has become, and what it should be.

Hazony laments, correctly, the expressly Marxist takeover of once liberal institutions, especially "mainstream media, universities, tech companies, philanthropies, and government bureaucracies." Marx, it turns out, has not been contained to the faculty lounge. Instead an identity-focused variant of Marxism, with new class jargon and new victims, finds support in newsrooms, corporate boardrooms, advertising agencies, arts, and every reach of politics. The rapidity of this illiberal shift worries him, and ought to worry all of us, as it threatens to replace favored Enlightenment doctrines of freedom, justice, and legal equality with rigid new forms of oppressor-oppressed class narratives.

Worse still, the Marxist campaign by definition destroys what came before it. This includes traditions, religion, and an intellectual landscape of open inquiry from which conservatives like Hazony

---

This article originally appeared August 26, 2020, on mises.org.

urge us to draw commonality. Once liberalism succumbs to Marxism, and not incrementally, the very way we organize society is cast into chaos:

> But while Marxists know very well that their aim is to destroy the intellectual and cultural traditions that are holding liberalism in place, their liberal opponents for the most part refuse to engage in the kind of conservatism that would be needed to defend their traditions and strengthen them. Indeed, liberals frequently disparage tradition, telling their children and students that all they need is to reason freely and "draw your own conclusions."
>
> The result is a radical imbalance between Marxists, who consciously work to bring about a conceptual revolution, and liberals whose insistence on "freedom from inherited tradition" provides little or no defense—and indeed, opens the door for precisely the kinds of arguments and tactics that Marxists use against them. This imbalance means that the dance moves only in one direction, and that liberal ideas tend to collapse before Marxist criticism in a matter of decades.

Certainly Hazony is correct in his analysis of Marxism's swift resurgence in America and the West, and rightfully concerned about it. But there is a nagging sense that Hazony does not quite get the antidote to Marxist revolution—liberalism—correct. Yes, an ersatz form of liberalism has failed in the West and appears to be in full retreat. That form, however, is mostly just a vague lump of beliefs today's liberals hold, or at least held twenty minutes ago. It is not the rigorous and definable conception Ludwig von Mises provided one hundred years ago. And I fear Hazony uses *liberalism* as a general catchall term for what today's liberals claim to believe, rather than a coherent doctrine.

This concern surfaced in my 2018 interview with Hazony, where I gently suggested he had superficially misread Mises as some avatar of hyperrational *homo economicus*. In fact, Mises took pains throughout his work to consider culture, language, nation-hood, religion, and intermediary institutions standing between individuals and uncaring markets. To Hazony's great credit, he agreed to read more and reconsider Mises.

The *Quillette* article, though, evinces Hazony's ongoing perspective of what we might call modal liberals. Absent moral grounding in religion, eschewing tradition and history, and hostile to individual nation-states, Hazony's liberals lack intellectual mooring against the mob. When Marxists come for them, it is far easier and professionally far wiser simply to stay quiet and hope for the best.

This vague kind of ungrounded liberalism explains Hazony's persistent tendency to take political and ideological pronouncements at face value. Thus self-appointed liberals, from Noam Chomsky to Hillary Clinton to Mises and Hayek, are all cut from the same cloth. If they say they're liberal, they are. But there is a big difference between Hillary Clinton and Ludwig von Mises which cannot be dismissed merely by broadly terming both liberals or even "neoliberals." This kind of imprecision does Hazony no favors.

Yet this Hazonyite caricature of liberalism is hardly made up out of whole cloth. It arose in the second half of the twentieth century, and persists in the twenty-first, among the self-proclaimed classical liberals populating many nonprofits, NGOs, media outlets, and Beltway think tanks. It is the liberalism of the Cato Institute and the Brookings Institution, of Professor Deirdre McCloskey and Professor Nadine Strossen, of David Brooks at the *New York Times* and David French at *National Review*. These quasi liberals, like left progressives, share a profound sense that history has an arc: everything will get better all the time, if only recalcitrant Americans stop resisting the program. It requires relentless political universalism, one set of rules and one kind of government for everyone, everywhere.

In this view, liberalism is a *way of thinking*, a kind of enlightened worldview adopted by *good people*. Liberalism becomes almost undefinable by its breadth: an interconnected passel of open-minded and tolerant attitudes across a swath of "social" issues. Cosmopolitanism, reason, tolerance, feminism, antiracism, and a healthy degree of support for egalitarian democracy are at the fore; economics is not the focus. Yes, free markets and property rights play a supporting role, but modal liberalism is more concerned with human self-actualization made possible only with the correct kinds of left-cultural attitudes. Markets work, they make people better off materially, and most of all they yield the kinds of societies and people liberals like.

The questions for this brand of liberalism write themselves. Do its adherents really think the twentieth century represents a liberal triumph in the West? Has mass democratic voting produced liberal societies? Are Brexit and the Trump presidency illegitimate per se, or merely because liberals didn't like the outcomes? Looking at the last century, should we count two bloody world wars, central banking and fiat currencies, income taxes, the rise of managerial superstates, vast social insurance and welfare programs, and diminutions of property rights unimaginable to our grandparents as liberal successes? What exactly is liberal, and what is not?

The aforementioned Mises explained this one hundred years ago. His conception of liberalism, particularly found in his interwar books *Nation, State, and Economy* (1919) and *Liberalism* (1927), show Mises grounding the organization of society in property and market cooperation:

> The program of liberalism, therefore, if condensed into a single word, would have to read: property, that is, private ownership of the means of production (for in regard to commodities ready for consumption, private ownership is a matter of course and is not disputed even by the socialists and communists). All the other demands of liberalism result from this fundamental demand.
>
> Side by side with the word "property" in the program of liberalism one may quite appropriately place the words "freedom" and "peace."

Here we condense Misesian liberalism down to its definable essence: property, freedom, and peace. There is nothing mushy or fuzzy here. For those willing to read on, Mises provides definitions.

- Without property we are utterly vulnerable and without agency, standing naked on a patch of earth. The first calorie, the first drop of water, the first stitch of clothing all represent property. What we create or produce from nature represents our will and actions made manifest in physical (or digital) form. Property, not vague ideals of personal liberties or individual rights, sets the stage for all human activity.

- Without freedom, by which Mises meant independence from the arbitrary state power, we lose mastery over our lives and labors. For Mises, freedom is not some inchoate aspiration or muddled set of conditions to "live your best life." It is not liberation from worldly wants, from unhappiness, or from social opprobrium. It is the ability to live and direct one's life largely free of state coercion, nothing more and certainly nothing less. Misesian liberalism recognizes involuntary servitude as a tremendous evil, but it also necessarily recognizes *partial* servitude to a rapacious government as contrary to our nature.

- Without peace, man loses his ability to enjoy property or exercise freedom. War symbolizes the refusal of men to deal with one another cooperatively and the descent into an animalistic state of nature. "War, carnage, destruction, and devastation we have in common with the predatory beasts of the jungle; constructive labor is our distinctively human characteristic."

This Misesian program, supplemented with his endorsement of aggressive self-determination and national secession to deal with inevitable political disputes, presents a very different and far more precise form of liberalism.

Would Hillary Clinton or Paul Krugman, both Hazonyite "liberals," hold property as sacrosanct and argue against zoning or redistributive taxes? Would Kamala Harris or Rachel Maddow argue that freedom ought to include the ability to enact localized abortion or gun laws? Would Joe Biden, supporter of Black Lives Matter, condemn the burning of auto dealerships in Kenosha as dangerous preludes to that most illiberal possibility, namely outright civil war?

Dr. Hazony's overly broad conception of liberalism as simply the worldview of liberals may render it meaningless. I am sure he would agree that we don't fight Marxism with platitudes or displays of tolerance; we fight it with a robust and better set of clearly defined principles: property, self-determination, markets, and peace. Mises—not vague platitudes about tolerance emanating from the dying political class—provides the polarity opposite Marx. Mises's "mere" economics is in fact the understanding of human cooperation and choice in the face of scarcity, and it gives us the blueprint for organizing a wealthy and just society. To the extent conservatives like Hazony can agree with this blueprint, Misesian liberalism is the robust counter to Marxist authoritarianism. But Hazony must give up a significant degree of state if he hopes to preserve any degree of nation.

Pandemic Government

16

The Absurdity
of Covid "Cases"

Today's headlines announced Donald and Melania Trump "tested positive" for covid-19. Another claims nineteen thousand Amazon workers "got" covid-19 on the job. Both of these pseudostories are sure to ignite another absurd media frenzy.

As always, the story keeps changing: Remember ventilators, flatten the curve, the next two weeks are crucial, etc.? Remember Nancy Pelosi in Chinatown back in February, urging everyone to visit? Remember Fauci dismissing masks as useless? Why should we believe anything the political/media complex tells us now?

So what do these headlines really mean? What exactly is a covid "case"?

Since the beginning of the coronavirus outbreak, most US media outlets have been exceedingly credulous and complicit in their reporting. Journalists almost uniformly promote what we can call the "prolockdown" narrative, which is to wildly exaggerate the

---

This article originally appeared October 2, 2020, on mises.org.

risks from covid-19 to serve a political agenda. They may be motivated to hurt Trump politically, to promote a more socialist "new
normal," or simply to drive more clicks and views. Bad news sells.
But the bias is clear and undeniable.

This explains why media outlets use the terms "case" and "infection" so loosely, to the point of actively misinforming the public. All
of the endless talk about testing, testing, testing served to obscure
two important facts. First, the tests themselves are almost laugh-
ably unreliable in producing both false positives and negatives.
And what is the point? Are we going to test people again and again,
every time they go out to the grocery or bump into a neighbor?
Second, detecting virus particles or droplets in a human's respiratory tract tells us very little. It certainly does not tell us they are
sick, or transmitting sickness to anyone.

Take a perfectly healthy person with no particular symptoms
and swab the inside of their nose. If the culture shows the pres-
ence of *staphylococcus aureus*, do we insist they have a staph infection? When someone drives to work without incident or accident,
do we create statistics about their exposure to traffic?

A virus is not a disease. Only a very small percentage of those
exposed to the virus itself—SARS-CoV-2—show any kind of
acute respiratory symptoms, or what we can call "coronavirus disease."

The only meaningful statistics show the incidence of serious
illness, hospitalizations, and deaths. The single most important
statistic among these is the infection fatality rate (IFR). Data col-
lected through July shows that the IFR for those under age forty-
five is actually *lower* than that of the common flu. The covid-19
IFR rises for those over fifty, but it is hardly a death sentence. And
the data does not segregate those with preexisting health issues
caused by obesity, diabetes, and heart disease. If we could see data
only for reasonably healthy people under fifty, the numbers would
be even more reassuring.

Mild or asymptomatic covid cases are effectively meaningless. The world is full of bacteria and viruses, and sometimes they make us a bit sick for a few days. There are millions of them in the world all around us, on our skin, in our nose and respiratory tract, in our organs. We are meant to live with them, which is why we all have immune systems designed to help us coexist and adapt to ever-changing organisms. We develop antibodies naturally, or we attempt to stimulate them through vaccines, but ultimately our own immune systems have to deal with covid-19. The virus will always be out there waiting, on the other side of any lockdown or mask—so we might as well get on with it.

From day one the focus should have been on boosting immunity through exercise, fresh air, sunlight, proper dietary supplementation, and the promotion of general well-being. Instead our politicians, bureaucrats, and media insisted on business lockdowns, school closures, distancing, isolation, masks, and the mirage of a fast, effective vaccine. As with almost everything in life, state intervention made the situation worse. We can only hope many governors are removed from office, either by impeachment or at the next election. Several, including Andrew Cuomo in New York and Gretchen Whitmer in Michigan, should face criminal charges for their lawless edicts. There is no due process exception for "public health."

Lockdowns were never justified, either in terms of the covid-19 risk or the staggering economic tradeoffs, which will be felt for decades. They certainly are not justified now, given seven months of additional data showing that the transmission and lethality of covid-19 are not particularly worse than previous SARS, swine flu, or Ebola pandemics. We still don't know how many of the reported two hundred thousand US covid-19 deaths were *actually caused* by the SARS-CoV-2 respiratory disease, or simply reflect people who died of other causes after exposure to covid-19. We do know that the harms caused by the lockdowns far outweigh the harms posed by the covid-19 virus.

17

Unmask America

We have had nearly eight months of life and liberty stolen from us by politicians and their hysteria-promoting accomplices in media. How much more will we accept?

Enough is enough. It is time to stop wearing masks, or at the very least to eliminate mask mandates in all settings.

This is especially urgent for children in schools and universities, who suffer the effects of masks for long hours each day despite being at exceedingly low risk for death or serious illness from covid.

We have a responsibility, once and for all, to reject the ludicrous, ever-shifting narratives underpinning masks as effective impediments to the spread of covid infections.

> Seriously people—STOP BUYING MASKS! They are NOT effective in preventing general public from catching #Coronavirus
> —former US Surgeon General Jerome Adams in February 2020.

The story changed from "masks don't work" to "masks may work," to "masks work and you must wear one." Now the narrative switches yet again: "Cloth masks don't work, so you should wear a surgical or 'well-fitted' mask," or even wear two!

Note that even as covid evolves into a *less* dangerous omicron variant, we are supposed to *increase* the hysteria level by wearing masks intended for surgeons maintaining a sterile environment

---

This article originally appeared January 20, 2022, on mises.org.

over open wounds. We are told this by the same political, medical, and media figures who have been "frequently wrong but never in doubt" about all things covid over the past two long years. And they spoke with just as much bogus certainty then as they do now.

Perversely, the Biden administration recently ordered 400 million surgical N95 masks for distribution across the country. Since N95 masks are considered disposable, and meant to be worn at most for perhaps forty hours, it is unclear what happens in a week or two when 330 million Americans run out of their "free" personal protective equipment.

The UK has sensibly ended its mask mandates, both in public places (offices and other workplaces, bars, restaurants, sporting events, theaters) and thankfully schools. One young university student broke down in tears at the news, lamenting the inhumanity of her experience over the past two years. As British health secretary Savid Javid stated, "We must learn to live with covid in the same way we live with flu."

Amen.

The arguments against masks are straightforward.

- Masks don't work. Or at least cloth masks don't.

Even the Centers for Disease Control and Prevention now admits what Dr. Anthony Fauci told the world in February 2020: cloth masks don't work and there is no reason to wear one:

> "The typical mask you buy in the drug store is not really effective in keeping out virus, which is small enough to pass through material. It might, however, provide some slight benefit in keep out gross droplets if someone coughs or sneezes on you."
>
> I do not recommend that you wear a mask, particularly since you are going to a very low risk location.

CNN's dubious medical expert Dr. Lena Wen, previously an übermasker, now tells us cloth masks are "little more than facial decorations. And heroic skeptic Dr. Jay Bhattacharya cites both a Danish study and a Bangladeshi study which found cloth masks show little efficacy in preventing covid.

Are we seriously prepared to wear tight and uncomfortable surgical masks all day to evade omicron?

- Masks are filthy.

Humans lungs and our respiratory system are designed to inhale nitrogen and oxygen and exhale carbon dioxide. Carbon dioxide is literally a waste product, removed from the blood via our lungs. Masks may not trap injurious levels of carbon dioxide against our nose and mouth, but they certainly get filthy very quickly unless changed constantly. They also encourage mouth breathing, which can cause "mask mouth" symptoms including acne, bad breath, tender gums, and lip irritation.

Why would we ever interfere with natural breathing unless we felt sick, displayed symptoms, and were worried about infecting others? And in that case, why not just stay home?

- Masks are dehumanizing.

Humans communicate verbally and nonverbally, and masks impede both forms. Masks muffle and distort our words. Our facial expressions are important cues to everyone around us; without those cues, communication and understanding suffer. Infants and toddlers may be most affected, as a lack of facial engagement with parents and loved ones impedes the human connections and attachments formed during childhood.

Perhaps most disturbing, however, are the symbolic effects when millions of Americans dutifully wear masks based on flimsy evidence provided by deeply unimpressive people. Facelessness—the lack of individual identity, personality, and looks—is inherently dehumanizing and dystopian. Like prison or military uniforms, masks reduce our personal characteristics. Mask are muzzles, symbols of rote acquiescence to an ugly new normal nobody asked for or voted for.

- Risk is inevitable.

Risk is omnipresent, and heavily subjective (e.g., covid risk var-
ies enormously with age and comorbidities). Nobody has a right to
force interventions like masks on others, just as nobody has a right
to a hypothetical germ-free landscape. Exhalation is not aggression,
short of purposefully attempting to sicken others. People wearing
masks arguably shed slightly fewer covid virus particles than those
not, but this does not justify banning the latter from public life. As
always, the overwhelming burden of justification for any intervention—including mask mandates—must rest on those proposing it,
not those opposing it.

In sum, Americans are not children. Tradeoffs are part of every
policy, whether government officials admit this or not. We know
how to coexist with flu, just as we live with countless bacteria and
viruses in our environment. We will similarly coexist with covid.
The goal is not to eliminate germs, and zero covid is an absurdity.
A healthy immune system, built up through diet, exercise, and sunlight, will always be the best frontline defense against communicable disease. But diet, exercise, and sunlight cannot be outsourced
to health officials or mandated by politicians.

Whatever slight benefits masks may provide are a matter for
individuals to decide for themselves. People who feel sick with
symptoms should stay home. We can all wash our hands frequently
and thoroughly. Otherwise it is time for Americans to assert themselves against the dubious claims and nonexistent legality of government covid measures.

It is time to get back to normal life, and that starts with visible
human faces.

18

Babbitt Is Back

Is Babbittry alive and well in twenty-first-century America?

George F. Babbitt is novelist Sinclair Lewis's protagonist in the novel of the same name. Babbitt is a real estate man, which is to say a salesman, but the newfangled 1920s term is "Realtor™." Incurious, smug, self-satisfied, and utterly predictable, Babbitt is well pleased with his life in fictional Zenith. As a strident booster of his hometown, he urges displays of "Zip for Zenith" among his delegation to the convention of real estate boards. Like all glad-handers, Babbitt is neither particularly concerned with life's mysteries or how he came to enjoy his own comfortable place in the world. Things which benefit him are good; things which threaten the unexamined ease of his career, family, town, and, above all, social status are bad.

Babbitt is thus an avatar of know-nothingness, and "Babbittry" is a descriptive term similar to H. L Mencken's "booboisie." Both denote uncultured and material impulses, the kind of ugly provincialism we all imagine ourselves above.

Murray Rothbard in *The Betrayal of the American Right* devotes a worthwhile chapter to "The Tory Anarchism of Mencken and Nock." Here Rothbard discusses the origins of Old Right thinking in the early twentieth century, with Baltimore journalist and social critic Mencken as a leading light. Mencken is revisionist, having opposed US entry into the Great War. He is also a strong critic of 1920s culture, the do-gooderism of Prohibition, and the general left-over stench of Woodrow Wilson's zeal for state planning. Given this,

This article originally appeared May 11, 2021, on mises.org.

Mencken sees *Babbitt* as a literary triumph, capturing the amalgamated essence of many American businessmen of the era:

> I know of no American novel that more accurately presents the real America. As an old professor of Babbittry, I welcome him as an almost perfect specimen. Every American city swarms with his brothers. He is America incarnate, exuberant and exquisite.

Mencken was no leftist, and was certainly a scathing skeptic of government in all forms. Lewis was a dyed-in-the-wool socialist who dabbled in commune life. But both identified in George Babbitt a dangerous underbelly beneath the superficial bonhomie. In the credulous Babbitt, Mencken saw the seeds of censorship and attacks on civil liberties. Lewis saw an archetype of protofascism in the guise of civic chauvinism. The analogies to American society today, one hundred years after Lewis published *Babbitt,* are readily apparent.

Surely today's Left would cast Trumpists as modern Babbitts, purposefully ignorant rubes who clamor against the rapid changes of a new progressive era. But this is inaccurate precisely because the polarity of smugness and self-certainty have shifted so rapidly toward the woke monoculture. Babbitts certainly exist across politics and across red and blue America. But the open hatred and contempt afforded to Deplorables, *Fox News* viewers, Karens of all stripes, covid deniers, antimaskers, antivaxxers, and other assorted lepers in America today go far beyond even Sinclair Lewis's scathing social criticism. And if we define provincialism as the inability to imagine or sympathize with a life and world view much unlike one's own, then blue America is anything but cosmopolitan. Make America Great Again grates on progressive ears as jingoism, but what are *Sí se puede* and Build Back Better if not pure Babbittry?

Lewis is at least somewhat sympathetic to his main character. Babbitt shows humanity when he falls in with a fast set and pursues an unrequited love affair with a young party girl. He even defends his new Bohemian friends against the raised eyebrows down at the athletic club. Deep down, rebellion against his many responsibilities and financial obligations and encroaching middle age stirs something in him. Carrying on in late-night speakeasies, Babbitt is for a brief moment the conservative who has been to jail. Lewis does not exactly redeem him; Babbitt in the end chooses to stay with his dutiful wife and unexciting job. But at least he ventures outside his comfortable bubble, to catch a glimpse of (presumably) a more beautiful and aspirational life. Lewis didn't hate Babbitt in the way many seem to hate Trump America.

Babbittry is here to stay. As the political world grows in importance, civil society necessarily and inexorably shrinks. But civil society is where the results are. Yes, our superficial, nonintellectual, and media-drenched culture produces plenty of incurious Babbitts. But there they remain, localized and anodyne. The political world, by contrast, gives us Mencken's charlatans, mountebanks, and bunco artists: people who create no value but live quite comfortably off those who do. People without skin in the game, who are rewarded time and again for the grossest misdeeds and failures. Politics weaponizes the Babbitts, turning them into monsters—otherwise harmless men and women who become true believers in their own mythology. If politics mattered less, the Joe Bidens and George W. Bushes of the world might have chosen to sell real estate like George Babbitt. We should have been so lucky.

Babbittry is a feature of mass democracy, not a bug. Unthinking acceptance is at the heart of what politicians sell, by necessity, in a country of 330 million people. If democracy is sacred, bunkum is sacred. The people selling us democracy believe in it the same way George F. Babbitt believes in a new listing from the Babbitt-Thompson Realty Company: in the most hollow and self-serving way imaginable.

19

YouTube Attempts to Silence the Mises Institute

YouTube, the dominant video platform owned by Google, decided yesterday to remove a Mises Institute video. This decision apparently lasts for all eternity, cannot be appealed to an actual human, and comes with this friendly admonition: "Because it's the first time, this is just a warning. If it happens again, your channel will get a strike and you won't be able to do things like upload, post, or live stream for 1 week."

The video, a talk by Tom Woods titled "The Covid Cult" with more than 1.5 million views, was recorded at our live event in Texas two weeks ago. It offered challenges to the official narrative surrounding the coronavirus, particularly with respect to mask mandates. Woods's talk featured several charts showing rises in Covid "cases" across multiple cities and countries not long after imposing mask rules, demonstrating how such rules apparently have little effect on slowing transmission of the virus.

This is what YouTube sent us to tell us of their actions:

This article originally appeared November 25, 2020, on mises.org.

Hi misesmedia,

Our team has reviewed your content, and, unfortunately, we think it violates our medical misinformation policy. We've removed the following content from YouTube:

Video: The Covid Cult | Thomas E. Woods, Jr.

We know that this might be disappointing, but it's important to us that YouTube is a safe place for all. If content breaks our rules, we remove it. If you think we've made a mistake, you can appeal and we'll take another look. Keep reading for more details.

How your content violated the policy

YouTube doesn't allow content that explicitly disputes the efficacy of local health authorities' or World Health Organization (WHO) guidance on social distancing and self isolation that may lead people to act against that guidance. Learn more here.

The speech was nothing less than a heartfelt tour de force against the terrible lockdowns and pseudoscience plaguing the debate over covid, and a call to reexamine tradeoffs and priorities. It was, as you might imagine, a mix of unassailable data combined with our friend Tom's strong prescription for liberty and personal choice rather than centralized state edicts.

In other words, YouTube had no earthly business removing it. This kind of discourse seems to me the best and highest use for YouTube, its most important function.

"Big Digital," as Professor Michael Rectenwald terms tech companies, have become "governmentalities": supposedly private enterprises turned into instruments of state power and state narratives. This sordid process is different for each company (some are more complicit than others, a few are heroically non-compliant), but it involves a mix of early start-up funding; connections and contracts with state agencies, particularly relating to defense and surveillance; and propaganda campaigns in service of state narratives. Rectenwald explains this phenomenon in his own recent talk titled "The Google Election":

> In short, Google, Facebook and others are not strictly private sector entities; they are governmentalities in the sense that I have given to the term. They are extensions and apparatuses of the state. Furthermore, these platforms are governmentalities with a particular interest in the growth and extension of governmentality itself. This includes championing every kind of "subordinated" and newly created identity class that they can find or create, because such "endangered" categories require state acknowledgement and protection. Thus, the state's circumference continues to expand. Big Digital is partial to the interests and growth of the state. It not only does business with statists but also shares their values. This helps makes sense of its leftist bent and their preference for the deep state Democrats. Leftism is statism.

We encourage readers to consider the entirety of Rectenwald's talk, and his sobering book *Google Archipelago* for his thorough treatment of the facts and realities behind tech companies and the US state. This is not alarmism or conspiracies, but documented examples of how Google, Facebook, YouTube, Twitter, Instagram, LinkedIn and others actively participate—including financially—in a melding of corporate and state power.

This, then, is real fascism. Big Digital—what writer Ilana Mercer calls "Deep Tech"—is not a collection of private companies in the sense we think of such. They are partners of the federal government, committed to ideological service as part and parcel of their own bottom line.

Thankfully, the sneering call to "build your own platforms" is being answered. Companies like Bitchute and LBRY (its video platform is Odysee) continue to host Mises Institute content, and promise to continue doing so. In fact, you can view Dr. Woods's forbidden talk at those respective sources.

Truth tellers matter more than ever. It's time for our own institutions and platforms, which is precisely why the Mises Institute exists.

Immigration and Borders

20

Market Borders,
Not Open Borders

The attack on a Christmas market in Berlin earlier this week, apparently carried out by a Tunisian immigrant, is just the latest in a series of violent and disturbing terrorist incidents in Germany. The event raises uncomfortable questions about immigration, culture clashes, Islam, and identity: what does it mean to be German, rather than someone who merely lives in Germany? It also raises pragmatic questions about how to provide physical security in public spaces, given such dramatic failures by the German government.

Libertarians can duck these questions, or dismiss them. We can sniff about how everyone is an individual, how Islam is not to blame, or how Tunisians are not any more prone to murderous violence than Germans. We can argue for a holistic approach to welfare statism, foreign policy, and human migration. None of these arguments will help Germans deal with horrific criminality here and now, however. Rather than virtue-signaling to deeply illiberal and hostile audiences in government, media, and academia, we should make populist arguments for radical privatization of property and

---

This article originally appeared December 20, 2016, on mises.org.

security. Imagine the actions a private shopping mall, theme park, or stadium would take immediately in response to a terrorist incident on their private property!

We also should argue for localized decision-making regarding immigration, as with every political matter. Germans, like everyone else, want and deserve true self-determination. The smaller the political unit, the closer we come to Mises's concept of granting this power to every individual. Mass state-sponsored immigration from Islamic countries is being imposed on Germans, as a political project created by the EU and the German government. It is not the result of market demand. We are not witnessing some kind of heroic movement of labor toward welcoming employers and family relatives, but rather a coordinated and staged relocation of people who mostly are not true refugees. Libertarians are right to criticize this political project, while supporting average Germans who simply want to enjoy their cities rather than "learning to live with terrorism" as part of everyday life.

If not, we risk irrelevance or worse: the conjoining (in the public's mind) of libertarianism with all of the useless "public policy" ideas issuing from Brussels, Washington, and Berlin. The common criticism of libertarianism is that it sounds great in theory, but fails to offer concrete solutions to real-world problems. This criticism is wrong. Libertarianism offers the most pragmatic, proportional, and efficacious solutions imaginable: marketplace solutions. It is modern governments, with their political intrigue, sclerotic monopolies, inefficient bureaucracies, and perverse incentives, that cannot competently address tough problems like border control and terrorism. It is precisely because these problems are so complex and intractable that they should be sorted by the market.

The thorny issue of immigration, rife with very real externalities and distorted by "public property," calls for market order. There is a market for immigration, just as there is a market for security. Open borders advocates ignore the in-group preferences of the marketplace, just as they ignore the tremendous externalities caused by sudden influxes of migrants. The real question is not whether borders are open or restricted, but rather who decides. When someone asks for the libertarian position on immigration, my response is that libertarians want as much or as little immigration as the market demands.

Immigration and borders have been debated at length, and vociferously, by libertarians. Probably no better examples exist than several exchanges by open borders advocate Walter Block and restricted immigration advocate Hans-Hermann Hoppe. There is little to say about the subject that is novel or more insightful than what Block and Hoppe already have provided. That said, certain points bear repeating or elaboration:

- Borders satisfy innately human desires for order and separation. Borders arise and exist naturally, without being created or enforced by political entities (although they were generally less rigidly defined and more porous prior to the era of modern governments).

- Nation is not state, as Murray Rothbard reminded us. Nations can and do emerge naturally, while states tend to be late-arriving artifices that do injury to earlier, more natural borders.

- In-group preferences are strong. Provided groups coexist without coercion or violence, libertarianism has nothing particular to say about such preferences.

- Humans are not all good and well-intentioned, nor are they fungible. People with money, intelligence, or in-demand skills are better immigrants than people without these attributes. Poor and criminal immigrants impose huge costs. Any worldview that denies this, or downplays this, fails to comport with reality. Libertarianism, rooted in natural law, should by definition accord better with reality than worldviews requiring positive law. Why do we lose sight of this?

- Humans naturally want to live in safe areas, i.e., in "good neighborhoods" on a macro scale. And they want to know their neighbors are not a threat. In other words, there is a market for security beyond one's own property—not everyone can own and control vast areas of property like Ted Turner. This is why gated communities exist. Simply stating that "nobody has a right to control any property they don't own" does not address reality.

- Almost no instances of rapid mass migration occur as natural marketplace phenomena. Instead, they usually occur due to wars, famine, and other state-created disasters. So it does not follow that resistance to mass migration is anti-market.

- Every human has a natural right to control his body and movement. No human should be falsely imprisoned, enslaved, or held in a place against his will. But the right to leave a physical place is different than the right to enter one. Entry should be denied or permitted by the rightful owner of the property in question. But when vast areas of land are controlled (and/or ostensibly owned) by government, the question becomes much more complex—and the only way to make it less complex is to privatize such land. Unless and until this happens, it is facile for libertarians simply to insist that everyone has a right to go wherever they wish.

- The concept of open borders is mostly a big-government construct. Without state-provided incentives (food, housing, clothing, schooling, mobile phones, etc.), and frequent NGO funding for actual travel, immigration naturally would be far more restricted.

- As stated in an earlier article, a libertarian society has no commons or public space. There are property lines, not borders. When it comes to real property and physical movement across such real property, there are owners, guests, licensees, business invitees, and trespassers.

- Libertarianism, to borrow a phrase from Judge Napolitano, is not a suicide pact. It does not require us to ignore history, tradition, culture, family, and self-preservation. It does not require us to live as deracinated, hyper-individualized actors who identify with nothing larger than ourselves and have no sense of home.

Immigration is a complex and antagonistic issue. But facile slogans won't help libertarians have a bigger voice in the debate.

21

An Immigration Roundtable with Ludwig von Mises, Murray Rothbard, Walter Block, and Hans-Hermann Hoppe

Immigration remains a contentious issue in the US and across the West. Libertarians have not been immune. While the reflexive tendency favors freedom of movement, this reflex is not dispositive wherever private property exists. The right to *leave* a place—the right not to be imprisoned or enslaved—is different than the right to *enter* a place, at least in a society with any degree of private-property norms.

This roundtable by the editors of the Mises Wire originally appeared August 30, 2018, on mises.org.

The Mises Institute offers more intellectual diversity on the topic than most organizations, although our writers and scholars generally do not favor "open borders" in the current sense of the term. Their views range from complete elimination of borders and open homesteading of unowned land (Block) to fully private property societies permitting access only according to covenants (Hoppe). Others focus on reducing welfare state inducements, decentralizing immigration policy and border controls, exploring market-based sponsorship programs and alternatives to current lottery systems, and decoupling immigration from naturalization, citizenship, and voting.

Any discussion of immigration benefits from the following caveats:

- No truly libertarian approach to immigration is possible when governments at all levels own (i.e., control) vast amounts of "public" land, including coastlines and ports, highways, airports, roads, military installations, parks, and common spaces.

- Thus, the debate, at present, centers around the question of *what government should do under current conditions* with regard to immigration.

- There are no easy answers to how government agents should control government property such as roads and other "public" commons. Real economic calculation is impossible when the state controls resources, and "non-economic" considerations are impossibly subjective.

- "Welfare," in the form of various taxpayer-provided goods and services, makes the issue more complex.

- Democratic voting, coupled with high-time-preference politicians, makes the issue more complex.

Our goal is to present each thinker's views on immigration by excerpting his or her writing on the subject.

Ludwig von Mises

We begin with Ludwig von Mises. Mises first addressed the topic of human migration at length in *Liberalism*, published in 1927 during the interwar period and influenced by the death and destruction he witnessed a decade earlier as an officer in the Austro-Hungarian Army.

In a section from *Liberalism* titled *Freedom of Movement*, Mises approaches immigration from both economic and social perspectives: "First, as a policy of trade unions, and then as a policy of national protectionism":

> Attempts to justify on economic grounds the policy of restricting immigration are therefore doomed from the outset. There cannot be the slightest doubt that migration barriers diminish the productivity of human labor. When the trade unions of the United States or Australia hinder immigration, they are fighting not only against the interests of the workers of the rest of the countries of the world, but also against the interests of everyone else in order to secure a special privilege for themselves. For all that, it still remains quite uncertain whether the increase in the general productivity of human labor which could be brought about by the establishment of complete freedom of migration would not be so great as to compensate entirely the members of the American and Australian trade unions for the losses that they could suffer from the immigration of foreign workers.

Immigration restrictions, then, are un-economic impediments on labor in the same manner as restrictions on goods. They operate to keep wages artificially high, just like protective tariffs.

But Mises was not blind to the cultural concerns surrounding mass immigration:

The workers of the United States and Australia could not succeed in having restrictions imposed on immigration if they did not have still another argument to fall back upon in support of their policy. After all, even today the power of certain liberal principles and ideas is so great that one cannot combat them if one does not place allegedly higher and more important considerations above the interest in the attainment of maximum productivity. We have already seen how "national interests" are cited in justification of protective tariffs. The same considerations are also invoked in favor of restrictions on immigration.

In the absence of any migration barriers whatsoever, vast hordes of immigrants from the comparatively overpopulated areas of Europe would, it is maintained, inundate Australia and America. They would come in such great numbers that it would no longer be possible to count on their assimilation. If in the past immigrants to America soon adopted the English language and American ways and customs, this was in part due to the fact that they did not come over all at once in such great numbers. The small groups of immigrants who distributed themselves over a wide land quickly integrated themselves into the great body of the American people. The individual immigrant was already half assimilated when the next immigrants landed on American soil. One of the most important reasons for this rapid national assimilation was the fact that the immigrants from foreign countries did not come in too great numbers. This, it is believed, would now change, and there is real danger that the ascendancy, or more correctly, the exclusive dominion of the Anglo-Saxons in the United States would be destroyed. This is especially to be feared in the case of heavy immigration on the part of the Mongolian peoples of Asia.

These fears may perhaps be exaggerated in regard to the United States. As regards Australia, they certainly are not. Australia has approximately the same number of inhabitants as Austria; its area, however, is a hundred times greater than Austria's, and its natural resources are certainly incomparably richer. If Australia were thrown open to immigration, it can be assumed with great probability that its population would in a few years consist mostly of Japanese, Chinese, and Malayans.

Despite being a strong anti-nationalist and anti-colonialist, Mises understood the natural fears of those who worried about "inundation" while also acknowledging a Lockean settlement argument:

> The aversion that most people feel today towards the members of foreign nationalities and especially towards those of other races is evidently too great to admit of any peaceful settlement of such antagonisms. It is scarcely to be expected that the Australians will voluntarily permit the immigration of Europeans not of English nationality, and it is completely out of the question that they should permit Asiatics too to seek work and a permanent home in their continent. The Australians of English descent insist that the fact that it was the English who first opened up this land for settlement has given the English people a special right to the exclusive possession of the entire continent for all time to come.

But Mises, a son of the former patchwork Austro-Hungarian Empire, also clearly understood the value of self-determination as something very different from jingoist or insular nativism. The concerns of ethnic or linguistic minorities could not be dismissed:

> The present inhabitants of these favored lands fear that some day they could be reduced to a minority in their own country and that they would then have to suffer all the horrors of national persecution to which, for instance, the Germans are today exposed in Czechoslovakia, Italy, and Poland.

It cannot be denied that these fears are justified. Because of the enormous power that today stands at the command of the state, a national minority must expect the worst from a majority of a different nationality. As long as the state is granted the vast powers which it has today and which public opinion considers to be its right, the thought of having to live in a state whose government is in the hands of members of a foreign nationality is positively terrifying. It is frightful to live in a state in which at every turn one is exposed to persecution—masquerading under the guise of justice—by a ruling majority. It is dreadful to be handicapped even as a child in school on account of one's nationality and to be in the wrong before every judicial and administrative authority because one belongs to a national minority.

As Dr. Joe Salerno points out in his seminal article "Mises on Nationalism, the Right of Self-Determination, and the Problem of Immigration," Mises was exceedingly careful to distinguish between "militant" or "aggressive" nationalism and a peaceful, liberal nationalism that did not seek to subjugate at home or expand abroad:

Thus for Mises, the choice was never between nationalism and a bland, atomistic "globalism"; the real choice was either nationalism that was cosmopolitan and embraced universal individual rights and free trade or militant nationalism intent on subjugating and oppressing other nations. He attributed the rise of anti-liberal nationalism to the failure to apply the right of self-determination and the nationality principle consistently and to the utmost degree possible in the formation of new political entities in the wake of the overthrow of royal despotism by war or revolution. The consequence was peoples differentiated by language, heritage, religion, etc. artificially and involuntarily bound together by arbitrary political ties. The inevitable outcome of these polyglot, mixed-nation-states was the suppression of minorities by the majority nationality, a bitter struggle for control of the state apparatus, and the creation of mutual and deep-seated distrust and hatred.

Salerno also points out Mises's strong view that only liberal, laissez-faire governments could accept the notion of completely free immigration:

> Thus, Mises views immigration as always and everywhere a "problem" to which there is "no solution," as long as interventionist political regimes are the norm. Only when the crossing of state borders by members of a different nation portend no political dangers for the indigenous nationality will the "problem of immigration" disappear and be replaced by the benign migration of labor that creates unalloyed and mutual economic advantages for all individuals and peoples. From Mises's perspective, then, the solution to the immigration problem is not to legislate some vague, ad hoc right to the "freedom of movement" between existing fixed-boundary states. Rather, it is to complete the laissez-faire liberal revolution and secure private property rights by providing for the continual redrawing of state boundaries in accordance with the right of self-determination and the nationality principle. Then—and only then—can the continual and wealth-creating reallocation of labor throughout the world required by a dynamic capitalist economy be peacefully accommodated without precipitating political conflict.

As Lew Rockwell states, in these important senses Mises cannot be claimed by advocates for "open borders" today. He believed in a form of liberal nationhood, but nationhood nonetheless—and advocated for political subdivisions along cultural, linguistic, and historical lines. He was a democrat, a utilitarian, and a realist; his cosmopolitanism did not extend to a vision of a borderless and stateless world. But it's safe to assume his experiences in the Great War, and the freedom he enjoyed taking trains from Vienna to

London without showing a passport, strongly affected his views on immigration.

For further reading from Mises on immigration, see *Nation, State, and Economy* from 1919 and "Mises on Protectionism and Immigration" by Matt McCaffrey, highlighting selected readings. Surprisingly, his magnum opus *Human Action* contains few direct references to the immigration issue, save for his observations that migration barriers could not be removed for aggressors during wartime.

Murray Rothbard

Rothbard, despite having written millions of words on economics, philosophy, ethics, history, politics, and culture, wrote relatively little directly addressing immigration per se.

His 1962 economic treatise *Man, Economy, and State*, specifically the *Power and Market* chapters he intended to publish with the original work, deals at length with various government interventions. In chapter 3 of *Power and Market* Rothbard discusses "triangular interventions," defined as government interference with actions between two or more private actors—i.e., the state compels or prohibits certain transactions between private parties.

Section 3, subsection E of that chapter deals with immigration restrictions, and represents Rothbard's longest and most specific writing on the topic. Rothbard, much like Mises, views state interference with immigration in the context of supply and demand for labor—and the effects restrictionism had on wages and prices:

> Laborers may also ask for geographical grants of oligopoly in the form of *immigration restrictions*. In the free market the inexorable trend is to equalize wage rates for the same value-productive work all over the earth. This trend is dependent on two modes of adjustment: businesses flocking from high-wage to low-wage areas, and workers flowing from low-wage to high-wage areas.

Immigration restrictions are an attempt to gain *restrictionist* wage rates for the inhabitants of an area. They constitute a restriction rather than monopoly because (a) in the labor force, each worker owns himself, and therefore the restrictionists have no control over the whole of the supply of labor; and (b) the supply of labor is large in relation to the possible variability in the hours of an individual worker, i.e., a worker cannot, like a monopolist, take advantage of the restriction by increasing his output to take up the slack, and hence obtaining a higher price is not determined by the elasticity of the demand curve. A higher price is obtained in any case by the restriction of the supply of labor. There is a connexity throughout the entire labor market; labor markets are linked with each other in different occupations, and the *general* wage rate (in contrast to the rate in specific industries) is determined by the total supply of all labor, as compared with the various demand curves for different types of labor in different industries. A reduced total supply of labor in an area will thus tend to shift all the various supply curves for individual labor factors to the left, thus increasing wage rates all around.

Immigration restrictions, therefore, may earn restrictionist wage rates for all people in the restricted area, although clearly the greatest relative gainers will be *those who would have directly competed in the labor market with the potential immigrants.* They gain at the expense of the excluded people, who are forced to accept lower-paying jobs at home. (italics original)

For Rothbard, immigration restrictions represented pure protectionism—favoring domestic workers over foreign in what ought to be an international division of labor, while creating inefficiencies and harming consumers in the process:

Immigration barriers confer gains at the expense of foreign workers. Few residents of the area trouble themselves about that. They raise other problems, however.

The process of equalizing wage rates, though hobbled, will continue in the form of an export of capital investment to foreign, low-wage countries. Insistence on high wage rates at home creates more and more incentive for domestic capitalists to invest abroad. In the end, the equalization process will be effected anyway, except that the location of resources will be completely distorted. Too many workers and too much capital will be stationed abroad, and too little at home, in relation to the satisfaction of the world's consumers. Secondly, the domestic citizens may very well lose more from immigration barriers as consumers than they gain as workers. For immigration barriers (a) impose shackles on the international division of labor, the most efficient location of production and population, etc., and (b) the population in the home country may well be below the "optimum" population for the home area. An inflow of population might well stimulate greater mass production and specialization and thereby raise the real income per capita. In the long run, of course, the equalization would still take place, but perhaps at a higher level, especially if the poorer countries were "overpopulated" in comparison with their optimum. In other words, the high-wage country may have a population *below* the optimum real income per head, and the low-wage country may have excessive population *over* the optimum. In that case, *both* countries would enjoy increased real wage rates from the migration, although the low-wage country would gain more. (italics original)

Rothbard also attacks the cranky but faddish 1960s concerns about world overpopulation, but he does so applying economics:

It is fashionable to speak of the "overpopulation" of some countries, such as China and India, and to assert that the Malthusian terrors of population pressing on the food supply are coming true in these areas. This is fallacious thinking, derived from focusing on "countries" instead of the world market as a whole. It is fallacious to say that there is overpopulation in some parts of the market and not in others. The theory of "over-" or "under-population" (in relation to an arbitrary maximum of real income per person) applies properly to the market as a whole. If parts of the market are "under-" and parts "over" populated, the problem stems, not from human reproduction or human industry, but from artificial governmental barriers to migration. India is "overpopulated" only because its citizens will not move abroad or because other governments will not admit them. If the former, then, the Indians are making a voluntary choice: to accept lower money wages in return for the great psychic gain of living in India. Wages are equalized internationally only if we incorporate such psychic factors into the wage rate. Moreover, if other governments forbid their entry, the problem is not absolute "overpopulation," but coercive barriers thrown up against personal migration.

The advocate of immigration laws who fears a reduction in his standard of living is actually misdirecting his fire. Implicitly, he believes that his geographic area now exceeds its optimum population point. What he really fears, therefore, is not so much immigration as *any* population growth. To be consistent, therefore, he would have to advocate compulsory birth control, to slow down the rate of population growth desired by individual parents.

It's interesting to note that Rothbard sticks strictly to economics throughout this five-page subsection. Rothbard wanted *Man, Economy, and State* to serve as an overarching Austro-Misesian treatise that would stand the test of time. Thus he avoids the kind of political polemics frequently delivered later in his career, and offers no examination of vested interests or cronyism behind immigration policy. But his full-fledged political anarchism, already developed when writing the book, placed him squarely in the "no borders" camp.

In the 1970s and 1980s Rothbard dived into libertarian ethics with gusto, producing *For a New Liberty* and *The Ethics of Liberty*. The former contains scant reference to the immigration issue, either in the context of labor policy, foreign policy, or personal liberty. The latter, however, briefly addresses the issue over two short pages in the context of property rights:

> In the libertarian society, however, where the streets would all be privately owned, the entire conflict could be resolved without violating anyone's property rights: for then the owners of the streets would have the right to decide who shall have access to those streets, and they could then keep out "undesirables" if they so wished.
>
> Of course, those street-owners who decided to keep out "undesirables" would have to pay the price—both the actual costs of policing as well as the loss of business to the merchants on their street and the diminished flow of visitors to their homes. Undoubtedly, in the free society there would result a diverse pattern of access, with some streets (and therefore neighborhoods) open to all, and others with varying degrees of restricted access.

Here we see a shift: his analysis of immigration moves away from the supply and demand for labor discussed in *Man, Economy, and State* toward questions of private property and freedom of association:

> Similarly, the private ownership of all streets would resolve the problem of the "human right" to freedom of immigration. There is no question about the fact that current immigration barriers restrict not so much a "human right" to immigrate, but the right of property owners to rent or sell property to immigrants. There can be no human right to immigrate, for on whose property does someone else have the right to trample? In short, if "Primus" wishes to migrate now from some other country to the United States, we cannot say that he has the absolute right to immigrate to this land area;

for what of those property owners who don't want him on their property? On the other hand, there may be, and undoubtedly are, other property owners who would jump at the chance to rent or sell property to Primus, and the current laws now invade their property rights by preventing them from doing so.

The libertarian society would resolve the entire "immigration question" within the matrix of absolute property rights. For people only have the right to move to those properties and lands where the owners desire to rent or sell to them. In the free society, they would, in first instance, have the right to travel only on those streets whose owners agree to have them there, and then to rent or buy housing from willing owners. Again, just as in the case of daily movement on streets, a diverse and varying pattern of access of migration would undoubtedly arise.

In the late 1980s and early 1990s Rothbard developed a more populist political outlook that caused critics to claim he had made an "about-face on immigration." Still, in a 1992 *Rothbard-Rockwell Report* article laying out a strategy for effective "rightwing populism," restricting immigration doesn't make it into Rothbard's list of tactics for dismantling state power and rule by elites. Nor does immigration play much role at all in Rothbard's articles during his "paleo" period, so-called because he called for a return to pre-Cold War noninterventionism on the Right.

Yet in this period he became more vocal about political self-determination, the distinctions between nation and state, the practical and strategic case for supporting secession movements, and especially about the relationship between various groups and the state (in contrast to a rigid either/or analysis of single individual vs. leviathan state).

The most often cited evidence for Rothbard's shift on immigration is his article "Nations by Consent," written in the fall of 1994 only shortly before his death. Here he begins to consider the reemergence of "nation" as opposed to "nation-state" in the wake of the Soviet Union's collapse:

> Libertarians tend to focus on two important units of analysis: the individual and the state. And yet, one of the most dramatic and significant events of our time has been the reemergence—with a bang—in the last five years of a third and much neglected aspect of the real world, the "nation." When the "nation" has been thought of at all, it usually comes attached to the state, as in the common word, "the nation-state," but this concept takes a particular development of recent centuries and elaborates it into a universal maxim. In the last five years, however, we have seen, as a corollary of the collapse of communism in the Soviet Union and in Eastern Europe, a vivid and startlingly swift decomposition of the centralized State or alleged nation-State into its constituent nationalities. The genuine nation, or nationality, has made a dramatic reappearance on the world stage.

Rothbard senses an opportunity to use the breakup of the USSR as a teaching moment, one that encourages further breakups of sclerotic governments laying claim to set geographic regions:

> The crucial flaw is the implicit assumption of the entire analysis: that every nation-state "owns" its entire geographical area in the same just and proper way that every individual property owner owns his person and the property that he has inherited, worked for, or gained in voluntary exchange. Is the boundary of the typical nation-state really as just or as beyond cavil as your or my house, estate, or factory!
>
> It seems to me that not only the classical liberal or the libertarian, but anyone of good sense who thinks about this problem, must answer a resounding "No." It is absurd to designate every nation-state, with its self-proclaimed boundary as it exists at any one time, as somehow right and sacrosanct, each with its "territorial integrity" to remain as spotless and unbreached as

your or my bodily person or private property. Invariably, of course, these boundaries have been acquired by force and violence, or by interstate agreement above and beyond the heads of the inhabitants on the spot, and invariably these boundaries shift a great deal over time in ways that make proclamations of "territorial integrity" truly ludicrous.

Again, he bases his argument against large and powerful states on an aspirational society of pure private property:

> I raise the pure anarcho-capitalist model in this paper, not so much to advocate the model per se as to propose it as a guide for settling vexed current disputes about nationality. The pure model, simply, is that no land areas, no square footage in the world, shall remain "public"; every square foot of land area, be they streets, squares, or neighborhoods, is privatized. Total privatization would help solve nationality problems, often in surprising ways, and I suggest that existing states, or classical liberal states, try to approach such a system even while some land areas remain in the governmental sphere.

Finally, he extends the fully privatized real property approach to the immigration issue:

> the question of open borders, or free immigration, has become an accelerating problem for classical liberals. This is first, because the welfare state increasingly subsidizes immigrants to enter and receive permanent assistance, and second, because cultural boundaries have become increasingly swamped. I began to rethink my views on immigration when, as the Soviet Union collapsed, it became clear that ethnic Russians had been encouraged to flood into Estonia and Latvia in order to destroy the cultures and languages of these peoples. Previously, it had been easy to dismiss as unrealistic Jean Raspail's anti-immigration novel *The Camp of*

the Saints, in which virtually the entire population of India decides to move, in small boats, into France, and the French, infected by liberal ideology, cannot summon the will to prevent economic and cultural national destruction. As cultural and welfare-state problems have intensified, it became impossible to dismiss Raspail's concerns any longer.

However, on rethinking immigration on the basis of the anarcho-capitalist model, it became clear to me that a totally privatized country would not have "open borders" at all. If every piece of land in a country were owned by some person, group, or corporation, this would mean that no immigrant could enter there unless invited to enter and allowed to rent, or purchase, property. A totally privatized country would be as "closed" as the particular inhabitants and property owners desire. It seems clear, then, that the regime of open borders that exists de facto in the US really amounts to a compulsory opening by the central state, the state in charge of all streets and public land areas, and does not genuinely reflect the wishes of the proprietors.

Under total privatization, many local conflicts and "externality" problems—not merely the immigration problem—would be neatly settled. With every locale and neighborhood owned by private firms, corporations, or contractual communities, true diversity would reign, in accordance with the preferences of each community. Some neighborhoods would be ethnically or economically diverse, while others would be ethnically or economically homogeneous. Some localities would permit pornography or prostitution or drugs or abortions, others would prohibit any or all of them. The prohibitions would not be state imposed, but would simply be requirements for residence or use of some person's or community's land area. While statists who have the itch to impose their values on everyone else would be disappointed, every group or interest would at least have the satisfaction of living in neighborhoods of people who share its values and preferences. While neighborhood ownership would not provide Utopia or a panacea for all conflict, it would at least provide a "second-best" solution that most people might be willing to live with.

Ultimately, Rothbard was consistent in viewing property rights as the best yet imperfect way to deal with thorny questions of nationhood, self-determination, and immigration. Ironically, both his fans and detractors alternatively claim he favored open borders or statist restrictions on immigration. In fact, his thoughts on immigration evolved over the years, as one might expect from any scholar with a long career. And he always favored peaceful, private solutions to the problems created by governments in the first place.

Walter Block

Professor Block has written several substantial academic and popular articles on the topic of immigration, beginning in the 1980s and extending into the 2010s. Dr. Block is probably the best-known pure "open borders" advocate among Senior Fellows at the Mises Institute; and while his primary arguments are robustly deontological he does not shy away from addressing pragmatic questions raised by critics. And unlike Mises and Rothbard in the main, Block from the outset extends the doctrine of *laissez-faire* movement of workers and goods from the context of economics into normative libertarian philosophy.

His 1998 article in the *Journal of Libertarian Studies* titled "A Libertarian Case for Free Immigration" begins with characteristic Blockean bluntness:

> I shall contend that emigration, migration, and immigration all fall under the rubric of "victimless crime." That is, not a one of these three per se violates the non-aggression axiom. Therefore, at least for the libertarian,

no restrictions or prohibitions whatsoever should be placed in the path of these essentially peaceful activities.

Immigration across national boundaries should be analyzed in an identical manner to that migration which takes place within a country. If it is non-invasive for Jones to change his locale from one place in Misesania to another in that country, then it cannot be invasive for him to move from Rothbardania to Misesania. Alternatively, if migration across international borders is somehow illegitimate, this should apply to the domestic variety as well. As long as the immigrant moves to a piece of private property whose owner is willing to take him in (maybe for a fee), there can be nothing untoward about such a transaction. This, along with all other capitalist acts between consenting adults, must be considered valid in the libertarian world. Note that there is no freedom of movement of the person per se. This is always subject to the willingness of property owners in the host nation to accept the immigrant onto their land.

Block continues this approach in making perhaps his best-known argument for free immigration: homesteading of previously unowned land:

The case is equally clear for allowing immigrants to settle on unowned land. When there is virgin territory, there is no legitimate reason for immigrants (or domestic citizens) to be prevented from bringing it into fruitful production. States Rothbard: "Everyone should have the right to appropriate as his property previously unowned land or other resources." "Everyone," presumably, includes immigrants as well as citizens or residents of the home country.

And here Block addresses the "paleo" argument regarding public or common real property and buildings, property ostensibly owned and definitely controlled by government:

Take the case of the bum in the library. What, if anything, should be done about him? If this is a private library, then the plumb-line or pure libertarian would agree fully with his paleo cousin: throw the bum out! More specifically, the law should allow the owner of the library to forcibly evict such a person, if need be, at his own discretion. Cognizance would be taken of the fact that if the proprietor allowed this smelly person to occupy his premises, he would soon be forced into bankruptcy, as normal paying customers would avoid his establishment like the plague.

But what if it is a public library? Here, the paleos and their libertarian colleagues part company. The latter would argue that the public libraries are per se illegitimate. As such, they are akin to an unowned good. Any occupant has as much right to them as any other. If we are in a revolutionary state of war, then the first homesteader may seize control. But if not, as at present, then, given "just war" considerations, any reasonable interference with public property would be legitimate. The paleos or postponement libertarians take a sharply divergent view: one should treat these libraries in as close an approximation as possible to how they would be used in the fully free society. Since, on that happy day, the overwhelmingly likely scenario is that they will be owned by a profit maximizer who will have a "no bums" policy, this is exactly how the public library should be treated right now. Namely, what we should do to the bum in the public library today is exactly what would be done to him by the private owner: kick him out.

Block alludes to arguments made by Professor Hans-Hermann Hoppe and others that proper ownership (and thus decisions about access) of taxpayer-funded property resides with taxpayers, who presumably would treat "their" property like any private owner. But he does not agree that imperfect present conditions, i.e., government ownership of land and buildings, warrant restrictions on immigration any more than imperfect conditions with respect to welfare or public schools warrant illibertarian approaches:

> There are difficulties with this stance. First, as we have already seen, it is extremely likely that in the fully free society, virtually all immigrants would be taken in by a landowner in the host country. Therefore, if the paleos are to remain consistent with their own position, they should eschew all legislated immigration barriers. Secondly, and even apart from this consideration, the postponement libertarian perspective is vulnerable to rebuttal by *reductio ad absurdum*. If we should not allow unrestricted immigration until we have achieved the free society, but instead should curtail immigration in an effort to approximate what would take place under a fully libertarian society, let us apply this insight to other realms of controversy.
>
> Public schooling is a disaster. Certainly, in the present journal, there is no need to document such a claim. That being the case, the libertarian position is clear: get rid of public education, forthwith, even if we have not attained complete liberty in other sectors of society.
>
> The US welfare policy is a disaster. The libertarian position is once again crystal clear: abolish welfare forthwith, no matter what the status of the remainder of the economy. But the paleo or postponement libertarians are once again precluded from embracing so clear, just, and simple a solution.

Dr. Block is equally adamant on the question of immigrants voting for more government or more welfare, insisting the core issue of voting should be the focus:

> The real difficulty here concerns promiscuous voting, not immigrants who might vote "incorrectly." The problem, even apart from new entrants to our country, is that those who are already citizens now have the "right" to vote on, not whether or not, but how much of other people's property they can legally steal through the ballot

box. This is the real threat to liberty. In a free society, all the wrong-thinking immigrants in the world would be powerless to overturn (what is left of) our free institutions, for there would be no possibility of voting to seize other people's property.

Block concludes his paper with a rhetorical flourish about the anti-immigration policies of Left and Right—but note the Blockean proviso regarding property and sponsorship of migrants:

> Are libertarians moderates or extremists on the issues of emigration, migration, and immigration? The libertarian position on migration does not constitute a compromise in that it is indubitably an all-or-none proposition: either migration is totally legitimate, in which case there should be no interferences with it whatsoever, or it is a violation of the non-aggression axiom, in which case it should be banned, fully. I have argued in this paper that the former position is the only correct one. But libertarianism constitutes a compromise position on this issue in two other senses. First, immigration is allowed if and only if there are property owners willing to sponsor (presumably for a fee, but not necessarily so) the new entrants, and not otherwise. Second, there are people on both Right and Left who oppose borders totally open to peaceful settlement (Chavez, Buckley), and libertarians find themselves safely on the other side of this unholy alliance.

Fast forward to 2011, and Dr. Block continues to advocate "free movement of goods, capital" in another seminal *Journal of Libertarian Studies* article titled "Hoppe, Kinsella, and Rothbard II on Immigration: A Critique." Here he attempts to rebut certain arguments made by the aforementioned Dr. Hoppe, libertarian legal theorist Stephan Kinsella, and the late Dr. Rothbard—in particular the argument that the free movement of goods and capital requires a different analysis than the free movement of people. In some cases he responds to rebuttals put forth by Hoppe and Kinsella regarding his *JLS* article quoted at length above. "Rothbard II" as used by Dr. Block refers to Rothbard's later writings, especially the article "Nations by Consent."

Block starts by questioning Rothbard's claim that full privatization of real property would entirely resolve the question of immigration:

> It is tempting to think that the private ownership of all streets, (plus every other single solitary square inch of land) would resolve the immigration issue, at least among libertarians. Alas, not even this is so. Worse, there is also the question of whether or not, given circumstances as they presently are with regard to land ownership, the government is justified in interfering with the free movement of people. That is, it cannot be denied that at present, such a salutary state of affairs (complete private ownership of all property) simply does not exist. To wit, there are vast land holdings on the part of the government (streets, parks, forests, etc.), and, further, there are other vast tracts that have need been so much as trod on by a human foot (mainly in Alaska, Nevada, and other western states).

He also dismisses Rothbard's concern, in the wake of the Soviet Union's collapse, that artificial languages and cultures might be imposed by mass and sudden immigration:

> There is simply nothing incompatible with libertarianism and destroying "cultures and languages," provided only that the latter is done without the initiation of violence. And this goes not only for Latvia and Estonia, but for the US as well.
>
> The point is, there is no such thing as anyone's "own country." This is a notion incompatible with libertarianism. What happened to the doctrine of allowing free competition in all matters? Certainly, this should apply to languages and cultures.

He then goes on to quote Hoppe's argument that long-suffering taxpayers in a country, not recent immigrant arrivals, have the highest and most just claim to control government property or "unowned" common areas:

> Given Block's undeniable credentials as a leading contemporary theoretician of libertarianism, it is worthwhile explaining where his argument goes astray and why libertarianism requires no such thing as an open-door policy. Block's pro-immigration stand is based on an analogy. "Take the case of the bum in the library," he states.
>
> What, if anything, should be done about him? If this is a private library, . . . the law should allow the owner of the library to forcibly evict such a person, if need be, at his own discretion. . . . But what if it is a public library? . . . As such [libraries] are akin to an unowned good. Any occupant has a much right to them as any other. If we are in a revolutionary state of war, then the first homesteader may seize control. But if not, as at present, then, given "just war" considerations, any reasonable interference with public property would be legitimate. . . . One could "stink up" the library with unwashed body odor, or leave litter around in it, or "liberate" some books, but one could not plant land mines on the premises to blow up innocent library users.
>
> The fundamental error in this argument, according to which everyone, foreign immigrants no less than domestic bums, has an equal right to domestic public property, is Block's claim that public property "is akin to an unowned good." In fact, there exists a fundamental difference between unowned goods and public property. The latter is de facto owned by the taxpaying members of the domestic public. They have financed this property; hence, they, in accordance with the amount of taxes paid by individual members, must be regarded as its legitimate owners. Neither the bum, who has presumably paid no taxes, nor any foreigner, who has

most definitely not paid any domestic taxes, can thus be assumed to have any rights regarding public property whatsoever.

Block responds with reference to Rothbard, and an expansion of the "unowned" public library example into the idea of homesteading vast tracts of open land:

> First, the position I took is not really all that remarkable. Indeed, this was roughly Murray Rothbard's position for many years.
>
> Second, while Hoppe is undoubtedly correct in mentioning that I do indeed rely on the bum in the library analogy, this by no means exhausts my arguments. Let me briefly mention a few of them before returning to the analogy, as none of these others have been so far addressed by Hoppe. To wit: what about the vast open spaces in the Rocky Mountains and Alaska that no one has ever settled. What aspect of libertarianism could an immigrant possibly violate if he somehow catapulted himself to any of this terrain and began subsistence farming? Or, trading with other such immigrants, among themselves. Or, trading with the rest of us, on a totally voluntary basis?

What rights would pre-existing inhabitants, say Robinson Crusoe, have to bar newcomers in such a scenario? Block answers:

> The analogy is a pretty airtight one. Crusoe, and extant Americans, were here first. Friday, and the would-be immigrant who Hoppe wants to bar from this country, are attempting to come here second. If Crusoe (present occupants) bars Friday (would-be immigrants are not allowed to settle in unused desert and mountainous regions of the US), then he is in Rothbard's analysis, claiming more than homesteading would justifiably entitle him to. Crusoe is the illegitimate aggressor against Friday. No less is true of the present occupants of the US; by adopting the Hoppe analysis, they are

preventing entirely innocent people from going about their lawful business of homesteading empty territory.

Now, Hoppe could reply that the only reason these mountainous and desert areas are not presently occupied is due to the fact that the US government forbids its citizens to do so, and/or illegitimately occupies these lands itself through its agencies such as the Bureau of Land Management. There are two responses to any such defense. One, Hoppe must then acknowledge that the courageous immigrants, and not the docile citizens, had the ability to ignore these unjust governmental institutions. Two, land, happily, is a superfluous factor of production, compared to labor. Thus, at any given time, there will be sub-marginal land, precisely the territory that looks so attractive to the hypothetical immigrants we are now considering. But, with the advent of these people, the margin shifts. Terrain that was previously sub-marginal, before their arrival, becomes supra-marginal with their arrival. This means that before these new people came on the scene, there is a reason in addition to governmental proscriptions why the mountains of Wyoming and the tundra of Alaska was not homesteaded and settled; it was previously sub-marginal, even though it is no longer so under our assumptions.

And what about the children of current inhabitants, who burst on the scene much like immigrants? Should we worry about their propensity to grow up and consume welfare or engage in criminal activity?

What about immigrants from the "country" of Storkovia? That is, how does the Hoppe theory handle newborns? My claim here is that anything this author can say about an immigrant I can say concerning a brand new baby, with a lag of some 18 years, perhaps. If the one will commit crimes, so will the other, in a decade or so. Ditto for welfare. And it is the same for being allowed onto the roads of the nation. If illegal immigrants should not be allowed onto the highways, why should it be licit for a citizen of, say, Texas, to enter a road in Louisiana? Hoppe might reply that parents are responsible for their children in a way that does not apply to employers of immigrants. But this only gets him so far. Remember that time lag! After 15–18 years or so, parents are no longer liable for the evil doings of their children. Given the analogy, there is no justification for treating employers any differently. Hoppe says that anyone, such as an employer who invites an immigrant to this country must obligate himself to financially support them. But this is erroneous, since it would be unjustified to impose any such obligation on parents, for their newborn children.

And Block disagrees that taxpayers, in Hoppe's view the rightful owners of government property, should be accorded more say in the control of such property than immigrants:

> Let us return, for a moment to an illegal immigrant seizing a bit of Yellowstone Park, which Hoppe and I agree has been stolen from the taxpayers of America. This act, in splendid isolation from everything else, must necessarily be justified. It is a necessary precondition to returning it to its rightful owners. But Hoppe would object. What reason does he offer? That I confuse *de facto* and *de jure*? That since this land is in justice really owned by the long-suffering taxpayers, it is illegitimate for anyone else, a third party, to even so much as touch it? This will not do.
>
> To return to the illegal immigrant who is now perched on a part of Yellowstone Park and refuses to give it back to a taxpayer, the rightful owner. In like manner we may say of him that he really should return this property to its proper owner. However, we may also say that of the two options, one the status quo where the evil state retains this property, and the other where the robber is relieved of his illicit gains, the latter

is certainly a better second-best scenario. Thus, illegal immigration, Hoppe to the contrary notwithstanding, is justified on libertarian grounds not only for unowned property, but also for that stolen from the taxpayers of the country.

My response is that I do not at all claim that property such as government roads or libraries is "unowned." Rather, I claim these holdings were stolen. I agree that the state now possesses them; I argue, only, that this is unjustified. And, yes, I insist, the same libertarian analysis can be applied, in this context, to virgin and stolen land. Why? This is because for the libertarian, at least as I construe him, stolen land is *de jure* virgin land, ready for the next homesteader to seize it (on the assumption that the rightful original owner cannot be located, or he acquiesces in the state's seizure, or that, arguendo, we can ignore this rightful owner.)

Dr. Block also responds to arguments made by Kinsella regarding the complexity of free immigration in a situation where government owns and controls so much land and infrastructure. Quoting Kinsella:

> Coming back to immigration, let's take the case of the federal government as owner-caretaker of an extensive network of public roads and other facilities. If the feds adopted a rule that only citizens and certain invited outsiders are permitted to use these resources, this would in effect radically restrict immigration. Even if private property owners were not prohibited from inviting whomever they wish onto their own property, the guest would have a hard time getting there, or leaving, without using, say, the public roads. So merely prohibiting non-citizens from using public property would be one means of establishing *de facto* immigration restrictions. It need not literally prohibit private property owners from having illegal immigrants on their prop-

erty. It need only prevent them from using the roads or ports—which it owns.

Given this reality, what sort of rules for access and use should libertarians support? Quoting Kinsella:

> It seems to me establishing rules as to how public roads are to be used is not inherently unlibertarian. Even libertarians who say the state has no right to make any rules at all regarding property it possesses—even speed limits, etc.—really advocate the following rule: allow anyone to use it, and/or return it to the people. This is a way of using a piece of property. But most libertarians don't seem to have a principled opposition to the very idea of rule-setting itself.

What rules, then, are defendable? It's an impossible question to answer, according to Block:

> Kinsella is saying, if I may paraphrase him, that government is our caretaker. As such, it must perforce set up reasonable rules. The state should act as if it were a (perhaps bumbling) private owner. In this way the people from whom the money to finance the swimming pool was stolen may at least get some services in return. But this is a fatally conservative outlook. The radical alternative is that the "rules" of the pool should be fashioned so as to eliminate these enterprises from governmental control. For example, everyone, anyone, should be "allowed" to walk off with the water in the pool, even the very bricks of which it is composed.

And Block goes further in opposing the "caretaker" or rightful owner argument:

> It seems to me decidedly unlibertarian to advocate these sorts of "reasonable" rules. A more libertarian stance would be to welcome actual chaos on all property statists steal from victims. The likelihood is that pure bed-

lam and pandemonium on all such terrain would deter the thieves from their evil deeds.

All I can say is that majority vote is no litmus test of libertarianism. Most Americans also favor minimum wage laws, taxes, government, affirmative action, yet no one would assert that these policies are therefore libertarian. I certainly support Kinsella's contention that "99 percent of my fellow taxpayers would . . . prefer some immigration restrictions." This might well enhance restitution, as he contends, but, as I have argued, restitution is a far less important libertarian concern than stopping the violence that lead to the need for the restitution in the first place.

Ultimately, Dr. Walter Block is a vociferous and prolific defender of the stateless society—and thus brooks no restrictionist immigration arguments regarding state-owned property, voting, or the welfare state. His open borders position, however, is built on an unstinting foundation of private property rights, Lockean homesteading, and the full privatization of *everything* government does or owns.

Hans-Hermann Hoppe

Hans-Hermann Hoppe is well-known in Austro-libertarian circles as a critic of "open borders" and an advocate for purely private communities. In his earlier works (1980s and 1990s) on socialism, private property, and argumentation ethics, Hoppe demonstrates his unyielding support for absolute property rights. This perspective informs his later work on trade, immigration, and borders, in well-known publications like *Democracy: The God that Failed.*

We start with his seminal 1998 article from the *Journal of Libertarian Studies* titled "The Cases for Free Trade and Restricted Immigration," where Hoppe first challenges the analogy between trade restrictions on goods and immigration restrictions:

I will argue that this thesis and its implicit claim are
fundamentally mistaken. In particular, I will demonstrate that free trade and restricted immigration are not
only perfectly consistent but even mutually reinforcing
policies. That is, it is not the advocates of free trade and
restricted immigration who are wrong, but rather the
proponents of free trade and free immigration. In thus
taking the "intellectual guilt" out of the free-trade-and-
restricted-immigration position and putting it where
it actually belongs, I hope to promote a change in the
present state of public opinion and facilitate substantial
political realignment.

Because goods and people are not the same thing, Hoppe argues,
even a provable overall increase in national income does not address
the subjective nature of "wealth":

From the outset, it must be emphasized that not even
the most restrictive immigration policy or the most
exclusive form of segregationism has anything to do
with a rejection of free trade and the adoption of protectionism. From the fact that one does not want to
associate with or live in the neighborhood composed of
Mexicans, Haitians, Chinese, Koreans, Germans, Catholics, Moslems, Hindus, etc., it does not follow that
one does not want to trade with them from a distance.
Moreover, even if it were the case that one's real income
would rise as a result of immigration, it does not follow
that immigration must be considered "good," for material wealth is not the only thing that counts. Rather,
what constitutes "welfare" and "wealth" is *subjective*, and
one might prefer lower material living standards and a
greater distance from certain other people over higher
material living standards and a smaller distance. It is
precisely the absolute voluntariness of human association *and* separation—the absence of any form of forced
integration—which makes peaceful relationships—
free trade—between racially, ethnically, linguistically,
religiously, or culturally distinct people possible.

Furthermore, the incentive to emigrate from low-wage countries to higher-wage countries is *reduced* by free trade policies:

> The relationship between trade and migration is one of elastic substitutability (rather than rigid exclusivity): the more (or less) you have of one, the less (or more) you need of the other. Other things being equal, businesses move to low wage areas, and labor moves to high wage areas, thus effecting a tendency toward the equalization of wage rates (for the same kind of labor) as well as the optimal localization of capital. With political borders separating high- from low-wage areas, and with national (nation-wide) trade and immigration policies in effect, these normal tendencies—of immigration and capital export—are weakened with free trade and strengthened with protectionism. As long as Mexican products—the products of a low-wage area—can freely enter a high-wage area such as the US, the incentive for Mexican people to move to the US is reduced. In contrast, if Mexican products are prevented from entering the American market, the attraction for Mexican workers to move to the US is increased. Similarly, when US producers are free to buy from and sell to Mexican producers and consumers, capital exports from the US to Mexico will be reduced; however, when US producers are prevented from doing so, the attraction of moving production from the US to Mexico is increased.

Hoppe then makes his critical distinction between "invited" goods imported by a willing buyer and an individual's desire to move at will. Uninvited mass migration, he argues, frequently makes one party or parties (current inhabitants of the recipient nation) subjectively worse off in their view. Thus immigration is not always analogous to "win-win" trade exchanges.

> The phenomena of trade and immigration are different in a fundamental respect, and the meaning of "free" and "restricted" in conjunction with both terms is categori-

cally different. People can move and migrate; goods and services, of themselves, cannot.

Put differently, while someone can migrate from one place to another without anyone else wanting him to do so, goods and services cannot be shipped from place to place unless both sender and receiver agree. Trivial as this distinction may appear, it has momentous consequences. For *free* in conjunction with trade then means trade by invitation of private households and firms only; and *restricted* trade does not mean protection of households and firms from uninvited goods or services, but invasion and abrogation of the right of private households and firms to extend or deny invitations to their own property. In contrast, *free* in conjunction with immigration does not mean immigration by invitation of individual households and firms, but unwanted invasion or forced integration; and *restricted* immigration actually means, or at least can mean, the protection of private households and firms from unwanted invasion and forced integration. Hence, in advocating free trade and restricted immigration, one follows the same principle: requiring an invitation for people as for goods and services.

However, with respect to the movement of people, the same government will have to do more in order to fulfill its protective function than merely permit events to take their own course, because people, unlike products, possess a will and can migrate. Accordingly, population movements, unlike product shipments, are not *per se* mutually beneficial events because they are not always—necessarily and invariably—the result of an agreement between a specific receiver and sender.

Furthermore, the reality of modern welfare states means that an influx of people (unlike an influx of goods) can be disastrous:

According to proponents of unconditional free immigration, the US qua high-wage area would invariably benefit from free immigration; hence, it should enact a policy of open borders, regardless of any existing conditions, i.e., even if the US were ensnarled in protectionism and domestic welfare. Yet surely, such a proposal strikes a reasonable person as fantastic. Assume that the US, or better still Switzerland, declared that there would no longer be any border controls, that anyone who could pay the fare might enter the country, and, as a resident then be entitled to every "normal" domestic welfare provision. Can there be any doubt how disastrous such an experiment would turn out in the present world? The US, and Switzerland even faster, would be overrun by millions of third-world immigrants, because life on and off American and Swiss public streets is comfortable compared to life in many areas of the third world. Welfare costs would skyrocket, and the strangled economy disintegrate and collapse, as the subsistence fund—the stock of capital accumulated in and inherited from the past—was plundered. Civilization in the US and Switzerland would vanish, just as it once did from Rome and Greece.

What then, is Hoppe's answer to the essential conflict posed by immigration rules—i.e., the desires of some residents of a country to permit immigration, and the desire of others to prohibit it? Not open borders, he says, which are inconsistent and contradictory. Some immigration restrictions must exist, but what restrictions? The only consistent and workable answer to that question is nothing less than a full anarcho-capitalist model for property, where private owners invite immigrants onto their property after assessing the benefits and costs. Neither forced integration nor forced exclusion should be permissible:

> The guiding principle of a high-wage-area country's immigration policy follows from the insight that immigration, to be free in the same sense as trade is free, must be *invited immigration*. The details follow from the further elucidation and exemplification of the concept of invitation *vs.* invasion and forced integration.

For this purpose, it is necessary to assume first, as a conceptual benchmark, the existence of what political philosophers have described as a private property anarchy, anarcho-capitalism, or ordered anarchy: all land is privately owned, including all streets, rivers, airports, harbors, etc. With respect to some pieces of land, the property title may be unrestricted, that is, the owner is permitted to do with his property whatever he pleases as long as he does not physically damage the property of others. With respect to other territories, the property title may be more or less restricted. As is currently the case in some developments, the owner may be bound by contractual limitations on what he can do with his property (restrictive covenants, voluntary zoning), which might include residential rather than commercial use, no buildings more than four stories high, no sale or rent to unmarried couples, smokers, or Germans, for instance.

Clearly, in this kind of society, there is no such thing as freedom of immigration, or an immigrant's right of way. What does exist is the freedom of independent private property owners to admit or exclude others from their own property in accordance with their own restricted or unrestricted property titles. Admission to some territories might be easy, while to others it might be nearly impossible. Moreover, admission to one party's property does not imply the "freedom to move around," unless other property owners have agreed to such movements. There will be as much immigration or non-immigration, inclusivity or exclusivity, desegregation or segregation, non-discrimination or discrimination as individual owners or owners associations desire.

When government intrudes, however—with its arbitrary borders and sanctioned passports—bureaucrats rather than invested property owners make the immigration rules. Thus what ought to be a private system becomes political:

In order to realize what this involves, it is necessary to explain how an anarcho-capitalist society is altered by the introduction of a government, and how this affects the immigration problem. Since in an anarcho-capitalist society there is no government, there is no clear-cut distinction between inlanders (domestic citizens) and foreigners. This distinction appears only with the establishment of a government. The territory which a government's power extends over then becomes inland, and everyone residing outside of this territory becomes a foreigner. State borders (and passports), as distinct from private property borders (and titles to property), come into existence, and immigration takes on a new meaning. Immigration becomes immigration by foreigners across state borders, and the decision as to whether or not a person should be admitted no longer rests exclusively with private property owners or associations of such owners but with the government qua domestic security producer. Now, if the government excludes a person while there exists a domestic resident who wants to admit this very person onto his property, the result is forced exclusion; and if the government admits a person while there exists no domestic resident who wants to have this person on his property, the result is forced integration.

How would a process of "invited" immigrants work, per Hoppe? Through contractual admission, which in effect makes the inviting party the sponsor of such immigrants:

> Qua contractual admission, the inviting party can dispose only of his own private property. Hence, the admission implies negatively—similarly to the scenario of conditional free immigration—that the immigrant is excluded from all publicly funded welfare. Positively, it implies that the receiving party assumes legal responsibility for the actions of his invitee for the duration of his stay. The inviter is held liable to the full extent of his property for any crimes the invitee commits against

the person or property of any third party (as parents are held accountable for the crimes of their offspring as long as they are members of the parental household). This obligation, which implies practically speaking that invitors will have to carry liability insurance for all of their guests, ends once the invitee has left the country, or once another domestic property owner has assumed liability for the person in question (by admitting him onto his property).

The invitation may be private (personal) or commercial, temporally limited or unlimited, concerning only housing (accommodation, residency) or housing and employment (but there cannot be a valid contract involving only employment and no housing). In any case, however, as a contractual relationship, every invitation may be revoked or terminated by the invitor; and upon termination, the invitee—whether tourist, visiting businessman, or resident alien—will be required to leave the country (unless another resident citizen enters an invitation-contract with him).

Dr. Hoppe closes the article with an admonition against the automatic grant of voting and citizenship rights to immigrants:

Becoming a citizen means acquiring the right to stay in a country permanently, and a permanent invitation cannot be secured other than by purchasing residential property from a citizen resident. Only by selling real estate to a foreigner does a citizen indicate that he agrees to a guest's permanent stay (and only if the immigrant has purchased and paid for real estate and residential housing in the host country will he assume a permanent interest in his new country's well-being and prosperity). Moreover, finding a citizen willing to sell residential property and being prepared and able to pay for it, although a necessary requirement for the acquisition of citizenship, may not also be sufficient. If and insofar as the domestic property in question is subject to restrictive covenants, the hurdles to be taken by a prospective citizen may be significantly higher. In Switzerland, for instance, citizenship may require that the sale of residential property to foreigners be ratified by a majority of or even all directly affected local property owners.

We move forward to 2001, when Dr. Hoppe releases his famous political polemic *Democracy: The God that Failed*. Here he presents his full exposition of how and why democratic processes are incompatible with property and *laissez-faire*. He builds on his central arguments: trade protectionism and migration restrictions are not the same, neither forced integration nor forced exclusion are defendable, and only a system of fully private property can justifiably and practically resolve conflicts over immigration.

He opens chapter 7 of the book, titled "On Free Immigration and Forced Integration," with a synopsis of the classical liberal argument for free immigration as increasing overall standards of living:

> The classical argument in favor of free immigration runs as follows: Other things being equal, businesses go to low-wage areas, and labor moves to high-wage areas, thus affecting a tendency toward the equalization of wage rates (for the same kind of labor) as well as the optimal localization of capital. An influx of migrants into a given-sized high-wage area will lower nominal wage rates. However, it will not lower real wage rates if the population is below its optimum size. To the contrary, if this is the case, the produced output will increase over-proportionally, and real incomes will actually rise. Thus, restrictions on immigration will harm the protected domestic workers qua consumers more than they gain qua producers. Moreover, immigration restrictions will increase the "flight" of capital abroad (the export of capital which otherwise might have stayed), still causing an equalization of wage rates (although somewhat more slowly), but leading to a less than optimal allocation of capital, thereby harming world living standards all-around.

But again, the Austrian perspective requires us to understand value subjectively:

> The problem with the above argument is that it suffers from two interrelated shortcomings which invalidate its unconditional pro-immigration conclusion and/or which render the argument applicable only to a highly unrealistic—long bygone—situation in human history. The first shortcoming will only be touched upon. To libertarians of the Austrian School, it should be clear that what constitutes "wealth" and "well-being" is subjective. Material wealth is not the only thing that has value. Thus, even if real incomes rise due to immigration, it does not follow that immigration must be considered "good," for one might prefer lower living standards and a greater distance to other people over higher living standards and a smaller distance to others. Instead, a second, related shortcoming will be the focus here. With regard to a given territory into which people immigrate, it is left unanalyzed who, if anyone, owns (controls) this territory. In fact, in order to render the above argument applicable, it is implicitly assumed that the territory in question is unowned, and that the immigrants enter virgin territory (open frontier). Obviously, today this can no longer be assumed. If this assumption is dropped, however, the problem of immigration takes on an entirely new meaning and requires fundamental rethinking.

Hoppe expands the analysis to consider the likely differences in immigration policies under two scenarios, namely monarchy and democracy. First he considers a monarchical ruler:

> It is time to enrich the analysis through the introduction of a few "realistic" empirical assumptions. Let us assume that the government is privately owned. The ruler owns the entire country within state borders. He owns part of the territory outright (his property title is unrestricted), and he is partial owner of the rest (as landlord

or residual claimant of all of his citizen-tenants' real estate holdings, albeit restricted by some preexisting rental contracts). He can sell and bequeath his property, and he can calculate and capture the monetary value of his capital (his country). Traditional monarchies—and kings—are the closest historical examples of this form of government. What will a king's typical immigration and emigration policy be? Because he owns the entire country's capital value, he will tend to choose migration policies that preserve or enhance rather than diminish the value of his kingdom, assuming no more than his self-interest.

He contrasts this with democratic leaders, whose time preferences reflect only their tenure in office:

> Migration policies become predictably different once the government is publicly owned. The ruler no longer owns the country's capital value but only has current use of it. He cannot sell or bequeath his position as ruler; he is merely a temporary caretaker. Moreover, "free entry" into the position of a caretaker government exists. In principle, anyone can become the ruler of the country. As they came into existence on a worldwide scale after World War I, democracies offer historical examples of public government. What are a democracy's migration policies? Once again assuming no more than self-interest (maximizing monetary and psychic income: money and power), democratic rulers tend to maximize current income, which they can appropriate privately, at the expense of capital values, which they can not appropriate privately. Hence, in accordance with democracy's inherent egalitarianism of one-man-one-vote, they tend to pursue a distinctly egalitarian-nondiscriminatory-emigration and immigration policy.
>
> As far as immigration policies are concerned, the incentives and disincentives are likewise distorted, and the results are equally perverse. For a democratic ruler, it also matters little whether bums or geniuses, below

or above-average civilized and productive people immigrate into the country. Nor is he much concerned about the distinction between temporary workers (owners of work permits) and permanent, property owning immigrants (naturalized citizens). In fact, bums and unproductive people may well be preferred as residents and citizens, because they create more so-called "social problems," and democratic rulers thrive on the existence of such problems. Moreover, bums and inferior people will likely support his egalitarian policies.

He concludes the chapter with a robust call for radical decentralization of immigration policy as the least-bad approach in democratic systems:

The current situation in the United States and in Western Europe has nothing whatsoever to do with "free" immigration. It is forced integration, plain and simple, and forced integration is the predictable outcome of democratic one-man-one-vote rule. Abolishing forced integration requires the de-democratization of society and ultimately the abolition of democracy. More specifically, the power to admit or exclude should be stripped from the hands of the central government and reassigned to the states, provinces, cities, towns, villages, residential districts, and ultimately to private property owners and their voluntary associations. The means to achieve this goal are decentralization and secession (both inherently undemocratic, and anti-majoritarian). One would be well on the way toward a restoration of the freedom of association and exclusion as is implied in the idea and institution of private property, and much of the social strife currently caused by forced integration would disappear, if only towns and villages could and would do what they did as a matter of course until well into the nineteenth century in Europe and the United States: to post signs regarding entrance requirements to the town, and once in town for entering specific pieces of property (no beggars, bums, or homeless, but also no Moslems, Hindus, Jews, Catholics, etc.); to expel as trespassers those who do not fulfill these requirements; and to solve the "naturalization" question somewhat along the Swiss model, where local assemblies, not the central government, determine who can and who cannot become a Swiss citizen.

Finally, in articles like "A Realistic Libertarianism," Hoppe makes the case for treating the net taxpayers of any political jurisdiction as the rightful owners of "common" or government property—with political officials acting as *trustees* of that property. Those trustees should ensure that property owners who invite immigrants bear the full cost of their impact on taxpayer-funded commons:

> In a world where all places are privately owned, the immigration problem vanishes. There exists no right to immigration. There only exists the right to trade, buy or rent various places. Yet what about immigration in the real world with public property administered by local, regional or central State-governments?
>
> First off: What would immigration policies be like if the State would, as it is supposed to do, act as a trustee of the taxpayer-owners' public property? What about immigration if the State acted like the manager of the community property jointly owned and funded by the members of a housing association or gated community?
>
> At least in principle, the answer is clear. A trustee's guideline regarding immigration would be the "full cost" principle. That is, the immigrant or his inviting resident should pay the full cost of the immigrant's use made of all public goods or facilities during his presence. The cost of the community property funded by resident tax-payers should not rise or its quality fall on account of the presence of immigrants. On the contrary, if possible the presence of an immigrant should yield the resident-owners a profit, either in the form of lower taxes or community-fees or a higher quality of community property (and hence all-around higher property values).

What the application of the full cost principle involves in detail depends on the historical circumstances, i.e., in particular on the immigration pressure. If the pressure is low, the initial entry on public roads may be entirely unrestricted to 'foreigners' and all costs insofar associated with immigrants are fully absorbed by domestic residents in the expectation of domestic profits. All further-going discrimination would be left to the individual resident-owners (this, incidentally, is pretty much the state of affairs, as it existed in the Western world until WWI). But even then, the same generosity would most likely not be extended to the use made by immigrants of public hospitals, schools, universities, housing, pools, parks, etc. Entry to such facilities would not be "free" for immigrants. To the contrary, immigrants would be charged a higher price for their use than the domestic resident-owners who have funded these facilities, so as to lower the domestic tax-burden. And if a temporary visitor-immigrant wanted to become a permanent resident, he might be expected to pay an admission price, to be remitted to the current owners as compensation for the extra-use made of their community property.

He also rejects the "accelerationist" view of some libertarians, namely that free immigration rules would overwhelm modern Western welfare systems and thus hasten the demise of their respective governments:

Absent any other, internal or local entry restrictions concerning the use of domestic public properties and services and increasingly absent also all entry restrictions regarding the use of domestic private property (owing to countless anti-discrimination laws), the predictable result would be a massive inflow of immigrants from the third and second world into the US and Western Europe and the quick collapse of the current domestic "public welfare" system. Taxes would have to be sharply increased (further shrinking the productive economy) and public property and services would dramatically deteriorate. A financial crisis of unparalleled magnitude would result.

Yet why would this be a desirable goal for anyone calling himself a libertarian? True enough, the tax-funded public welfare system should be eliminated, root and branch. But the inevitable crisis that a "free" immigration policy would bring about does not produce this result. To the contrary: Crises, as everyone vaguely familiar with history would know, are typically used and often purposefully fabricated by States in order to further increase their own power. And surely the crisis produced by a "free" immigration policy would be an extraordinary one.

He concludes with another admonition regarding the incompatibility of mass immigration and democracy, where political leaders bear no cost when they subsidize immigrants rather than act as trustees for property owners:

> The immigration policies of the States that are confronted with the highest immigration pressure, of the US and Western Europe, have little resemblance with the actions of a trustee. They do not follow the full cost principle. They do not tell the immigrant essentially to "pay up or leave." To the contrary, they tell him "once in, you can stay and use not just all roads but all sorts of public facilities and services for free or at discounted prices even if you do not pay up." That is, they subsidize immigrants—or rather: they force domestic taxpayers to subsidize them. In particular, they also subsidize domestic employers who import cheaper foreign workers, because such employers can externalize part of the total costs associated with their employment—the free use to be made by his foreign employees of all resident public property and facilities—onto other domestic taxpayers. And they still further subsidize immigration

(internal migration) at the expense of resident-taxpayers in prohibiting—by means of non-discrimination laws—not only all internal, local entry restrictions, but also and increasingly all restrictions concerning the entry and use of all domestic private property.

Ultimately, Dr. Hans-Hermann Hoppe's positions on immigration and borders are logically consistent with a private property order—one where owners of said property bear the benefits and burdens of immigration. Government ownership of real estate, particularly in democratic welfare states, clouds the immigration issue and forces us to analyze the "least bad" policies.

22

A Libertarian Approach to Disputed Land Titles

The recent spate of bombing violence in Israel's West Bank, East Jerusalem, and Gaza demonstrates the enduring attachment both Israelis and Palestinians have to physical land in the country. Both sides make claims—legal, moral, and political—to land within Israel, from the southernmost tip of Gaza to the northernmost tip of the Golan Heights. This ongoing and often violent dispute is based on interrelated historical and religious events reaching back thousands of years, even before the origins of the biblical Holy Land. And while

---

This article originally appeared June 3, 2021, on mises.org.

ancient disputes are inherently more difficult to resolve, twentieth century events also weigh heavily on the current conflict. The Balfour Declaration in 1917, the official establishment of Israel by UN resolution in 1948, decisive domestic land wars in 1967 and 1973, and even recent peace accords all failed to settle the issue or at least bring an end to violence.

Fights over land are the norm in human affairs, and the impetus for most wars across time. This is unsurprising, because for most of human history land and wealth were virtually synonymous. Today, the ultimate landowner, Queen Elizabeth of England, at least symbolically controls 6 *billion* acres of British territories far beyond the Crown Estate. In theory, the wealthiest elites today, people like Jeff Bezos, derive most of their net worth from equity ownership in public or private companies. And unlike the blue-chip companies of fifty years ago, today's big tech firms operate mostly in the digital sphere—owning lots of servers, intellectual property, and lines of code, but little in the way of factories, offices, or fields. Yet several tech titans, including Bezos and Bill Gates, are found among the old-money crowd in *The Land Report's* list of top American landowners. The richest people in the world tend to hedge their bets, and one way they do so is selling stock to buy land rather than the other way around. This should tell us something.

So long as land remains valuable, we should expect people to fight over it. And not only in Israel. Similar disputes over historical claims are simmering in the West, including claims by American Indian tribes against the US federal government for land restoration and black Americans seeking land as partial reparations for slavery. Yet we view these claims almost entirely in political terms, as matters to be settled by legislatures representing "the people" and using public appropriations. Why should this be so? Why does modern positivist "land law" focus primarily on zoning issues and land use rather than defining ownership? *Black's Law Dictionary* appears to provide more guidance than the Supreme Court or international pseudotribunals. Why do we lack a method or road map for resolving land disputes in the modern context when land has been such a fixture in common law? One would think the basic rules of property titles would have been settled centuries ago.

What Land Titles Are "Just"?

So how do we address thorny land disputes in Gaza and elsewhere? Fortunately, both the late Murray N. Rothbard and his mentor, Ludwig von Mises, wrote at some length on the question of property titles, though from two different perspectives. In particular, we can look to Rothbard's *The Ethics of Liberty* and Mises's *Socialism* for their fullest treatments of law and justice as they relate particularly to real property. Rothbard's approach is normative, based strictly on natural law justice principles rather than economic efficiency. Mises, by contrast, is a strong critic of natural law. His "rule utilitarianism" views markets as a form of social cooperation, and seeks rules of conduct which encourage such cooperation for land disputes. But both men recognize the role that earlier aggression, whether force or fraud, played in creating property titles held today. Invasion, war, seizure, theft, trickery, and general violence are at least as prevalent in human history as heroic homesteading.

Mises, in *Socialism*, does not sugarcoat this reality:

All ownership derives from occupation and violence. When we consider the natural components of goods, apart from the labour components they contain, and when we follow the legal title back, we must necessarily arrive at a point where this title originated in the appropriation of goods accessible to all. Before that we may encounter a forcible expropriation from a predecessor whose ownership we can in its turn trace to earlier appropriation or robbery. That all rights derive from violence, all ownership from appropriation or robbery, we may freely admit to those who oppose ownership on considerations of natural law. But this offers not the

slightest proof that the abolition of ownership is necessary, advisable or morally justified.

Rothbard, in *The Ethics of Liberty*, rejects the notion of accepting current settled land titles under color of state authority. Defending things as they are, he says, causes the utilitarian to smuggle in
an implicit ethic:

> This, in fact, is the way utilitarian free-market econo-
> mists invariably treat the question of property rights.
> Note, however, that the utilitarian has managed to
> smuggle into his discussion an unexamined ethic:
> that all goods "now" (the time and place at which the
> discussion occurs) considered private property must
> be accepted and defended as such. In practice, this
> means that all private property titles designated by
> any existing government (which has everywhere seized
> the monopoly of defining titles to property) must be
> accepted as such. This is an ethic that is blind to all con-
> siderations of justice, and, pushed to its logical conclu-
> sion, must also defend every criminal in the property
> that he has managed to expropriate.
>
> (Libertarians) must take their stand on a theory of
> just versus unjust property; they cannot remain utili-
> tarians. They would then say to the king: "We are sorry,
> but we only recognize private property claims that are
> just that emanate from an individual's fundamental
> natural right to own himself and the property which
> he has either transformed by his energy or which has
> been voluntarily given or bequeathed to him by such
> transformers. We do not, in short, recognize anyone's
> right to any given piece of property purely on his or
> anyone else's arbitrary say-so that it is his own. There
> can be no natural moral right derivable from a man's
> arbitrary claim that any property is his. Therefore, we
> claim the right to expropriate the 'private' property of
> you and your relations, and to return that property to

the individual owners against whom you aggressed by
imposing your illegitimate claim."

So how, then, does a Rothbardian apply natural law theory
to determine just land titles? We start with self-ownership, the
idea that humans have an absolute right to own and control their
bodies. From that right, we derive the right to find and transform
unowned resources into owned property. Finally, owning property
means having the right to alienate such property, by exchange or
gift. So humans justly acquire property by mixing their labor with
unowned resources, or by contract and gift. All other methods of
ownership, variants of theft or fraud, do not create just property
titles. This is Rothbard's theory of the rights of property distilled:

> The right of every individual to own his person and the
> property that he has found and transformed, and there-
> fore "created," and the property which he has acquired
> either as gifts from or in voluntary exchange with other
> such transformers or "producers." It is true that exist-
> ing property titles must be scrutinized, but the reso-
> lution of the problem is much simpler than the ques-
> tion assumes. For remember always the basic principle:
> that all resources, all goods, in a state of no-ownership
> belong properly to the first person who finds and trans-
> forms them into a useful good (the "homestead" prin-
> ciple) . . . unused land and natural resources: the first
> to find and mix his labor with them, to possess and use
> them, "produces" them and becomes their legitimate
> property owner.

Mises alludes to the "is" and "ought" of later versus original
ownership, but takes an analytic rather than normative view:

> [T]he sociological and juristic concepts of ownership
> are different. This, of course, is natural, and one can
> only be surprised that the fact is still sometimes over-
> looked. From the sociological and economic point of
> view, ownership is the having of the goods which the

economic aims of men require. This having may be called the natural or original ownership, as it is purely a physical relationship of man to the goods, independent of social relations between men or of a legal order. The significance of the legal concept of property lies just in this—that it differentiates between the physical has and the legal should have. The Law recognizes owners and possessors who lack this natural having, owners who do not have, but ought to have. In the eyes of the Law "he from whom has been stolen" remains owner, while the thief can never acquire ownership.

The point here is not to reconcile Rothbard and Mises on just property titles, but rather to demonstrate their understandings of how and why property derives legal title. Any argument for the undoing of current land ownership starts with an understanding of the specific history of titles in question.

Four Scenarios for Land Title Disputes

As an analytic framework for considering the validity or criminality of land titles, Rothbard lays out four possible scenarios. He does so with the proviso that merely proving a title is criminal does not answer the question of to whom it should transfer:

> Suppose that a title to property is clearly identifiable as criminal, does this necessarily mean that the current possessor must give it up? No, not necessarily. For that depends on two considerations: (a) whether the victim (the property owner originally aggressed against) or his heirs are clearly identifiable and can now be found; or (b) whether or not the current possessor is himself the criminal who stole the property.

That said, each scenario suggests a remedy to Rothbard.

- **Scenario 1: Clear title.** In this instance we know a particular title is entirely valid and free of criminal origins.

This might readily apply to a brand-new subdivision in a remote area in which no humans have lived, farmed, built, or about which no humans have even known prior. In the modern context, however, even the rawest land must have been bought from someone (such as the state), and then recorded with someone (certainly the state). But clear and unchallenged title is the baseline for Rothbard's evaluation, and obviously requires no action.

- **Scenario 2: Unknown title.** In this situation we cannot assess or know whether a title has criminal origins, because we lack the ability to find out. Accordingly, Rothbard tells us, the "hypothetically 'unowned' property reverts instantaneously and justly to its current possessor."

- **Scenario 3: Criminal title, absent victim.** Here we know the title is criminal and defective, but we cannot identify or find the victim or the victim's heirs. This creates two possible just outcomes: (i) if the current titleholder was not the criminal,[1] title reverts to such holder as "first owner of a hypothetically unowned property" or (ii) if the current titleholder is the criminal aggressor, such holder is immediately deprived of title and it reverts to the first person who takes this land newly determined unowned and appropriates it for use under the homesteading principle outlined above.

- **Scenario 4: Criminal title, identifiable victim.** Finally, when we know a title is criminally defective and we can clearly identify the victim (or heirs), the title immediately reverts to the victim without compensation to the criminal (or unjust titleholders). This last scenario is a bit more

---

[1]In legal parlance, this is a bona fide purchaser for value. In other words, the purchaser does not know and has no reasonable reason to know that the land in question has a suspected stolen title. The purchaser obtains the land innocently, and for its full value—as opposed to the shady character who knowingly buys stolen goods at suspiciously low prices. This risk is of course mitigated by the marketplace, which creates experts in title research who sell title insurance.

fraught, as victims have immediate right to full ownership and possession even if after the criminal appropriation an innocent buyer came along.

These four examples, at least in theory, give us the clearest possible approach to working out land disputes. They apply to any scenario, including the worst atrocities in human history, provided proof can be produced which both identifies the original theft and the perpetrators and victims involved.

Who Bears the Burden of Proof?

In *The Ethics of Liberty* Rothbard does not discuss the burden of proof that plaintiffs should bear in disputes over land. Burden of proof requirements arise from common law, and require a suing party to put forth evidence at a certain level to prevail in their claim. This is not merely a technicality, but an evidentiary standard which often determines the outcomes of cases. In civil suits today, a plaintiff seeking money damages generally must demonstrate liability by a preponderance of the evidence, which means the judge or jury believes that the evidence shows the defendant "more likely than not" bears responsibility. By contrast, a prosecutor seeking to jail a defendant must demonstrate guilt beyond a reasonable doubt. Since Rothbard advocates "collapsing tort into crime," which is to say basing all actionable lawsuits on aggression against persons or property, is a much higher burden of proof required in land disputes?

Writing in the *Cato Journal* several years later on property rights and pollution, Rothbard appears to answer in the affirmative:

> Who, then, should bear the burden of proof in any particular case? And what criterion or standard of proof should be satisfied?
>
> The basic libertarian principle is that everyone should be allowed to do whatever he or she is doing unless committing an overt act of aggression against someone else. But what about situations where it is unclear whether or not a person is committing aggression? In those cases,

the only procedure consonant with libertarian principles is to do nothing; to lean over backwards to ensure that the judicial agency is not coercing an innocent man. If we are unsure, it is far better to let an aggressive act slip through than to impose coercion and therefore to commit aggression ourselves. A fundamental tenet of the Hippocratic oath, "at least, do not harm," should apply to legal or judicial agencies as well.

The presumption of every case, then, must be that every defendant is innocent until proven guilty, and the burden of proof must be squarely upon the plaintiff... for libertarians, the test of guilt must not be tied to the degree of punishment; regardless of punishment, guilt involves coercion of some sort levied against the convicted defendant. Defendants deserve as much protection in civil torts as in criminal cases.

This evidentiary burden decidedly colors the larger argument about justice and land titles. In this practical sense, Rothbard partially concedes Mises's view on the utilitarian value of continuity and the general sentiment that "possession is nine-tenths of the law." Rothbard is willing to overturn the apple cart, but only if and when a party seeking title to land makes a thoroughly persuasive case.

Is There a Statute of Limitations for Land Claims?

That persuasion may well depend on the age of such a claim: as years, decades, or even centuries go by, witnesses die and written records are hard to find. This is certainly the case in Israel, where current land titles are often traced to very old or even ancient provenance—with little in the way of official deeds. As evidence become harder to adduce with the passage of time, disputed title claims become harder and harder to prove. To be sure, Rothbard takes pains to deny any concept of a statute of limitation in libertarian legal theory. After all, statutes require legislatures, which he rejects altogether. And he is not the kind of thinker whose sense of normative justice shifts simply because an injury is long in the past. Yet Rothbard's four scenarios, outlined above, create bright lines for determining just outcomes for *proven* claims. Neither Rothbard nor any other theorist can solve the issue of proof, which means no system of justice is perfect. And it's important to repeat that Rothbard's analysis is based on *individual* cases and *specific* claims, not generalized calls for redistributive justice for past actions. For Rothbard, there is no generalized political justice for slavery, genocide, military land grabs, or groups with historical grievances.

Should Lineage Matter?

Finally, we have the difficult question of whether and why genetic lineage should allow any person to make (or collect on) a claim on behalf of their ancestor. At several points, Rothbard discusses victims and their heirs, as contrasted with criminal aggressors and their ancestors. This clearly indicates his agreement with the idea that property rights adhere to successive generations, as does the taint of theft.

Certainly, an individual who dies with a successful legal claim to land (but who has not yet taken possession) can assign that claim to heirs (or anyone else, of course). In many US states the operation of law effectively achieves this if the individual died without a will or without making such an assignment. But in a scenario like Israel, lineal heirs to people with just Rothbardian claims to land may be dozens of generations and thousands of miles removed from the dispute in question. Especially in Rothbard's fourth scenario above, why should a bona fide innocent purchaser (or the purchaser's heirs) not have a better or equal claim to the land? What if the heirs have no familial, geographic, or cultural ties to the original victim whatsoever? Why should they, in effect, step into the shoes of a long-dead and long-forgotten ancestor, even when the ancestor is a complete stranger? Why does the hyper-individualist Murray Rothbard think family relations should matter so much in legal theory?

The short answer is because we don't have a better way. Channeling Thomas Sowell, we must ask, "Compared to what?" Are hereditary rights to claims the best imperfect system we can devise? Do they give us a way to identify worthy claimants that no other system can? Yes and yes.

Conclusion

Henry George was correct: the amount of physical land on earth is inherently fixed and finite. Mark Twain told us to "buy land, they're not making it anymore." Of course, the amount of "usable" land (inhabitable, arable, reachable by humans) increases with technology, along with the amount of extractable resources and economic value. Someday the vast sea floors may be widely available to us. But land is indeed exhaustible, in a purely possessory sense. This simple reality inescapably benefits earlier generations, which came to possess land by dint of discovery, homesteading, legitimate purchase, inheritance, war, colonization, force, fraud, or just the sheer luck of being born at the right place and time. Young people may well resent this state of affairs. They may wonder if they'll ever be able to afford even modest property like their grandparents could, much less hellishly expensive homes in New York City or Singapore or Vancouver (never mind the role of central banks in this). They were late to the party—through no fault of their own—and now find themselves landless in a crowded world of over 7 billion people.

But does this apparent cosmic injustice make the case for upending and redistributing existing land titles? No, because a generalized sense of fairness, even if such an ideal were remotely possible to determine, would require mass injustice to implement. Justice should always be specific, individual, temporal, and local to the greatest extent possible. This is why Rothbard requires a great degree of specificity in identifying both perpetrators and victims of land appropriation, while Mises argues against abolishing current ownership simply because of the injustice or indifference of past legal orders. Land, like any capital good, will tend to move toward those who can find its best and highest use. Thieves and squatters, however much unjustly enriched, are unlikely to maintain ownership forever under a better system of market liberalism (i.e., a more just and less barbaric system of land acquisition). In the view of both Rothbard and Mises, markets tend toward justice in allocating titles to land over time, however imperfectly and slowly. Rothbard gives us the rough foundation of justice, but only common law juries—temporalized and local—can fill in the gaps. Justice is often found in the details, and this sets natural limits for any overarching theory of justice. In this sense the here and now always has the upper hand over the past.

Yet life is unfair. No legal code based even on the best libertarian principles found in common law can fix this entirely.

Economics

23

In Thrall to the Federal Reserve

P erhaps no economic pronouncement in history has been anticipated, discussed, predicted, dissected, and reported like the Federal Reserve's momentous decision today not to raise interest rates.

The outpouring of relief witnessed today by the financial press is nothing short of cathartic. Fear and anxiety, built up over months, is replaced by relief, even euphoria.

This is not to say the hype is unwarranted. On the contrary, the decision to raise interest rates even just 25 basis points would have represented nothing less than the end of an era, as one Bank of American analyst described (courtesy of *Zerohedge*):

> On Wall Street only 2 things matter: interest rates and earnings. Everything else is noise unless it impacts rates and earnings. No one impacts interest rates more than the Fed. So the . . . rate hike decision is a big deal.
>
> Should the Fed decide to raise interest rates, it will be the first Fed hike since June 29, 2006. In the 110

This article originally appeared September 17, 2015, on mises.org.

> months that have since passed, global central banks
> have cut interest rates 697 times, central banks have
> bought $15 trillion of financial assets, zero interest rate
> policies have been adopted in the US, Europe & Japan.
> And, following the Great Financial Crisis of 2008, both
> stocks and corporate bonds have soared to all-time
> highs thanks in great part to this extraordinary mon-
> etary regime.
>
> As noted above, a rate hike with a stroke ends this
> era.

A stroke indeed. By unelected, unaccountable, anti-market bureaucrats whose identities are completely unknown to virtually all Americans.

After so many years of the "new normal," we have to be reminded just how extraordinary—and unprecedented—the Fed's actions since 2008 have been. But does it not occur to bankers, much less the media breathlessly covering stock and bond markets, that these actions have set America on a hopelessly dangerous and unsustainable path? Or that placing so much economic power in the hands of a select few might not end well?

In a digital world, where information increasingly is decentral-ized and disseminated through multiple channels, it is astonishing to witness the degree to which a tiny group of individuals issues the single most important piece of information in the entire global economy.

By "tiny group" I mean the ten people who sit on the Fed's Open Market Committee: five Federal Reserve Board Governors (with two vacancies), and five of the twelve Federal Reserve Bank presidents on a rotating basis.

When the whole world waits with bated breath for the eco-nomic pronouncements of ten people sitting in one room, we might call that central planning. We might accurately call those ten people elites, since the shoe fits. And when those elites effectively determine the cost of borrowing money across whole economies, we might call that price fixing.

Interest rates are indeed prices, make no mistake about it. They are a critical component of economic calculation, providing instant information to entrepreneurs seeking to deploy capital to its best and highest uses. In a rational world, interest rates reflect the (ever-changing) relative time preferences of both lenders and borrowers.

But we live in an irrational world, where the judgments of real economic actors with skin in the game are thwarted by omniscient bureaucrats who openly seek to distort the price of money. Since the Crash of 2008, that distortion takes the form of suppressing interest rates below what Ludwig Mises called "originary" levels.

The FOMC explicitly targets a particular federal funds rate, the weighted average rate at which commercial banks lend their Fed reserves overnight. This hardly differs from explicitly targeting the price of a new Honda or a bushel of wheat.

Apologists bizarrely assure us that the Fed does not in fact "set interest rates" through this targeting, because the fed funds rate applies only to overnight lending of bank reserves that (by definition) cannot be lent commercially to the public.

But the fed funds rate is termed the "base" interest rate for a reason: it forms the baseline from which commercial banks apply cost-plus lending. The interest rate that borrowers with good credit pay commercial banks—the prime rate—absolutely is tied to the underlying overnight rate banks pay each other.

David Stockman calls the fed funds rate the most important price in all of capitalism. And since we don't know what interest rates should be thanks to central banks, Stockman argues, we really have no honest pricing of assets anywhere on the planet.

Since 2008 the Fed has kept the rate effectively at zero, and even pays interest on reserves at a .25 percent rate to forestall an environment of real negative rates and encourage banks to keep reserves higher.

But these many years of price fixing have failed to produce any-thing other than ersatz economic growth, mostly represented in overpriced equity markets, luxe housing, and bogus government spending. Average people are not better off than they were in 2008, and in many cases they are worse off.

In *The Theory of Money and Credit*, Ludwig Mises made the case more than 100 years ago—before the Fed and ECB ever existed—that monetary interventions cannot create prosperity:

> Attempts to carry out economic reforms from the mon-etary side can never amount to anything but an artificial stimulation of economic activity by an expansion of the circulation, and this, as must constantly be emphasized, must necessarily lead to crises and depression. Recur-ring economic crises are nothing but the consequence of attempts, despite all the teachings of experience and all the warnings of the economists, to stimulate eco-nomic activity by means of additional credit.

The key words here are "as must constantly be emphasized." It is incumbent on all of us to do everything in our power to make the case against central banking, one of the great evils of our time. We must make the case against the Fed loudly and repeatedly, even as the world is in thrall to it.

24

How to Think
about the Fed Now

The Great Crash of 2020 was not caused by a virus. It was *precipitated* by the virus, and made worse by the crazed decisions of governments around the world to shut down business and travel. But it was *caused* by economic fragility. The supposed greatest economy in US history actually was a walking sick man, made comfortable with painkillers, and looking far better than he felt—yet ultimately fragile and infirm. The coronavirus pandemic simply exposed the underlying sickness of the US economy. If anything, the crash was overdue.

Too much debt, too much malinvestment, and too little honest pricing of assets and interest rates made America uniquely vulnerable to economic contagion. Most of this vulnerability can be laid at the feet of central bankers at the Federal Reserve, and we will pay a terrible price for it in the coming years. This is an uncomfortable truth, one that central bankers desperately hope to obscure while the media and public remain fixated on the virus.

But we should not let them get away with it, because (at least when it comes to legacy media) the Fed's gross malfeasance is perhaps the biggest untold story of our lifetimes.

Symptoms of problems were readily apparent just last September during the commercial bank repo crisis. After more than

---

This article is an excerpt from the introduction to the Anatomy of the Crash *ebook, published by the Mises Institute, 2020.*

a decade of quantitative easing, relentless interest rate cutting, and huge growth in "excess" reserves (more than $1.5 trillion) parked at the Fed, banks still did not have enough overnight liquidity? The repo market exposed how banks were capital constrained, not reserve constrained. So what exactly was the point of taking the Fed's balance sheet from less than $1 trillion to over $4 trillion, anyway? Banks still needed money, after a decade of QE?

As with most crises, the problems took root decades ago. What we might call the era of modern monetary policy took root with the 1971 Nixon Shock, which eliminated any convertibility of dollars for gold. Less than twenty years later, in October 1987, Black Monday wiped out 20 percent of US stock market valuations. Fed chair Alan Greenspan promised Wall Street that such a thing would never happen again on his watch, and he meant it: the "Greenspan Put" was the Maestro's blueprint for providing as much monetary easing as needed to prop up equity markets. The tech stock crash of the NASDAQ in 2000 only solidified the need for "new" monetary policy, and in 2008 that policy took full flight under the obliging hand of Fed chairman Ben Bernanke—a man who not only fundamentally misunderstood the Great Depression in his PhD thesis, but who also had the self-regard to write a book titled *The Courage to Act* about his use of other people's money to reinflate the biggest and baddest stock bubble in US history.

In response to the coronavirus crisis, at least ostensibly, both the Fed and the US Treasury went into hyperdrive during March of 2020. The Fed's response to the crash strains credulity, simply because it has been so brazen. In fact, any article about the Fed becomes obsolete in just a few days, as it announces new programs, credit facilities, and purchases at a dizzying pace. In just the past six weeks the Fed announced $700 billion in new rounds of asset purchases from banks, to the point where the financial press has lost count of which "round" of quantitative easing we are in!

But more QE was just the beginning. Fed officials also cut the Federal Funds rate to nearly zero, and announced that bank reserve ratio requirements would be eliminated as of March 2020. This puts a new twist on fractional reserve banking, because it is hard to have a fraction when the numerator is zero.

Apart from this, the Fed also initiated a $1.5 trillion program of short-term lending facilities, with borrowers providing as collateral anything from Treasury debt to commercial paper to securities backed by student loans, auto loans, and credit-card loans. But there is more: for the first time in history, the Fed will spend billions purchasing corporate bonds, perhaps the biggest bubble of all in an economy full of debt-laden companies which took advantage of cheap interest rates to buy back equity and generally substitute financial engineering for real growth. Helpfully, the Fed chose the world's biggest asset management firm to run the corporate debt purchase program through various Exchange Traded Funds. And that firm, BlackRock, happens to be the world's largest provider of said ETFs.

As a result of all this, the Fed's balance sheet already has surged to over $6 trillion in mid-April 2020, and can anyone doubt it will soon be $10 trillion? Meanwhile, Congress managed to get involved with monetary policy through the backdoor in its $2 trillion "stimulus" bill called the CARES Act. The Act contains $454 billion to back an entirely separate Fed loan program for banks and corporations, a sum the Fed can leverage up to 10 times or $4.5 trillion. This is done using a "special purpose vehicle" under the auspices of the Treasury Department. This represents the melding of fiscal and monetary policy, the unholy blurring of any distinction (much less independence) of the Fed relative to Congress and the executive. It also represents the potential for another huge spike in the Fed's balance sheet.

Of course neither Congress nor the Fed can get the nation's fiscal house in order, no matter how much they print and spend. In fact, the 2020 federal deficit is projected at $4 trillion, which would represent more than 100 percent of likely tax revenue! $1,200 relief checks from the CARES Act will not go far when people are prohibited from working, and very little of the bill's spending will trickle down to individual Americans. The cascading effect across retail business and restaurants, landlords and mortgage companies, the travel industry, and local tax revenue will be overwhelming.

As this economic crisis unfolds, we will know the Fed has lost control if one of two things happen:

First, if the influx of new money and credit so rapidly created by the Fed causes (or at least worsens) rapid price inflation for consumers. Unlike 2008, this new money creation is not going primarily into the monetary base as commercial bank reserves. It is flowing out across the range of Fed purchases, and already in January and February the M2 money stock grew more than 15 percent. In 2008, economists of an Austrian bent warned, correctly, that a vast and sudden expansion of the Fed's balance sheet would have very harmful consequences. They were derided when hyperinflation did not materialize, but in fact there has been significant price inflation across a range of assets. Since the Fed has opened the floodgates far wider than in 2008, and since the residual effects of aggressive monetary easing since 2008 are still felt across markets, significant consumer price inflation is a real concern. If prices begin to rise noticeably, we will know the Fed has lost the ability to push off the day of reckoning.

Second, look for hiccups in the market for US Treasury debt which has implicitly relied on Fed backing since 2008. The Fed's willingness to buy up Treasuries in huge numbers from commercial banks signals to the world it will always act as a backstop and "make the market" as needed. Ultra-low interest rates engineered by the Fed ensure that debt service does not grow too large in the annual federal budget—less than $500 billion annually at present. This keeps Congress happy, knowing they can spend wildly beyond tax revenues without much pain. But this is perverse: if investors know the Fed will buy assets at a certain price no matter what markets do, they are not buying an "investment" but rather a guaranteed upside with socialized losses—every hapless dollar holder becomes a *de facto* surety for US Treasuries.

But what if they held a Treasury auction and no one bid? What if demand weakens, especially as Uncle Sam pays less than 1 percent interest on a ten-year bond? What if foreign buyers, representing almost 40 percent of US debt held by the public, simply lose faith that the profligate US government will ever get its fiscal house in order? If the Fed became the *primary* buyer at auction, that too would send a signal to the world—and a bad one. Rising interest rates for Treasury debt would be a calamity for the federal government budget, as even historically average rates above 5 percent would spike debt service above $1 trillion annually. The entire inflationary program, using monetary stimulus to prop up flagging demand, is utterly dependent on a steady market for US debt paying near zero interest. From Keynes to Krugman, this is the program. But like a game of musical chairs, nobody wants to hold low yield Treasuries if rates begin to rise no matter what the Fed does.

So what now? What should we make of the Fed today?

James Grant of *Grant's Interest Rate Observer* characterizes the Fed's recent actions as a "leveraged buy-out of the United States of America." The Fed is assumed to have an unlimited balance sheet, able to provide financial markets with "liquidity" as needed, in any amount, for any length of time. Pennsylvania senator Pat Toomey urges the Fed to do more, and Congress to spend more, all in the unholy name of liquidity.

But liquidity is nothing more than ready money for investment and spending. In the current environment it is a euphemism for free manna from heaven. It is "free" money—unearned, representing no increase in output or productivity. It has no backing and no redeemability. And not only are there no new goods and services in the economy, there are far fewer due to the lockdown.

So monetary "policy" as we know it is dead as a doornail. What central banks and Fed officials do no longer falls within the realm of economics or policy; in fact the Fed no longer operates as what we think of as a central bank. It is not a backstop or "banker's bank," as originally designed (in theory), nor is it a steward of economic stability pursuing its congressionally authorized dual mandate. It does not follow its own charter in the Federal Reserve Act (e.g., impermissibly buying corporate bonds). It does not operate based on economic theory or empirical data. It no longer pursues any identifiable public policy other than sheer political expediency. Fed governors do not follow "rules" or targets or models. They answer to no legislature or executive, except when cravenly collaborating with both to offload consequences onto future generations.

The Fed is, in effect, a lawless economic government unto itself. It serves as a bizarro-world ad hoc credit facility to the US financial sector, completely open ended, with no credit checks, no credit limits, no collateral requirements, no interest payments, and in some cases no repayments at all. It is the lender of first resort, a kind of reverse pawnshop which pays top dollar for rapidly declining assets. The Fed is now the Infinite Bank. It is run by televangelists, not bankers, and operates on faith.

That faith will be sorely tested.

25

MMT: Not Modern, Not Monetary, Not a Theory

Modern monetary theory (MMT) has a new champion, and a new bible. Stephanie Kelton, economics professor at SUNY Stony Brook, is the author of *The Deficit Myth: Modern Monetary Theory and the Birth of the People's Economy*. Professor Kelton was an advisor to the Bernie Sanders presidential campaigns, and her ideas increasingly find purchase with left progressives. It is certainly possible that she has a future either in a Biden administration or even on the Federal Reserve Board, which is a testament to how quickly our political and cultural landscape has shifted toward left progressivism. And left progressivism requires a "New Economics" to provide intellectual cover for what is essentially a political argument for painless free stuff from government.

Kelton's essential argument, first advanced by MMT guru Warren Mosler in the 1990s, is quite simple: federal spending is unconstrained by revenue. Taxes function only to regulate demand and hence inflation; federal borrowing functions only to regulate interest rates. Sovereign government treasuries can create and spend as much money as they like to stimulate growth, especially when the economy is underperforming. If inflation spikes, taxes can be imposed to take money out of the economy.

Thus the only constraints on unlimited government spending are political. Unleashing ourselves from these "self-imposed" constraints,

This article originally appeared June 24, 2020, on mises.org.

as Mosler puts it, is purely a matter of political will. Revenue is irrelevant to how you fund a government, so why not use government to fund the economy as a whole?

Dr. Bob Murphy has written a substantive review of Kelton's book and does a thorough and effective job of debunking MMT and providing Austrian rebuttals to her claims regarding money, debt, and deficits. But I would make three quick points of my own:

- **MMT is not modern.** Kings have used seigniorage and currency debasement for centuries to fund their endeavors, always at the expense of their subjects.

- **MMT is not monetary.** It is primarily a fiscal approach to state finance, focused on tax policy as the economic accelerator and brake. Its roots predate the US Federal Reserve Bank, and in fact predate the present notion of "monetary policy." MMT finds origins in early twentieth-century chartalism, whose proponents opposed gold in favor of paper money issued by government and mandated as legal tender. It is also a genealogical heir to the Greenbackers of the late 1800s, who believed Congress should direct the issuance of unbacked paper currency.

- **MMT is not a theory.** It is accounting. In fact, it relies on an accounting subterfuge which bizarrely claims government deficits represent private (societal) surpluses. Because government is the font from which currency springs, all financial assets (denominated in that currency of issue) exist thanks to government! Thus, under "national accounting," the more government spends, the richer we the people get. When tax revenue is $100 but government spends $120, Americans are richer by $20. And so on. This is not a theory; this is accounting gimmickry almost purposefully designed to obscure what's really going on.

In the relentlessly circular world of MMT, government is the source of all finance and in effect all wealth. Taxpayers don't fund government, because after all government first provides the "tokens" (currency) taxpayers need to pay their IRS bills! Government funds taxpayers, which is broadly speaking what the American left really believes. It's a version of Obama's "You didn't build that" rewritten into policy.

But let's not kid ourselves: the US federal government already finances its operations, at least in part, using conjured money. 2020 federal spending may exceed $8 trillion as Congress and the Trump administration blow the roof off the authorized $5 trillion budget with covid relief bills. *More than half* of that amount, maybe as much as $4 trillion, will be "deficit financed"—a nice way of saying not financed by tax revenue. This is a first in American history, to put it mildly.

This $4 trillion will not simply issue forth from Treasury Department printing machines, as Kelton would prescribe, but the effect is the same: the Treasury issues debt to cover the shortage, which the "public" buys, implicitly understanding that the Fed will always provide a ready market for such debt. And where does the Fed get the money to buy Treasurys? It creates it from nothing, in Keltonite fashion.

Chicagoites, market monetarists, supply-siders, NDGP targeters, and other free market proponents frankly don't have much to say about MMT. They already accept the premise of "monetary policy," i.e., that government or central banks should issue and control money in society. They already accept treating the money supply and interest rates as forms of policy tools. They already accept deficits and taxes as methods to prime or slow the economy. So although they may object to *how* Ms. Kelton wants to use money politically, they can't much object to *whether* money is used politically.[1]

---

[1] Austrians have always decried state-ordered or central bank monetary expansion per se, because it produces no new wealth in society but benefits those closely connected to the new money. And Austrians consistently apply Say's law to refute the entrenched idea that demand and consumption form the foundation of a healthy economy

Kelton deserves credit for writing a book aimed at lay audiences instead of for her peers in academic economics. Unlike most of those peers, she seems genuinely interested in helping us understand how the world works. And unlike most left progressive academics, she also seems interested in helping average people improve their lot in life. Perhaps most importantly, she does not display the kind of contempt and anger toward Red State America we see from the Paul Krugmans and Noah Smiths.

It's easy for those of a free market bent to dismiss MMT out of hand, but the impulse to create something from nothing resides deep in the human psyche, and politics is where this impulse finds expression. We should not underestimate the allure of MMT in the midst of our current upheavals, because it appears to make possible every left progressive program: unlimited public works and federal jobs, useless and uneconomic green energy schemes, reparations for black Americans, Medicare for All, free college, free housing, and a host of others. MMT is the perfect economic proposal for those who sincerely and deeply believe wealth simply exists in America, and will continue to exist, regardless of incentives. All we need to do is figure out how to more fairly divvy it up—and so why not through government spending?

The promise of something for nothing will never lose its luster. MMT should be viewed as a form of political propaganda rather than any kind of real economics or public policy. And like all propaganda, it must be fought with appeals to reality. MMT, where deficits don't matter, is an unreal place.

26

Negative Interest Rates Are the Price We Pay for De-Civilization

D o central bankers really think negative interest rates are rational?

"Calculation Error," which Bloomberg terminals sometimes display, is an apt metaphor for the current state of central bank policy. Both Europe and Asia are now awash in $13 trillion worth of negative-yielding sovereign and corporate bonds, and Alan Greenspan suggests negative interest rates soon will arrive in the US. Despite claims by both Mr. Trump and Fed Chair Jerome Powell concerning the health of the American economy, the Fed's Open Market Committee moved closer to negative territory today—with another quarter-point cut in the Fed Funds rate, below even a measly 2 percent.

Negative interest rates are just the latest front in the post-2008 era of "extraordinary" monetary policy. They represent a Hail Mary pass from central bankers to stimulate more borrowing and more debt, though there is far more global debt today than in 2007. Stimulus is the assumed goal of all economic policy, both fiscal and monetary. Demand-side stimulus is the mania bequeathed to us by Keynes, or more accurately by his followers. It is the absurd idea that an economy prospers by consuming and borrowing instead of producing and saving. Negative interest rates turn everything we know about economics upside down.

This article originally appeared September 18, 2019, on mises.org.

Under what scenario would anyone lend $1,000 to receive $900 in return at some point in the future? Only when the alternative is to receive $800 back instead, due to the predicted interventions of central banks and governments. Only then would locking in a set rate of capital loss make sense. By "capital loss" I mean just that; when there is no positive interest paid, the principal itself must be consumed. There is no "market" for negative rates. The future is uncertain, and there is always counterparty risk. The borrower might abscond, or default, or declare bankruptcy. Market conditions might change during the course of the loan, driving interest rates higher to the lender's detriment. Inflation could rise higher and faster than the agreed-upon nominal interest rate. The lender might even die prior to repayment.

Positive interest rates compensate lenders for all of this risk and uncertainty. Interest, like all economics, ultimately can be explained by human nature and human action.

If in fact negative interest rates can occur naturally, without central bank or state interventions, then economics textbooks need to be revised on the quick. Every theory of interest contemplates positive interest paid on borrowed capital. Classical economists and their "Real" theory say interest represents a "return" on capital, not a penalty. Capital available for lending, like any other good, is subject to real forces of supply and demand. But nobody would "sell" their capital by giving the buyer interest payments as well, they would simply hold onto it and avoid the risk of lending.

Marxists think interest payments represent exploitation by capital owners lending to needful workers. The amount of interest paid in addition to the capital returned was stolen from the debtor, because the lender did not work for it (ignoring, of course, the capitalist lender's risk). But how could a borrower be exploited by receiving interest payments for borrowing, i.e., repaying less than they borrowed? I suppose Marxists may in fact cheer the development of negative rates, and perversely see them as a transfer of wealth from lenders to borrowers (when, in fact, we know cheap money and credit overwhelmingly benefit wealthy elites, per the Cantillon Effect). So negative rates require Marxists to drastically rethink their theory of interest.

Austrians stress the time element of interest rates, comparing the lender's willingness to forego present consumption against the borrower's desire to pay a premium for present consumption. In Austrian theory interest rates represent the price at which the relative time preferences of lenders and borrowers meet. But once again, negative interest rates cannot explain how or why anyone would ever defer consumption without payment—or in fact pay to do so!

It should be noted that rational purchasers of negative-yield bonds hope to sell them before maturity, i.e., they hope bond prices rise as interest rates drop even lower. They hope to sell their bonds to a greater fool and generate a capital gain. They are not "buying" the obligation to pay interest, but the chance of reselling for a profit. So purchasing a negative-yield bond might make sense as an investment (vs. institutional and central bank bond buyers, which frequently hold bonds to maturity and thereby literally pay to lend money). But if and when interest rates rise, the losses to those left holding those $13 trillion of bonds could be staggering.

In the meantime, a huge artificial market for at least nominally positive US Treasury debt grows, strengthening the dollar and suppressing interest rates here at home. Once again, the dollar represents the least dirty shirt in the laundry. Congress loves this, of course, because even 5 percent rates would blow the federal budget to smithereens. Rising rates would cause debt service to be the largest annual line item in that budget, ahead of Social Security, Medicare, and defense. So we might say Congress and the Fed are in a symbiotic relationship at this point. The rest of the world might call it America's "exorbitant privilege."

Negative interest rates are the price we pay for central banks. The destruction of capital, economic and otherwise, is contrary to every human impulse. Civilization requires accumulation and production; de-civilization happens when too many people in a society borrow, spend, and consume more than they produce. No society in human history previously entertained the idea of negative interest rates, so like central bankers we are all in uncharted territory now.

Our job, among many, is to bring the insights of Austrian economics on money and banking to widespread attention before something truly calamitous happens.

27

The Terrible Economic Ignorance behind Covid Tradeoffs

Some of you may know the name Alex Berenson, the former *New York Times* journalist who comes from a left-liberal background. He has been absolutely fearless and tireless on Twitter over the past eighteen months, documenting the overreach and folly of covid policy—and the mixed reality behind official assurances on everything from social distancing to masks to vaccine efficacy. He became a one-man army against the prevailing covid narratives.

Mr. Berenson is famous for creating a viral (no pun intended) phrase which swept across Twitter last year: virus gonna virus.

Which means whether one is in Sweden or Australia, whether in New York or Florida, whether you have mask mandates or

---

This article is an excerpt from a talk delivered at the Ron Paul Institute conference on September 4, 2021.

lockdowns or close schools or require vaccine passports—or do NONE of these things—virus gonna virus. Covid hospitalizations and deaths will be concentrated among the obese and elderly. In almost any community, two-thirds or more of deaths are over age seventy, but even among the elderly more than 90 percent of those infected survive covid. And among all covid deaths, only about 7 percent are "covid only" without other serious contributing factors.

What we won't ever know, unfortunately—because we don't have a control group, at least in the West—is what would have happened in a society which simply did nothing in response to the virus. What if a country simply had encouraged citizens to build up their natural immunity through a healthy diet, exercise, vitamins, and natural sunlight? What if it had taken precautions for elderly and immune-compromised populations, while allowing younger and healthier people to live normally? Would such a country have reached a degree of natural immunity faster, with overall better outcomes for the physical and mental health of its citizens? And with far less economic damage?

All of this is the unseen. And no, it wasn't "worth it" to shut down the world.

Back to Mr. Berenson. Last week Twitter decided it had enough, and permanently suspended his account. This is no small thing for independent journalists—and God knows we need them—who reach a lot of people via Twitter and rely on it to make a living.

Search for his Twitter profile and you'll find something spooky. His name is still there, but with a quietly menacing "Account Suspended" warning. All other traces of his existence are erased: his header photo is gone, his profile photo is blank, and the descriptive bio is missing. Just blank. It's eerie and reminds me of that famous old photo of Stalin by the Moscow Canal. He's standing next to Nikolai Yezhov (I had to look him up), who fell out of favor with Stalin and was executed—then erased from the photo by Soviet censors.

Alex Berenson has been similarly unpersoned, removed, erased. But even if he ends up a casualty of this war—and whether you agree with him or not—people like him have managed to challenge the official narrative in ways unimaginable even twenty years ago. The financial journalist John Tamny made an interesting point last week: complain about social media all you want, but Facebook and Twitter have been great sources of information during this covid mess. And after thinking about it I had to agree. Most of the alternative information about covid I've consumed via social media. But of course, Mr. Berenson no longer has this luxury.

The Covid Economy and Tradeoffs

Speaking of narratives, we have especially lacked clear and sober thinking about the injuries to the US economy created by covid policies. We profoundly fail to understand the economics behind covid, because we so desperately want to kid ourselves that the economy will be "normal" soon.

Governments are good at two things, namely bossing us around and spending money. They do both in spades whenever a supposed crisis arises, and both Congress and the Fed went into hyperdrive beginning in March 2020. The Fed pumped more than $9 trillion to its primary dealers, estimates are that more than 20 percent of all US dollars ever issued were issued in 2020 alone. On the fiscal side, more than forty federal agencies have spent $3.2 trillion in covid stimulus spending. So that is $12 trillion of inflationary pressure introduced to our economy.

What the economy wants and needs during crises is of course deflation. When uncertainty rises, and it certainly did for millions of Americans worried about their jobs in 2020, people naturally and inevitably hold larger cash balances. They spend less. Meanwhile they were staying home, driving less, dining out less, traveling less, working less. All of this is naturally deflationary, so of course Congress and the Fed embarked on an effort to fight this tooth and nail with intentional inflation. So now we're in a wrestling match between two opposing forces, one natural and one artificial.

Dr. Hans-Hermann Hoppe has a famous dictum: markets produce goods, which are the things we want and willingly buy or consume. Government produces bads, which is to say things we don't want at all. Things like wars and inflation. They do this with our own money, reducing what we have to spend on actual goods and thus reducing production of those goods.

The past sixteen months we've had lots of government bads, to the point where we might call them "worsts," which are even worse than bads. The covid and Afghanistan debacles come to mind.

It may be facile and self-serving to compare the federal state's inability to manage Afghanistan with its inability to manage a virus, but the comparison is just too perfect to resist. So I won't resist.

Among the bads government produces is misinformation. One analogy between covid and Afghanistan is the phenomenon known as the fog of war: the uncertainty in situational awareness experienced by participants in military operations.

Paraphrasing Carl von Clausewitz: war is the realm of uncertainty; the factors on which action in war is based are wrapped in a fog of uncertainty. Fog and friction cloud the commander's judgment—even where the commander wholly shares our interests, which is hardly a given with covid. When we declared war on a virus, clarity went out the window. And so we've lived with sixteen months of fog, of covid misinformation. This happens in tandem with the media, which parrot official pronouncements from sources like the deeply compromised Fauci and stir up alarmism at every turn.

And we're still living with it. Consider we still don't have definitive answers to these simple questions:

Do masks really work?

Do kids really need masks? As an aside, our great friend Richard Rider reports that San Diego County—population 3.3 million—shut down its public schools for a year with *one* student death!

Is there asymptomatic spread?

Does the virus live on surfaces?

How long does immunity last after having covid?

How many vaccines will someone need to be "fully" vaccinated? How many boosters? Annual?

Aren't delta and other variants simply the predictable evolution of any virus?

How do we define a "case" or infection if someone shows no symptoms and feels fine?

Can covid really be eradicated like polio? If so, why haven't we eradicated flu by now?

And so on. We never get clear answers, but only fog.

But perhaps the most shocking thing about sixteen months is our childlike inability to consider tradeoffs! I'm not only talking about the tremendous economic consequence of shutting down businesses, and the horrific financial damage it has done and will do to millions of Americans. I'm not only talking about the depression, isolation from friends and loved ones, alcoholism, untreated illness, suicide, weight gain and obesity, stunted child development, and all the rest.

I'm talking about understanding the basic economic tradeoffs of covid policy: supply chain, food, energy, housing, unemployment. This is bread and butter economics.

I can't stress this enough: millions of Americans have no conception of economics, and simply don't believe tradeoffs exist. They think, and are encouraged by the political class to think, that government can simply print money in the form of stimulus bills and pay people enhanced unemployment benefits to stay home. That the CDC [Centers for Disease Control and Prevention], of all cockamamie federal agencies, can simply impose a rent moratorium and effectively vitiate millions of local contracts—it will just work itself out somehow. That Congress can simply issue forgivable PPP [Paycheck Protection Program] loans to closed or hobbled businesses so they can magically make payroll. That the Federal Reserve can simply buy up assets from commercial banks, lend them limitless funds, and command lower interest rates to stimulate housing and consumerism.

Millions of Americans, through sheer ignorance of economics, literally think these actions are costless and wholly beneficial—without downside.

And now we wonder why the economy can't just flip a switch and get back to normal. But that's not how an incredibly complex global supply chain, with just-in-time delivery, works. And that's why thousands of Ford F-150s are sitting unsold, and unsellable, in huge parking lots—there is a global semiconductor chips shortage. Many of them come from a single company in Taiwan. By the way, semiconductor chips are used in everything from iPhones to Xbox consoles to Surface laptops to refrigerators.

CNBC recently wrote about the supply chain interruptions. It gets the cause of inflation wrong, blaming it on the pandemic rather than central banks, but it paints a vivid picture of the serious problems facing a radically overstressed global manufacturing sector. Delays in delivery are said to be the longest in decades. And inflation plus delays is bad news, because it's so hard for buyers and sellers at all stages of production to know what to charge and what to pay for either capital goods or consumption goods. How many construction projects, for example were blindsided by the five-time rise in lumber prices last year? Ports are clogged awaiting trucks—not enough drivers—so containers sit for weeks rather than days. Empty containers have become scarce. Rail schedules are affected by the ports like dominos, and freight prices are spiking. Will West Coast longshoremen strike in 2022 when their contract is up? Will new emissions regulations which slow ships kill more capacity? Will key Chinese factories shut down again due to delta?

None of it is pretty, and may last into 2023. So buy your Christmas presents now!

We are starting to see the unseen, but economists, whose job it is to show us the tradeoffs, have been largely AWOL over the past year and a half. Consider this recent post by a famous libertarian free market economist:

> US GDP is now higher, in fact a fair bit higher, than when the pandemic began.
> US labor force participation is about 1.5% lower than when the pandemic began.
> Was there really slack to the tune of a few million people in Jan of 2020?
> Has inflation really changed enough to make the GDP numbers misleading?
> Has total factor productivity improved that much in that time, under those stresses? (i.e., more output from less input, labor & capital).
>
> Or is this all a sign that the structure of the economy is more stratified than we think—that there are millions of people in more-or-less filler jobs who can be cast out and the economy just keeps on running along? Yes, there are all sorts of reports of labor shortages, and all manner of supply chain hiccups which seem too often be associated with off shoring, but general activity is still high. (Or is it? Are the numbers reporting "vapor GDP?"—or are the inflation adjustments really out of whack so real GDP is not what we think it is?)

This is clever masquerading as smart, and it's the sort of thing which makes people dislike economists. It's *homo economicus* nonsense. This kind of navel-gazing—wondering aloud, as though we could shut down the world for a year, send everybody home, suspend rent payments, and not suffer tradeoffs—makes me think economics as a profession is not doing the world any good. People desperately need productive activity for their basic health and happiness, even if that activity doesn't much add to the national economy.

A friend who runs a large chain of retail stores across several states sent me this in response.

> It's amazing how [BLANKED]-up this person is. An economy is a way to get stuff. Is there much stuff, or less stuff, than when this all began? More cars or less? More computers and personal digital devices or less? More food or less? More oil or less? Greater business to business supply chain or less?
>
> But because this [BLANK] thinks the economy is a symbolic architecture, not a real thing for getting real stuff, he's absolutely flummoxed by a simple question. Go outside, moron. Step away from the keyboard and the spreadsheet.

I thought he was spot on. Economics is the study of choice in the face of scarcity, of how we get the goods and services we want in an environment of tradeoffs and uncertainty. Nothing could be more disastrous to that environment than vague, open-ended government lockdown measures. We don't need to move numbers around until they please us as some kind of substitute gnostic knowledge. We shut down the world over a virus, restarting it will be difficult, and the economic damage will be enormous and long lasting. Economists should be showing us the unseen damage, not cheering the juiced-up data.

My point here is to suggest the economics of our present situation are worse than advertised, and that economics is about what holds us together. What we think of as America is mostly an economic arrangement, not a social or cultural one—and certainly not a political arrangement. America is hardly a country anymore, and I take no pleasure in saying that. What happens when the economics unravel?

The Great Unraveling

But there is a happy upside to all of this. A silver lining, perhaps.

Over eighteen months we've learned that all crises are local. For eighteen months it has mattered very much whether you live in Florida or New York, whether you live in Sweden or Australia. And the physical analog world reasserted itself with a vengeance: no matter where you are, no matter how rich you may be, you must exist in corporeal reality. You need housing, food, clean water, energy, and medical care in the most physical sense. You need last-mile delivery, no matter what is happening in the broader world. Your local situation suddenly mattered quite a bit in 2020. It was the year localism reasserted itself.

Whether your local reality was dysfunctional or did not matter quite a bit in the terrible covid year. And people are waking up to the simple reality of this dysfunction. We know the federal government can't manage covid. It can't manage Afghanistan. It can't manage debt, or the dollar or spending, or entitlements. It can't even run federal elections, for God's sake, much less provide security, or justice, or social cohesion.

So how can it manage a country of 330 million people? How can it manage fifty states?

Whether we want to call it the Great Awakening or the Great Realignment, something profound is happening. Imagine if the twenty-first century reverses the dominant trend of the nineteenth and twentieth, namely the centralization of political power in national and even supranational governments? What if we are about to embark on an experiment in localism and regionalism, simply due to the sheer inability of modern national governments to manage day-to-day reality?

A kind of centrifugal force is at work. Here in the US, people are self-segregating—both ideologically and geographically—in what we should think of as a kind of soft secession. United Van Lines confirms what we already knew: people are fleeing California, New York, New Jersey, and Illinois for Texas, Idaho, Florida, and Tennessee. This is simple flight from the dysfunction of big cities and unworkable progressive policies, laid bare by the analog lessons of covid.

We should cheer this. If just 10 percent of Americans hold reasonable views on politics, economics, and culture they would constitute 33 million people—we could coalesce as a significant political force! And this nation within a nation would be larger and more economically powerful than many European countries.

Furthermore, we are witnessing a tremendous shift in political power away from cities toward exurbs and rural areas. There really is nothing like it in US history. America started in colonies and villages, before moving westward to farms and ranches. When factories began to replace farms as major employers, Americans moved to the old Rust Belt cities like Chicago and Pittsburgh and Detroit. When tech and finance began to overshadow manufacturing, Americans moved to Manhattan and Seattle and Silicon Valley for the best jobs. But that revolution in finance and tech means capital is more mobile than ever, and covid accelerated our ability to work from home. All of this could have huge beneficial effects for smaller cities and rural areas, which in turn could have profound effects for the congressional map and electoral college. If the angry school board meetings over masks are any indication, politics already has become more localized.

Covid policies ruined cities, at least for a while, and the Great Unraveling will reduce the political and economic power of those cities.

So, a once-in-a-generation opportunity is before us. The federal government is far and away the biggest, most powerful institution in America and faith in institutions is crumbling. And it should crumble. Washington, DC, has been the centerpiece around which we have organized society for a hundred years now, and that's a profoundly evil reality. So, we should cheer when Americans lose faith in it due to Trump or covid or Afghanistan or public opinion polls which show a deeply divided and skeptical country. There is a growing sense that DC is over, it's done, and it's time to turn our backs on it. We are losing our state religion.

Contra our political elites, covid and the disastrous reaction by governments may end up reducing their power and standing in society.

28

Inflation: State-Sponsored Terrorism

R emember the quaint old days of 2019? We were told the US economy was in great shape. Inflation was low, jobs were plentiful, GDP was growing. And frankly, if covid had not come along, there is a pretty good chance Donald Trump would have been reelected.

At an event in 2019, my friend and economist Dr. Bob Murphy said something very interesting about the political schism in this country. He said: If you think America is divided now, what would things look like if the economy was terrible, if we had another crash like 2008?

Well, we might not have to imagine such a scenario much longer.

If you think Americans are divided today, and at each other's throats—metaphorically, but more and more literally—imagine if they were cold and hungry!

The article is from a talk delivered on September 3, 2022, at the Ron Paul Institute in northern Virginia.

Imagine if we had to live through something like Weimer Germany, Argentina in the 1980s, Zimbabwe in the 2000s, or Venezuela and Turkey today? What would our political and social divisions look like then?

Ladies and gentlemen, we live under the tyranny of inflationism. It terrorizes us, either softly or loudly. I suspect it will get a lot louder soon.

As the late Bill Peterson explained, "Inflationism, in today's terms, is deficit-spending, deliberate credit expansion on a national scale, a public policy fallacy of monumental proportions, of creating too much money that chases too few goods. It rests on the 'money illusion,' a widespread confusion between income as a flow of money and income as a flow of goods and services—a confusion between 'money' and wealth."

Inflationism is both a fiscal and monetary regime, but its consequences go far beyond economics. It has profound social, moral, and even civilizational effects. And understanding how it terrorizes us is the task today.

Understanding Inflationism

I'll ask you to consider three things.

First, inflation is a policy. We should make them own it. Inflation is not something beyond our control that comes along periodically like the weather. Our monetary and fiscal regimes actually set out to create it and consider it a good thing. Let's not forget—both Trump and Biden signed off on covid stimulus bills which combined injected roughly $7 TRILLION dollars directly into the economy—even as actual goods and services were dramatically reduced due to lockdowns. Deflation was the natural order of things in response to a crisis, a bullshit crisis in my view, but still a crisis. So of course, Uncle Sam actively attempted to undo the natural desire to spend less and hold more cash during a time of uncertainty.

This $7 trillion was created on the *fiscal* side of things. It was not new Fed bank reserves exchanged for commercial bank assets as a roundabout monetization of Treasury debt, as we saw with quantitative easing. This was direct stimulus from the Treasury via Congress as express fiscal policy. Free money. This money went straight into the accounts of individuals (stimulus checks), state and local governments, millions of small businesses (PPP [Paycheck Protection Program] loans), the airline industry, and untold earmarks. This was actual cash, and it is being spent. So any economist who tells you today's inflation is somehow a surprise is either charitably misinformed or gaslighting.

This is a policy. Inflation is engineered. The difference between supposedly desirable 2 percent CPI [Consumer Price Index] and very bad, awful, no good 9 percent CPI is only one of degree. The same mindset produces both. But the inflationists insist a little bit of virus is good for us, like a vaccine. . . . So, an express policy of some inflation is the mechanism to forestall *too much* inflation. This is a curious position.

Second, inflation is nothing less than sanctioned state terror, and we ought to treat it as such. It's criminal. It makes us live in fear. Inflation is not just an economic issue, but in fact produces deep cultural and social sickness in any society it touches. It makes business planning and entrepreneurship—which rely on profit and loss calculations using money prices—far more difficult and risky, which means we get less of both. How do you measure money profits when the unit of measurement keeps falling in value? It erodes capital accumulation, the driver of greater productivity and material progress. So, inflation destroys both existing wealth and future wealth, which never comes into being and thus diminishes the world our children and grandchildren inhabit. And it makes us poor and vulnerable in our senior years.

After all, saving is for chumps. Current one-year CD rates are below 3 percent, while inflation is at least 9 percent. So, you're losing 6 points just by standing still! By the way, the last time official

CPI approached double digits, in the early '80s, a one-year CD earned 15 percent. I'd like to hear Jerome Powell explain that. By the way, ever since Alan Greenspan began this great experiment of four decades of lower and lower interest rates, guess who hasn't benefited? Poor people and subprime borrowers, who still pay well over 20 percent for their car loans and credit cards.

But here is an unspoken truth: inflation also makes us *worse people*. It degrades us morally. It almost forces us to choose current consumption over thrift. Economists call this high time preference, preferring material things today at the expense of saving or investing. It makes us live for the present at the expense of the future, the opposite of what all healthy societies do. Capital accumulation over time, the result of profit, saving, and investing, is how we all got here today—a world with almost unimaginable material wealth all around us. Inflationism reverses this.

So this very human impulse, to save for a rainy day and perhaps leave something for your children, is upended. Inflationism is inescapably an antihuman policy.

Third, hyperinflation can happen here. It may not happen, and it may not happen soon. But it might well happen. And even steady 10 percent inflation means prices double roughly every seven years. We can pretend the laws of economics don't apply to the world's leading superpower, or that the world's reserve currency is safe from the problems experienced by lesser countries. And it's certainly true our reserve currency status insulates us and makes the world need dollars. Governments and industry mostly use US dollars to buy oil from OPEC countries, hence the term "petrodollar." It's certainly true governments, central banks, large multinational companies, worldwide investment funds, sovereign wealth funds, and pension funds all hold plenty of US dollars—and thus in a perverse way share our interest in maintaining King Dollar. It's true we don't have easy historical examples of a world reserve currency, like gold, suffering a rapid devaluation across the world (even the Spanish silver devaluation of the 1500 and 1600s was not necessarily caused by a glut in circulating currency). So we're in uncharted territory, especially given the fiscal and monetary excesses of the last twenty-five years and especially the last two years. But this only means the potential contagion is greater and more dangerous. The whole world can be sickened at once.

A Story: When Money Dies

But as most of you surely know by now, we don't turn the ship around or win hearts and minds simply with logic and facts and airtight arguments. We need stories, or narratives, in today's awful media parlance, to gain influence. We need emotional reactions. So I will suggest a story with plenty of pathos to shake people out of their complacency and sound the warning.

That story is *When Money Dies*, Adam Fergusson's brilliant cautionary account of hyperinflation in Weimar-era Germany. It is the story Americans desperately need to hear today.

Fergusson's book should be assigned to central bankers' stat (we wonder how many of them know of it). It's not a book about economic policy per se—it's a story, an historical account of folly and hubris on the part of German politicians and bureaucrats. It's the story of a disaster created by humans who imagined they could overcome markets by monetary fiat. It's a reminder that war and inflation are inextricably linked, that war finance leads nations to economic disaster and sets the stage for authoritarian bellicosity. We think Versailles and reparations created the conditions for Hitler's rise, but without the Reichbank's earlier suspension of its one-third gold reserve requirement in 1914, it seems unlikely Germany would have become a dominant European military power. Without inflationism, Hitler might have been a footnote.

Most of all, *When Money Dies* is a tale of privation and degradation. Not only for Germans, but also Austrians and Hungarians grappling with their own political upheavals and currency crises in the 1910s and '20s. In a particularly poignant chapter, Fergusson describes the travails of a Viennese widow named Anna Eisenmenger. A friend of mine, @popeofcapitalism on Twitter, sent me her diary from Amazon.

The story starts with her comfortable life as the wife of a doctor and mother to a wonderful daughter and three sons. They are talented and cultured and musical and upper middle class. They even socialize with Archduke Franz Ferdinand and his wife, the Duchess of Hohenberg.

But in May 1914 their happy life is shattered. Ferdinand is assassinated at Sarajevo, and war breaks out. Wars cost money, and the gold standard wisely adopted by Austria-Hungary in 1892 is almost immediately seen as an impediment. So, the government predictably begins to issue war bonds in huge numbers, and the central bank fires up the printing presses. This results in a sixteenfold increase in prices just during the war years.

But the human effects are catastrophic, even apart from the war itself.

Frau Eisenmenger is luckier than most Viennese women. She owns small investments which produce modest income—fixed in kronen. Her banker quietly urges her to immediately exchange any funds for Swiss francs. She demurs, as dealing in foreign currency has been made illegal. But soon she realizes he was right. There is probably a lesson here for all of us!

As the war unfolds, she is forced into black markets and pawning assets to procure food for her war-damaged children. Her currency and Austrian bonds become almost worthless. She exchanges her husband's gold watch for potatoes and coal. The downward spiral of her life, marked by hunger and hoarding anything with real value, happens so quickly she barely has time to adjust.

But her misery doesn't stop with the end of the war. On the contrary, the Saint-Germain Treaty in 1919 gives way to a period of hyperinflation: the money supply increases from 12 to 30 billion kronen in 1920, and to about 147 billion kronen at the end of 1921 (does this sound like America 2020, by the way?). By August 1922, consumer prices are fourteen thousand times greater than before the start of the war eight years earlier.

In just a few short years she endures countless tragedies, all made worse by privation, cold, and hunger. Her husband dies. Her daughter contracts tuberculosis and dies, leaving Frau Eisenmenger to take care of her infant daughter and young son. One son goes missing in the war, one son is blinded, and her son in law becomes crippled following the loss of both legs. Food and coal are rationed, so her apartment is a miserable hovel—and she is forced to dodge searches by the "Food Police" looking for illegal hoarding. Ultimately, she is shot in the lung by her own Communist son, Karl, in a fit of rage.

There is a haunting and historically accurate silent film about conditions in Vienna during this era called *The Joyless Street*, starring a young Greta Garbo. Her character sees everything deteriorate around her; even her father beats her with his cane for returning home without food. Once friendly neighbors become suspicious of each other's stores of bread and cheese, while prostitution becomes rampant. Angry people jostle in line, waiting for the butcher to open; when he does, only the most attractive women receive the scraps of meat available that day. Fistfights become common. Starving children beg for food in front of restaurants and cafes like stray dogs. Everything familiar and beautiful in society becomes degraded and cheapened seemingly overnight.

Like a Stephen King horror movie, something very familiar changes into a strange and menacing place. Your neighborhood takes on a different light. People you thought you knew became malevolent strangers. Scapegoating, blame, and snitching become commonplace.

Is this beginning to sound familiar, especially after Biden's sick speech the other night?

So, next time one of these sociopaths in our political class wants to spend a few trillion more to pay for a green new deal or a war with China or free college, remember Frau Eisenmenger's story.

The Lessons for Today

How do we apply this grim historical lesson from the Weimar period to America today? How do we tell this story?

First, we explain inflationism in human terms, to personalize it and debamboozle it. Make monetary policy vital and immediate, not boring, and dry and technocratic. Again, there are enormous moral and civilization components to monetary policy. Inflation not only harms our economy, *it makes us worse people*: profligate, shortsighted, lazy, and unconcerned with future generations. Professor Guido Hülsmann literally wrote the book on this. It's called *The Ethics of Money Production*. This is maybe the greatest untold story in America today: the story of not only how the Fed fundamentally shifted our economy from one of production to consumption, *but what it did to us as people.* Don't let them hide behind complex Fed speak the simple reality: monetary policy is nothing less than criminal theft from future generations, from savers, and from the poorest Americans, who are furthest from the money spigot. The idea that reasonably intelligent laypeople cannot understand monetary policy, that it is too important and complex for anyone but experts, is nonsense. We should expose it.

Second, ridicule the absurd idea that "policy" can make us richer. More goods and services produced more and more efficiently, thanks to capital investment—and thereby creating price deflation—make us richer. That's the only way. Not legislative or monetary edicts.

So we should attack any notion of "public policy" and especially "monetary policy." Inflationism creates a fake economy, a "make-believe" economy, as Axios recently put it. A fake economy depends on enormous levels of ongoing fiscal and monetary intervention. We call this "financialization," but we all have a sense that our prosperity is borrowed. We all feel it. Capital markets are degraded: a lot of money moves around without creating any value for anyone. Companies don't necessarily make profits or pay dividends; all that matters to shareholders is selling their stock for capital gains. It always requires a new Ponzi buyer. But we know intuitively this isn't right: consider a restaurant or dry cleaner which operated without profit for years in the hope of selling for a gain years or decades later. Only the distorted incentives created by inflationism make this mindset possible. So down with "policy"—what we need is sound money!

Finally, let us not fear being accused of hyperbole or alarmism. Let me ask you this: what happens if we're wrong, and what happens if they're wrong? What they are doing, meaning central bankers and national treasuries, is unprecedented. Fake money is infinite, real resources are not. Hyperinflation may not be around the corner or even years away; no one can predict such a thing. But at some point, the US economy must create real organic growth if we hope to maintain living standards and avoid an ugly inflationary reality. No amount of monetary or fiscal engineering can take the place of capital accumulation and higher productivity. More money and credit is no substitute for more, better, and cheaper goods and services. Political money can't work, and we should never be afraid to attack it root and branch. We need private money, the only money immune from the inescapable political incentive to vote for things now and pay for them later. If this is radical, so be it.

History shows us how money dies. Yes, it can happen here. Only a fool thinks otherwise.

Strategy

29

Welcome to
Post-Persuasion America

Welcome to 2021 in post-persuasion America!

I first heard this term used by Steve Bannon, architect of the surprising 2016 Trump campaign, in a PBS *Frontline* documentary titled *America's Great Divide*. Speaking way back in the pre-covid days of early 2020, Bannon asserted the information age makes us less curious and willing to consider worldviews unlike our own. We have access to virtually all of humanity's accumulated knowledge and history on devices in our pockets, but the sheer information overload causes us to dig in rather than open up. Anyone who wants to change their mind can find a whole universe of alternative viewpoints online, but very few people do (especially beyond a certain age). For Bannon this meant the Trump campaign, and politics generally, was about mobilization rather than persuasion.

Because we can always find media sources which confirm our perspective and biases—and dismiss those which don't—the notion of politics by argument or consensus is almost entirely lost.

This article originally appeared January 1, 2021, on mises.org.

And no matter what our political or cultural perspective, there is someone creating content tailored to suit us as stratified consumers. Thus liberals, conservatives, and people of every other ideological stripe live in vastly different digital media worlds, even when they live in close physical proximity.

This overwhelming amount of curated and segregated white noise comes at us every day, from 24-hour news to Facebook, Twitter, and YouTube. Idiotic platforms like TikTok and Discord vie with video games for the attention of our children. All of it leaves us numb and exhausted. Our attention spans suffer. We slowly lose our aptitude for deep thinking and serious reading. We attempt to replace wisdom and understanding with data and facts.

But because information is so abundant and readily available, it becomes worth less and less. Information is cheap, literally.

For our grandparents, knowledge was analog and came with a price. Gatekeepers, in the form of media, universities, libraries, and bookstores, acted as editors and filters. Walter Cronkite, the most trusted propagandist in America, delivered one version of the news every night. The local newspaper did the same every morning. Even just thirty years ago it was often no easy task, and there was no small cost, to obtain books and literature not easily found in local or university libraries.

If someone today wants to read Austrian economics, for example (a particular bogeyman of Bannon's), they can do so at virtually no cost other than time. They don't even need to leave home. The smartphone in their palm holds a lifetime of reading and learning in just this one discipline. No physical books, no college, no tuition, and no librarian required.

So why don't more people do so? The short answer is: most people are beyond persuasion.

This does not mean we should surrender to the forces of economic illiteracy, or give up trying to win hearts and minds for political liberty. On the contrary, we should redouble our efforts to cultivate anyone interested in civil society, real economics, markets, property, and peace—especially those under thirty. But this is not a numbers game. We should focus on those who can be reached, not some mythical majority. Our task is to reach some people narrowly and deeply, not a majority of people superficially. We stand in contrast to the white noise, and opposed to the superficiality and anti-intellectualism of our age. Mobilizing the few is far more important and far more effective than foolishly trying to persuade the many.

H. L. Mencken was right about believing in liberty but not believing in it enough to force it upon anyone. Just as we oppose foreign interventionism, we should stop trying to remake those US cities and states which are beyond help. We need to recognize that tens of millions of Americans are likely beyond persuasion in the direction of sensible political or economic views. Millions more are committed socialists who would readily agree to nationalize whole industries and radically redistribute property. By definition these are unreasonable views, so how does one use persuasion where reason is lacking?

Post-persuasion America requires us to think about how to separate and unyoke ourselves politically from DC. Our immediate future lies in hard federalism, which dovetails with the soft secession which is happening already as millions of Americans vote with their feet. Mobilization and separation, not persuasion, is the way forward.

30

The Sober Political Reality
for Libertarians

What do I mean by better understanding and accepting reality? What I mean is this: libertarians should understand the numbers, and tailor goals and expectations accordingly. First, recognize that America is no longer a country of natural or reflexive libertarians which it once was—to put it mildly.

Sometimes we forget that the twentieth century was the progressive century, because progressivism has become part of the landscape. Central banking, adventurous foreign policy, income taxes, Social Security, Medicare, welfare programs, housing programs, food stamps—all of these would have sounded outrageous to most Americans at the turn of the twentieth century. By the turn of the twenty-first century, all of these progressive programs were entrenched. They are merely the *baseline* for the next program. Both major parties are thoroughly and irretrievably progressive.

The entrenched mindset, the default position in American politics today is for government to "do something." This is the activist view of the state—held by both Democrats and Republicans—that no area of human activity is not the state's business.

We can blame pandering politicians for this, we can blame the cronyist patronage system, we can blame mainstream media and government schools for this—and they are all to blame. But

This article is from a talk given at the 2016 Texas Libertarian Party Convention.

it doesn't change the fact: most Americans are now reflexively progressive, meaning they want government to *do something*, rather than reflexively libertarian.

This explains so much. As I mentioned, the internet and social media have been great levelers. But they also tend to create echochambers, where we all live in bubbles of content tailored to fit our viewpoint. We live in bubbles with friends who share that viewpoint.

That's why a few million dedicated people can feel like a huge movement online—we saw this during Ron Paul 2012—but have little impact on electoral politics. When libertarians are scattered around fifty states, their political impact is severely diluted.

Let's also not forget that America is much larger than it was when the Libertarian Party began in 1971. The US was 207 million people then, compared to nearly 330 million people today. This raises an uncomfortable question: has the population grown faster than interest in libertarian ideas has grown?

It's also important to accept the extent to which the two-party system has locked down certain deep advantages at every level of government. We're not just talking about ballot access laws or campaign finance rules that benefit those parties.

We're talking about a bicameral federal legislature that is fundamentally structured to maintain the status quo. The Constitution simply says that the US House and Senate may determine the rules for their proceedings. The Constitution simply says that a census for apportioning representatives will be taken every ten years. The Constitution simply gives Congress power over the time, place, and manner of *elections*.

It says nothing about political parties, or congressional committees, or congressional leadership, or gerrymandering, or how campaigns are financed.

But today we have this incredible system of party power and party apparatus that doesn't allow for a single Libertarian, Green,

214 A Strange Liberty

Peace & Freedom, or any other third party in Congress. Not a single one, in a country of 330 million people! Think about that.

Now I'm not particularly enamored of the Constitution. My point here is that the parties have set up a wildly extra-constitutional system of patronage for themselves, using the legislative process to funnel money and power to themselves. The political class is not going to be persuaded to give this all up in the face of superior libertarian arguments!

I think we'd be far better off today with a parliamentary system, at least it would allow for minority parties, strategic alliances, and coalition building.

My point here is not to discourage anyone, but rather to counsel acceptance of the numbers and the facts and make tactical decisions based on that reality.

And there are bright spots. For example, a 2014 Gallup poll suggests that roughly 24 percent of Americans could be characterized as libertarian, in a category distinct from conservatives, liberals, and populists.

My own highly unscientific opinion is that perhaps a quarter of the US population is sympathetic to libertarian ideas—regardless of how they identify themselves, and regardless of how they vote. Perhaps 5 percent to 10 percent of the population is actual libertarians, people who agree to a large extent with the idea of serious reductions in the size and scope of government.

So take heart, knowing that we're still talking about 10 or 20 or 30 million people. That's quite a vanguard, and if history is any guide, vanguards are just that: a small but highly influential and highly energized group of individuals who lead new developments and new ideas. Take heart, but be realistic about the numbers and the system itself. It's OK to have modest short-term goals, and it's OK if progress is slower than we'd like. Not everybody sees the world the way we do. Progressives have built their political victories over 100 years! It may not be popular, but every great society was built by people with time horizons beyond their own lifetimes.

31

Against the Zeitgeist

Ladies and gentlemen, the first task for any intellectual or ideological effort is to understand the environment surrounding it. Whether we like it or not, we live in a decidedly illiberal age: an age hostile to private property, individualism, civility, speech, academic freedom, culture, even to civilization itself. The spirit and tenor of our time are not at all conducive to liberal arguments; in fact such arguments are perverted into justifications for state action. Because of this sober reality we should resist the zeitgeist, and resist the language, narratives, issue framing, incivility, and purported egalitarian ends of the anti-intellectual landscape around us.

If you've read Murray Rothbard on the Progressive Era, you know he hated a reformer. And he especially hated a Yankee pietist reformer. No one embodied this kind of reformer like John Dewey, the psychologist who earned Rothbard's wrath through his evangelical though secular zeal for saving the world through progress and statism.

Dewey had what Rothbard called a "seemingly endless" career, with significant influence—which he bolstered with frequent columns in *The New Republic*—a new magazine in 1914, created as an unholy alliance between big business and leftwing public intellectuals.

An astonishing article Dewey produced for *The New Republic* in 1917 bore the perfect title for our discussion today: "The Conscription of Thought." Dewey, like his colleagues at the magazine, urged the US to enter the Great War in Europe, and

This article is excerpted from a talk delivered at the 2018 annual meeting of the Property and Freedom Society, in Bodrum, Turkey.

they did everything they could to encourage a "war spirit" among stubbornly doubtful Americans.

Now his pro-war perspective had nothing to do with the realities on the ground in Germany or Britain or France, or even US interests in those areas. His focus was entirely domestic—war would help lead America to socialize its economy and greatly expand the powers of the state. War collectivism in Europe should be admired and emulated. War could be used as an "aggressive tool of democracy" at home and help "foist innovation upon the country."

For Dewey, then, rejecting neutrality had nothing to do with the outcome of the war per se, but instead was critically important for his quest to achieve National Greatness—America could not afford to miss out on an opportunity to join an historic war and unite its citizens as a world power rather than a provincial observer.

In other words, he adopted a pro-war view solely to advance the Progressive program at home. And he knew that once "Conscription of Thought" was achieved—once American minds were conscripted for the war effort or any other Progressive cause—then their bodies and wallets would follow.

What an astonishingly honest phrase: "Conscription of Thought." It applies in spades to America and the West still today, even more so today. We have accepted the premises and framework of the state, and thus we accept the degradations that follow from statism. The only corrective, in Dewey's time and our own, was a full-throated intellectual challenge to those premises and framework.

Yet it is precisely this challenge from which the Zeitgeister shrinks.

Succumbing to The Zeitgeist

Lew Rockwell brings up the old adage, the smaller the movement the more—and louder—the factions. Now I know what you're thinking, but this is not a talk about libertarian factions: Left vs. Right, thick vs. thin, modal vs. paleo, or Beltway vs. populist.

No, this is not about factions. The Zeitgeist Libertarian transcends these categories by accepting the purported *ends* of Progressivism and state action while only suggesting different *means*—and in most cases only slightly different means.

Like John Dewey hectoring stubborn Americans still stuck on WWI neutrality, the Zeitgeisters hector us to give up the old modes of thinking—that dreary talk about rights and property and the state—and instead happily accept the spirit and tenor of the age. The details matter less than being in the game. In this sense the Zeitgeister accepts the Conscription of Thought—accepts the parameters set by the political world, and focuses on influence within those parameters over all other considerations.

There is a great story involving David Gordon, whom I'm sure many of you know, and the late Ronald Hamowy, who was a wonderfully funny un-PC scholar and a member of Murray Rothbard's Circle Bastiat group in New York City.

David and Ronald attended a conference at Stanford University in the 1980s, and were walking to their car when a scraggly looking person approached them obviously hoping for a ride. Upon being asked by the stranger "Which way are you going?" Ron rushed to answer: "The other way. We're going the other way."

And so it is for many of us in this room I suspect: we feel at odds not only with the dominant Western politics and economics of our day, but also with the cultural landscape. We don't want to be, in Mises's term, "historians of decline," but we are clear-eyed and honest about where we are after a progressive century of war, central banking, and statism.

Not so for the Zeitgeisters, who as their name suggests are not only caught up in the spirit and tenor of our age, but mostly approve of it. They cheer, even advance the prevailing narratives: America and the West are deeply racist, sexist, homophobic, and transphobic. Western wealth is the result of colonialism and conquest. Climate change is an immediate civilizational threat. Income inequality is the most pressing economic issue of our time. And so forth.

218 A Strange Liberty

Above all the Zeitgeisters go along to get along. Unlike the happy radicals Murray Rothbard, David Gordon, and Ron Hamowy—all going the other way—they treat radicalism—at least libertarian radicalism—with reflexive suspicion and contempt.

Recall how Murray Rothbard used the term "libertarian movement," a phrase we might regret him using. It's a loaded term, certainly. Of course by "movement" he meant a multi-pronged approach involving top-down intellectualism, bottom-up right-wing populism, leftwing antiwar instincts, and libertarian political action—mostly educational, mind you, and always purist—all combined with a healthy dose of bourgeois sensibility and a willingness for ordinary people to engage in a bit of Irish Democracy when the state oversteps. Above all he called for radicalism and real opposition to state power.

Yet "movement libertarianism" must be seen as a failure today, in the political sense. And it is in every way political; how could it not be? The Zeitgeisters pushing political libertarianism accept the politicization of everything just as they accept other injuries to liberty. They take what ought to be a radical nonpolitical movement—one dedicated not only to reducing the size and scope of the state, but to diminishing politics itself, *a movement to make society less political*—and reduce it to a set of watered-down "public policy" choices.

And as a result of this neutering, political libertarianism has crashed, as all political movements must, on the rocky shoals of compromise, dilution, and ultimately co-option.

The Horseshoe: Neoliberalism and Neoconservatism

Now to be fair to the Zeitgeist Libertarians, and to understand that Zeitgeist, we must take a look at where we are and how we got here.

You're probably familiar with the horseshoe theory. While we would reject the Left-Right continuum, the horseshoe theory takes this linear concept and bends it into a horseshoe shape.

It's used in a facile way to suggest that the far Left and far Right have so much in common that they almost come together, like the two ends of a horseshoe. The Left veers toward radical socialism or Communism; the Right toward virulent nationalism or fascism. Both movements, if left unchecked and taken to their logical extremes, lead to violent suppression of freedom, devolving economies, and an authoritarian ruling class that badly mistreats or even kills its subjects.

Again, it's a facile argument, but useful for making the larger point that widely divergent political motivations can lead to similar destinations. Quoting from a progressive website called *The Conversation*:

> When fascists reject liberal individualism, it is in the name of a vision of national unity and ethnic purity rooted in a romanticised past; when communists and socialists do so, it is in the name of international solidarity and the redistribution of wealth.

Well thanks for clearing that up! Yet it remains true, at the policy level, when it comes to what governments actually do, there is a great degree of convergence—regardless of the motivations behind those policies.

That's why we might view the horseshoe today as having been cut off on the end and shaped into two parallel tracks: neoliberalism and neoconservatism. These are the two dominant political views of our time, we might almost call them default ideologies because they represent devolutions of older, better versions of left-liberalism and conservatism. The old ideological causes and motivations scarcely seem to matter anymore, the only fight now is over who controls the political apparatus and turf.

And by parallel we mean neoliberalism and neoconservatism appear to be converging rather than diverging:

- Both purport to represent "Third Way" thinking between fully planned economies and complete laissez-faire;

- Both are fully globalist and universalist in outlook, elitist, technocratic, hostile to populism; and both treat political decentralization and breakaway sentiments as dangerous developments to be quashed;

- Both hate Trump and Brexit, and far more importantly, Trump and Brexit voters, while viewing Hillary Clinton and Remainers as self-evidently preferable to anyone other than an exasperating child;

- Both advocate a robust global role for the US as the chief, even unilateral enforcer of a global world order—a militarily order courtesy of US armed forces and NATO, and an economic order courtesy of the US Federal Reserve Bank and the US Treasury market;

- Both support nation building as an obvious and just endeavor for Western nations, oblivious to their own neo-colonialist impulses;

- Both support the legitimacy of supra-national organizations like the EU, UN, IMF, and various trade bodies;

- Both give lip service to market capitalism as a necessary ingredient for a wealthy society, but only within a robust regulatory environment and with robust restrictions on private property rights;

- Both advocate some variant of social democracy as the accepted way to organize society, with a robust social safety net—the current vogue term is "welfare capitalism"—and plenty of taxes to fund it;

- Both support political correctness over robust free speech and academic truth-seeking;

- Both support activist governance, i.e., both see the state as an active participant in society rather than a referee or neutral arbiter; and

- Both purport to be pragmatic rather than ideological.

Today, accordingly, the differences between neoliberals and neoconservatives are more tone and style than substance. Yet shockingly, or perhaps not shockingly, our Zeitgeist Libertarians are right there with them, on a parallel track between them: sharing their ends and only quibbling about means.

Today's Zeitgeist Libertarians:

- Are similarly globalist and universalist in outlook—and not the good kind of globalist, the market globalist who cheers when commerce triumphs over government, but the bad kind of *political* globalist;

- Hate Trump and consider Hillary Clinton the lesser of evils—when they aren't openly praising her;

- Accept, or at least fail to be exercised by, US interventionism, nation building, and Pax Americana—foreign policy always takes a distant back seat to social and cultural issues. They dislike Ron Paul, for example, but offer only muted criticisms of "statesmen" like the late John McCain;

- Accept the role of the Federal Reserve, and merely advocate tinkering with "rules-based" reforms;

- Accept the legitimacy of supra-national organizations— even as such organizations clearly attenuate supposedly cherished democracy—lest they be lumped in with those reactionary "Get Out of the UN" types;

- Accept regulated capitalism and the regulatory state as pragmatic, and not only dismiss property rights absolutism but reject the concept of property as the core element of libertarian thought;

- Dismiss concerns about PC overreach and campus intolerance;

- Accept the overarching narrative that liberals are well-intentioned but only misguided as to means, while conservatives are evil almost by definition; and as a result they obsess about the tiny, fringe "alt-Right"—with no institutional support, money, or influence—even as Bernie Sanders and Alexandria Ocasio-Cortez win elections running on openly socialist platforms; and

• Perhaps most importantly, Zeitgeist Libertarians increasingly seek to minimize the intellectual and philosophical components of libertarianism in favor of pragmatic and empirical approaches.

In other words, they sound a lot like neoliberals and neoconservatives—and thus they push political libertarianism toward a convergence with those doctrines. In doing so they take the marrow out of the bone, and reduce liberty to a variant of "public policy." And by this we mean *approved* public policy—nothing too radical or intellectual. They make a fetish of appearing neither Left nor Right, and engage in endless "whataboutism," but end up with a milquetoast message that sounds to ordinary people precisely like a mishmash of Left and Right.

The Progressive Triumph

Why should this be so?

Why does movement libertarianism lack the stomach to present a truly radical, anti-state program to the world—a program bold enough to defy government as the central organizing principle in society?

Yes, there is a sense of wanting to be in the game, in the fray, in Washington, DC and New York and Brussels, of being taken seriously and invited to the right parties. That's why they are happy to write progressive-friendly articles for the *Washington Post* or *New York Times*, hoping for that next step up to *The Atlantic* or *The New Yorker*. That's fine in a sense, and understandable.

But there is more to all of this. We need to view the Zeitgeist Libertarians through the lens of recent history, and perhaps judge them leniently. They are, after all, creatures of their environment. Over the past 140 or so years, Progressivism went from, say, 10 on a scale to 100 on that scale today. Anyone who suggests dialing the state back to 95, or merely proceeding from 100 to 105 more slowly, risks immediate branding as a reactionary. And that is the one thing Zeitgeisters seek to avoid being called above all.

Progressivism has been the overwhelming force in Western politics for the last one-hundred-odd years. Political progressives—defined not by their party, but by their desire to remake man into a more obedient political animal, absolutely dominated the twentieth century.

Consider: anti-trust legislation, central banking, income taxes, the League of Nations giving way to the UN, two world wars, the rejection of economic freedoms by the Supreme Court, the New Deal with its old age pensions and public works, the Great Society with its welfare entitlements and food stamps, healthcare schemes, and finally the absolute triumph over each and every culture war issue by the Left.

What kind of movement libertarianism should we expect to emerge from this?

In every meaningful way, progressives control politics, government, business, and culture in America and the West. The twentieth century was so irretrievably progressive that we've stopped paying attention to the baseline state all around us. Thanks to that progressive century—a century of war and socialism—government has become like the furniture or potted plants around us: we're so accustomed to it we no longer even see it.

- Progressives overwhelmingly control both major political parties in the US;
- Progressives control the federal judiciary, along with all federal departments and agencies;
- Progressives dominate academia, universities, and K-12 education, both government and private;
- Progressives run the American Medical Association and the American Bar Association, and thus the traditionally

"conservative" professions of medicine and law are now steered Leftward;

- Major corporations, both global and domestic, are run by progressives. Their boards are progressives. Their corporate branding and messaging is progressive;

- Progressives run Wall Street, and give far more campaign money to progressive candidates;

- Silicon Valley and the tech industry are dominated by progressives, from Google to Apple to Microsoft; also donating overwhelmingly to Left politicians;

- Progressives overwhelmingly control traditional media, including broadcast news and print publications (virtually all journalists self-identify as progressive);

- Progressives overwhelmingly run important social media outlets like Facebook, and Twitter;

- Progressives run Hollywood: they hold sway over the film, TV, and video industries, including the growing market for streaming content from HBO, Netflix, and others; and

- All major religious institutions in the West, from the Vatican to mainline Protestant churches to virtually all synagogues, are now thoroughly progressive both politically and doctrinally.

Conclusion

The point here is that modern libertarianism did not evolve separate and apart from this Progressive juggernaut—and how could it? Our point is to understand the impossibility of political or movement libertarianism within the current progressive framework. No truly libertarian movement will advance when it accepts the wrong premises, asks the wrong questions, and cedes the terms of the debate. It's not a matter of selling out principles for influence, it's a matter of preemptively accepting the organizing principle of the state.

Our responsibility to libertarians is the same as our responsibility to the world at large: to truth, wherever it takes us, and to promoting the timeless ideas that yield peace and human flourishing. We are not required to engage in watered-down political movements, or to engage in politics at all. We are not required to participate in ideological or intellectual movements that accept Progressive ends. We are not required to append a set of left-wing cultural precepts onto political liberty any more than we are required to append rightwing militarism. What matters is getting first principles right. Without that nothing good follows.

32

What Should Politically Vanquished People Do?

What should politically vanquished people do? Should they resist the political status quo no matter what, or accept it in the spirit of civil comity and bide their time for the next election? What if their political fortunes are waning, and they are ever less likely to prevail politically? What rights and powers do seemingly permanent political minorities (e.g., libertarians) possess? At what point is open rebellion permitted in a supposed democracy, and how do we judge principled resistance as opposed to sour grapes from political losers?

This article originally appeared June 19, 2018, on mises.org.

Furthermore, what can political majorities rightfully do—in spite of a minority's strident opposition—and what policies cannot be altered regardless of majority consensus? What spoils rightfully belong to political victors, and what longstanding rules should not be upended?

These are uneasy questions in the Age of Trump, especially since Western governments long ago abandoned constitutional restraints and the cliched "rule of law" in favor of administrative governance by bureaucratic managers. Democracy, at least the mass variety practiced in modern Western welfare states, provides no satisfactory answers. Are those unelected managers bound by popular will, or much of anything? What restrains the state?

Ludwig von Mises, a robust social theorist in addition to his staggering work in economics, saw these issues clearly. Despite—or perhaps because—he witnessed the ravages of actual combat in the Great War, he chose to use the language of warfare in describing the plight of political minorities:

> It was liberalism that created the legal form by which the desire of the people to belong or not to belong to a certain state could gain expression, viz., the plebiscite. The state to which the inhabitants of a certain territory wish to belong is to be ascertained by means of an election. But even if all the necessary economic and political conditions (e.g., those involving the national policy in regard to education) were fulfilled in order to prevent the plebiscite from being reduced to a farce, even if it were possible simply to take a poll of the inhabitants of every community in order to determine to which state they wished to attach themselves, and to repeat such an election whenever circumstances changed, some unresolved problems would certainly still remain as possible sources of friction between the different nationalities. *The situation of having to belong to a state to which one does not wish to belong is no less onerous if it is the result of an election than if one must endure it as the consequence of a military conquest. . . . To be a member of a*

national minority always means that one is a second-class citizen. (italics added)

The almost unbelievable rancor surrounding the Trump administration demonstrates precisely how little even rich Westerners really revere democracy when they don't like its results. Anti-Trump forces indeed consider themselves conquered, feeling suddenly like second-class citizens in a country they thought they knew (one where an inevitable "progressive" arc would of course elect Mrs. Clinton). They don't accept Trump any more than they would accept the head of a hostile and occupying foreign power. But rejecting the outcome of elections is a strange position for Clinton supporters, a candidate who frequently gushed about "our sacred democracy."

The same can be said for the Brexit referendum in the UK and rising anti-immigration sentiment across continental Europe—both pilloried as sinister and ill-intentioned populism as opposed to noble expressions of "the people" exercising their democratic rights. But populism is just democracy delivered good and hard, and technocratic administrators are correctly portrayed as gross hypocrites who use the veneer of democratic support only when it bolsters what they plan to do anyway.

Democracy, far from yielding compromise and harmony, pits Americans against each other while creating a permanent bureaucratic class. All of this is understandable and predictable from a libertarian perspective. Only libertarians make the consistent case against democratic mechanisms, and consider freedom from state power as far more important than majority consensus. Freedom isn't up for a vote, as the hopeful saying goes. Liberty—properly understood as nothing more and nothing less than freedom from the state—is the highest political end.

But we don't live in a free world, and most people are not ideological libertarians. Most people, though far less thoughtful, are (small d) democrats like Mises himself. In the interwar years, following the collapse of European monarchies and the rise of

Nazism in Germany, Mises saw democracy as nothing short of the societal mechanism for avoiding further wars and bloodshed:

> Democracy is that form of political constitution which makes possible the adaptation of the government to the wishes of the governed without violent struggles. If in a democratic state the government is no longer being conducted as the majority of the population would have it, no civil war is necessary to put into office those who are willing to work to suit the majority. By means of elections and parliamentary arrangements, the change of government is executed smoothly and without friction, violence, or bloodshed.

Nearly one hundred years later we might wonder if he would still write those words today, having seen the twentieth and now twenty-first centuries unfold. In hindsight they seem unduly optimistic. We'll never know, of course, and even the most doctrinaire anarchist can admit democracy played a part in the success of America and the West.

But there have been both literal and figurative casualties along the way, and more will become apparent in the coming decades. The elite Western consensus, favoring globalism, a vague "neoliberalism," and social democracy will butt up against nationalist and breakaway impulses. Whether "democracy" will be permitted when it goes against elite sentiment is very much an open question, and people are not so easily fooled that globalist projects are in any way democratic.

It's vitally important to understand that Mises saw self-determination as the highest political end, and thus strongly argued against universalism and in favor of political subdivision wherever needed and feasible. Reordering political arrangements by creating smaller units, or abandoning them altogether via secession, was Mises's answer to the question of how political minorities could be protected. Breakaway movements were the safety valve in Mises's conception of democracy:

The right of self-determination in regard to the question of membership in a state thus means: whenever the inhabitants of a particular territory, whether it be a single village, a whole district, or a series of adjacent districts, make it known, by a freely conducted plebiscite, that they no longer wish to remain united to the state to which they belong at the time, but wish either to form an independent state or to attach themselves to some other state, their wishes are to be respected and complied with. This is the only feasible and effective way of preventing revolutions and civil and international wars.

At some point, Americans of all ideological stripes have to ask themselves a question: if one really believes 30 or 40 or 50 percent of the population is beyond redemption, utterly immoral, stupid, fascist, racist, or communist, what should be done? Should they be killed? Deported? Herded into camps? Re-educated against their will until they vote correctly? Forced into low-caste status, politically, socially, and economically? Tolerated, but punished in future elections?

Or should we listen to Mises, and elevate political separation, federalism, and localism to the highest political principles?

Top-down rule from DC isn't working, and in fact it's making people miserable and ready to think unthinkable thoughts about civil war. Pro-Trump and anti-Trump sentiment is destroying social cohesion, the real "law" in any society. And for what? Miniscule policy differences between two parties that will never lift a finger against war, state power, entitlements, or the Fed?

It takes 70 million votes to control the White House, and the (deep) administrative state may be beyond the reach of even an overwhelming political majority. No matter where you sit ideologically, the risk of becoming a marginalized political minority grows as state power grows. It is time to stop trying to capture DC and start talking about realistic breakaway or federalist solutions, even under the umbrella of an ongoing federal state. The elections of 2018 and 2020 won't settle our problems, but only make them

230 A Strange Liberty

worse. At least 50 or 60 million Americans, a group far larger than most countries, will be politically disenfranchised and ruled by a perceived hostile government no matter what candidates or parties prevail.

If breaking up seems unthinkable, so does civil war. Is it written in stone that 330 million people must live under one far-flung federal jurisdiction, no matter what, forever?

33

The Case for Optimism

I promised you some optimism today. Perhaps one of the most optimistic libertarians ever was Murray Rothbard, a happy intellectual warrior if ever there was one. And he was very enthusiastic about the revolution of libertarian ideas, because he understood fundamentally that liberty is the only manner of organizing society that is compatible with human nature and human action. And it was this optimism, this unshakeable belief that we're right and the statists are wrong, that drove him to produce a staggering body of work in defense of personal liberty. Now let me stress that Rothbard, despite his reputation as an uncompromising intellectual, saw his efforts as pragmatic, not utopian. He understood quite clearly that utopianism was the hallmark of the state's intellectual champions, not the state's detractors. He understood that utopianism and statism, not liberty, produced the great monsters and the great wars of the twentieth century.

This article is adapted from a speech delivered at the Costa Mesa Mises Circle, held November 8, 2014.

Most of all, he understood that the true utopians are the central planners who believe they can overcome human nature and steer human actors like cattle. To quote Murray: "The man who puts all the guns and all the decision-making power into the hands of the central government and then says, 'Limit yourself'; it is he who is truly the impractical utopian." In Rothbard's eyes a libertarian world would be better, not perfect. So while our revolution is indeed intellectual, it is also optimistic and pragmatic. We should talk about liberty in terms of first principles, and how those principles make for a better society precisely because they accord with the innate human desire for liberty. Let the statists explain their grand schemes, while we offer a realistic vision of a world organized around civil society and markets.

Now, all of us who are liberty-minded have heard at least some version of the "unrealistic" accusation, "Oh, libertarianism would be great but it's unrealistic," they say. It's one thing to talk about anarcho-capitalism in a dorm room discussion or philosophy lecture, but such a society is too impractical and idealistic for the real world. States have existed for as long as human societies, you'll never get rid of them. Some might even go so far as to claim that a market exists for government "services," seeing how states seem to keep cropping up in human history.

But let's examine this. If you believe the state is harmful rather than benevolent; if you believe that the state threatens individual rights and property rights, rather than protects them; if you believe that the state decreases our chances for peace and prosperity; if you believe, in sum, that the state is an overwhelming force for ill in our society, a force that makes all of us far worse off, why in the world is it unrealistic to work toward its elimination?

Notice that the charge of being unrealistic, impractical, or overly idealistic is never applied to medicine or crime prevention. Nobody says to the cancer researcher, "you should be more realistic, cancer and infectious disease will always exist. Why not just work on making the common cold a bit less severe?" Nobody says to the criminal investigator, "gee, organized crime and violence are just part of human nature, it's useless to try to prevent them. Maybe you should just focus on reducing bike thefts."

So why should we be apologetic or timid or less than fully optimistic in our fight against the state? We should not. Like the cancer researcher, like the crime fighter, we should be bold, we should be optimistic, and we should be vigorous in our opposition to government. We should be every bit as certain as Murray Rothbard was in the eventual success of our mission.

I'm Optimistic Because the State Is Fiscally Unsustainable

Rest assured we will win. The state, at least as currently constituted in the US and most Western nations, is dying under the weight of its sheer fiscal unsustainability.

I'm curious as to whether some of you have heard of Herbert Stein. You may know *Ben* Stein from "Win Ben Stein's Money" and *Ferris Bueller's Day Off*. Herbert Stein was his dad. Herbert Stein was an economist, and chairman of the Council of Economic Advisors, a kind of cheerleading squad, for presidents Richard Nixon and Gerald Ford. He's not my kind of economist, and was only faintly free market, but he was still an economist. And apparently an interesting man: in his later years he briefly wrote an anonymous "Dear Prudence" advice column for *Slate* and print papers.

Herbert Stein came up with his own law, known as Herbert Stein's law. It goes like this: "If something cannot go on forever, it will stop." It sounds simple. He used it to describe economic trends like balance of payments deficits. He meant that no program was needed to stop something that would stop by itself, something that could not be sustained. And clearly, the US federal government, the largest and most powerful government that ever existed, cannot be sustained. Not in the fiscal sense. No way, no how.

We're not talking simply about the $17 trillion in Treasury bond debt the federal government owes its creditors. We're talking about unsustainability on a much larger level. Economist Laurence Kotlikoff uses a concept known as the fiscal gap, which is much more accurate, and much more depressing, than tracking Treasury debt. The fiscal gap basically measures the present value of future tax revenues against the present value of future government obligations. So not just Treasury bond debt, but also Social Security, Medicare, welfare entitlements, etc. And Kotlikoff came up with a fiscal gap of more than $200 *trillion*. Let me repeat that: $200 *trillion*. Now we don't have time today to discuss the details of the federal government's fiscal situation, and how this fiscal gap came to be. But rest assured the reality is wildly worse than virtually anyone in government or the mainstream press will admit.

Understand that there is zero political will in Washington to cut the big ticket items like Social Security, Medicare, welfare, and defense. Zero. Remember the howls during the sequestration debates? Witness the outrage when Congress merely considers cuts in the rate of growth of certain programs! There is zero political will in Washington for huge tax increases, which wouldn't help anyway. Politics will not solve this problem. Our federal government's fiscal reality cannot be fixed, politically or economically. We cannot grow our way out of it. The numbers behind Kotlikoff's fiscal gap simply cannot be overcome, they can only be put off—and made worse—by endless monetary expansion.

It may seem almost funny, but this reality should give us cause for optimism. We know the current arrangement cannot continue, so we—as liberty minded people—have a tremendous opportunity to recognize this and begin building the future. We don't have to labor under the delusion that everything will continue as usual, that the system will work if only we reform it or tinker with it or elect the right people. We can be honest and recognize that democracy doesn't work, it can't work, and the sooner it is exposed as a failure the better. We should celebrate this understanding, because

234   A Strange Liberty

no progress toward liberty can occur until we understand reality and understand the problem at hand.

I'm Optimistic Because the State Is Intellectually Unsustainable

But there is a deeper and more satisfying reason for us to be optimistic. The state is not only fiscally unsustainable, it's intellectually unsustainable as well. We should be optimistic because we're living at the beginning of what Hans-Hermann Hoppe calls a "bottom-up" revolution. Bottom-up because it starts at the individual and hyper-local level. Bottom-up because it relies on radical decentralization and political secession. Bottom-up because it bypasses politics and traditional power structures. Bottom-up because it bypasses state schools, state intellectuals, and state media.

Governments, and the political classes who run them, are facing a nonviolent revolution of ideas that was scarcely imaginable just twenty years ago. And this revolution will strike at the heart of these states' only true asset: their legitimacy in the eyes of those they would govern. The bottom-up revolution is based on informed individuals who increasingly don't need elites, political, academic, or scientific, to run their lives. It is based on the recognition that national and global governance schemes have failed to solve, or even address, huge structural problems like hunger, medical care, energy, and economic development. It is based on radical decentralization, political and otherwise, because the vast diversity of individual interests demands an end to top-down government edicts and bullying by 51 percent of the electorate.

This can happen—and is happening—without even a tacit acceptance or understanding of liberty among the majority of people necessarily. They simply see with their own eyes that the state doesn't work, so naturally they seek another way. I think this is especially true of millennials, who are not particularly libertarian but yet still deeply distrustful of government.

Technology plays a huge role in this bottom-up revolution. Technology has given us the ability to find fellow travelers anywhere in the world, and to compare notes on what our would-be rulers are doing. It has taken the monopoly over the marketplace of ideas away from traditional media outlets. It has enormously lowered the cost of learning and acquiring knowledge. It has literally brought the vast store of human knowledge to our fingertips! Governments will have an awfully hard time keeping all this information, not to mention the ideas of liberty, away from people who are increasingly connected and hungry for a better life.

The toothpaste is out of the tube, so to speak. To be absolutely clear: technology is not an ideology. And technology is used by the state, just as it is used against the state. Imagine J. Edgar Hoover with today's NSA apparatus available to him! And technology can never change the fundamental choice before us: liberty or statism. There is no "third way." Either humans deal with one another voluntarily, through civil society and markets, or they deal with each other using compulsion, through crime or government. Economic means or political means, the age-old choice remains the same.

But the free and virtually instantaneous flow of information has radically transformed the world. Governments like to talk about democracy. Well, they're about to get it good and hard. *Real* democracy, where people vote with their feet, their wallets, and their mobile devices, across borders.

I'm optimistic that this global interconnectedness will pose a huge threat to the viability of many nation-states, and to their political ruling classes as a result. People are now connected by ideas, by interests, by shared values, by commerce and not only by geography and nationality. In fact, geography and nationality are shrinking in importance every day.

Perhaps the greatest legacy of the online revolution will be the demise of state education systems. Teacher unions, lousy and compulsory schools, huge administrative bureaucracies, outlandish pensions, and crushing student loan debt clearly are unsustainable. Government schools clearly cost too much and teach too little of importance, like classical languages, rigorous math and science, skilled trades, and money management. What they do teach is often harmful and statist—the whole panoply of victim's studies.

Liberty is not possible in a society filled with ill-educated, state-indoctrinated people. So the need for separation of education and state has never been greater, and it's at our doorstep. The online education revolution, still in its infancy, will make learning cheaper, easier, more efficient, and—most importantly—accountable. Market-based education will produce actual results—the antithesis of government education. We should all be happy to witness the state's education model crumbling.

All of these happy developments will take place at their own pace, sometimes quickly—as with the fall of the former Soviet Union—and sometimes slowly. There is great cause for optimism that this bottom-up revolution can take place inexorably, and non-violently. There are no guarantees, of course, and political interests can be expected to react violently when threatened. But many of these seismic shifts are already underway, and one gets the sense that power is flowing away from the political classes, slowly but surely. States and statists are losing their greatest asset, legitimacy.

None of this withering away of state legitimacy should surprise us. Just as Mises conclusively explained the impossibility of socialism as an economic system, the great Spanish economist Jesús Huerta de Soto and others make the case for the impossibility of statism as a social, legal, and political system. As Huerta de Soto explains, it simply is not possible intellectually to defend a coercive central state with a monopoly on aggression. Such a state cannot achieve its coordination goals, just like central economic planners cannot know the price to place on a bushel of wheat or the number of automobiles to produce. The huge volume of information an all-encompassing state would need is too dispersed, too tacit, too quickly changing, and too distorted when commanded by the state rather than received by markets.

It's not liberty that's impossible ladies and gentlemen, it's statism.

Conclusion

Personally, I don't care if you call yourself a conservative, a constitutionalist, a classical liberal, a libertarian, a minarchist, an anarcho-capitalist, a progressive or whatever—this message is for you. All that matters is you recognize and agree that the state is out of control, even if just in one area, like drug laws or foreign policy—we can work out the details later! We are so far from what anyone in this room envisions as a free society that many of these labels and differences seem petty, to say the least.

Murray Rothbard used a freedom train metaphor that I think applies quite well today; he actually borrowed it from the late Gene Burns, who was a phenomenal talk radio host for years in San Francisco.

The freedom train metaphor for building a movement is very simple: if you want more freedom, join us. Get on the train. You can get off whenever you like. Maybe you favor 60 percent of our ideas, or 80 percent, or 90 percent, or whatever. Just join us and go as far as you like, get off when you like. As I said earlier, we are so far from what anyone in this room considers a free society that we hardly should concern ourselves about it now. Let's just get the train moving in the right direction! I really like this metaphor; it sure beats endlessly putting ourselves in narrow boxes.

So in closing let me encourage you to embrace an optimistic strategy for liberty. Understand that we simply don't have to convince everyone, or even a majority of people, that liberty is better. We certainly don't have to convince our opponents. Today, just as in colonial America during our revolution, most people are fence sitters.

As talk radio host Herman Cain recently said to a caller, we can only save those who would be saved. Far too often we let the statists frame the debate. Far too often liberty-minded people are defined by what we oppose—government—rather than by what we propose: liberty.

So propose liberty, and make the case for optimism. After all, despite the state and its depredations we still lead magnificent lives compared to virtually every human who ever walked the earth— kings and queens included. If we let the state make us unhappy or pessimistic about our future, we will have failed not only our children and grandchildren, but our ancestors as well.

34

The New Rules of Engagement

Not that long ago, my grandparents explained to me why they never discussed politics, religion, or sex in mixed company. Politeness was their currency. And why antagonize people or create ill will over private matters?

Fast-forward to 2023, and their advice seems needed more than ever. Today nothing is private; everything is political. And American politics is characterized by a perverse degree of bad faith.

This article originally appeared January 23, 2023, on mises.org.

Whether the country really is more divided than any time since the Civil War or this is merely our perception—thanks to social media rancor, nonstop cable news, and rabid political partisanship—scarcely matters. Either way, the psychology is clear. Anger directed toward the "other" delivers the desired dopamine hit. Under conditions of extreme distrust, scapegoating is far easier and more satisfying than cooperation. We see this clearly with attitudes toward Brexit, Hillary versus Trump, covid lockdowns, vaccines, Ukraine, Antifa, January 6, the 2022 midterm elections, and a host of other manufactured issues. Americans are watching at least two different movies.

So does this political polarization cause, or merely reflect, broader social and cultural rifts? The late Andrew Breitbart insisted politics is downstream from culture, which seems broadly correct when we observe the progressive near monopoly over cultural institutions. But there has been a concurrent quiet revolution in law and politics, creating a "rival constitution" and placing politics more squarely at the center of American life. Today we live in a crass and hyperpoliticized reality where every facet of life—race, sex, sexuality, family, marriage, money, career—is seen as a political statement. This aids and abets the progressive project, which leverages the Leninist/Stalinist "Who, Whom?" distinction as carrot and stick.[1]

Operating effectively in this environment requires us to be clear eyed and honest about the rules of engagement. Politics is not war, but it suggests violence. People who simply don't want to fight, or who don't recognize the fight taking place, are at a tremendous disadvantage. Ideas, debate, logic, and persuasion satisfy our sense of fairness and honor. But they are effective only when

---

[1] "Progressive" generally connotes "left wing" today, as most progressive impulses are animated by leftist cultural ambitions. But there are right progressives (neoconservatives) in the broader sense of the word. Both varieties believe mankind can and should be perfected to serve broader state or societal goals.

widely accepted and their results adhered to. We are not required to delude ourselves about this or to turn the other cheek to retain our humanity.

These rules of engagement may seem obvious and common-sense but nonetheless may be helpful for your family and friends who do not fully grasp the situation.

- **Assume bad faith in political matters.**

    Many politicians, especially at the federal level, have dropped any pretense of working to achieve democratic consensus. Lying, gaslighting, and subterfuge are the operative tools to win elections and vanquish the other side. This is not the simple cynicism of my grandfather's day, when the whole political charade might well have been viewed as a gang of crooks fighting over spoils. This is not a period scandal like Watergate, Iran-Contra, or Teapot Dome. Today we must entirely rework our understanding of modern US politics, understanding it as a precursor to violence rather than a mechanism for governance and dispute resolution. Americans acutely feel this brutal winner-take-all element in our politics. Consensus has nothing to do with it. "Democracy" is nothing more than a cheap moniker for "when progressives win." So your default position regarding any political statement or proposal must be disbelief.

- **Assume institutions are politicized.**

    Like it or not, the nonmarket, nongovernmental institutions of civil society no longer operate as a buffer between individual and state. They have been almost entirely captured by progressive ideology, from mainline Protestant denominations and Catholic leaders to the American Civil Liberties Union and Boy Scouts of America. We no longer can assume their stated purpose is their actual purpose or that their public stances can be separated from politics. Thus, Robert Conquest's third law can be updated slightly to reflect bureaucratic control of institutions that not only places them at odds with their original raison d'être but tasks them with an entirely new agenda of serving the progressive project.

- **Assume business is politicized.**

  Medicine, education, law, banking, accounting, insurance, pharmaceuticals, arms manufacturing, and much of the tech world have been enormously affected. Firms operating in these industries often resemble what Michael Rectenwald terms "governmentalities," in which ostensibly private market actors willingly take on the role and imperatives of the state. Add DEI (diversity, equity, and inclusion) and ESG (environmental, social, and governance) to the mix, and virtually all US public companies now at the very least toe the government line when it comes to all manner of political positions. This means heroic smaller and privately held companies must be the true "private sector" drivers of the economy, a bright spot where real win-win social cooperation can take place.

- **Treat public policy as politics.**

  Beware of those advancing a particular agenda under the guise of "public policy." In a hyperpolitical environment, this is simply code for preferred politics. There may have been a time in American history when there actually were nonpartisan policy wonks laboring away in the basements of federal agencies or in think tanks, but that time clearly is past. Politics, not policy, drives federal lawmaking and the administrative state. If Joe Biden manages to enact his student loan forgiveness bill, for example, it won't have anything to do with some study or statistical analysis provided by the Brookings Institution. It will reflect raw politics and patronage toward younger voters, just as George W. Bush's Medicare Part D bill pandered to older voters. And remember, we don't need "policy" at all, whether monetary policy or housing policy or energy policy. We need markets. This is not to say we cannot participate in policy debates or support a particular measure (e.g., an actual tax cut) and oppose another. But we should no longer allow a pseudo-professional class of people in and around DC to claim an expertise or neutrality they don't possess. And we should never elevate politics with the window dressing of "policy."

- **Assume religiosity, not reason, in public discourse.**

  We like to think logic rules the day, but every indication says otherwise. Consider Al Gore's unhinged rant at Davos last week, a fire-and-brimstone homily which would have elicited mirth from attendees had it been delivered by an evangelical preacher. Or consider the religious zeal with which a National Hockey League player was attacked not for any action or statement concerning LGBT (lesbian, gay, bisexual, and transgender) issues, but merely for his forbearance—refusing to wear a rainbow flag jersey before a designated game. Progressives live in an emotional, faith-based universe, every bit as removed from pure reason as the religious observers they mock. Simply appealing to reason rather than hearts and minds is a surefire way to lose in the current environment. This is especially true for young people. Effective argumentation today recognizes and adjusts for this reality without sacrificing principle or truth.

- **Never confuse the imposers with the imposed upon.**

  Progressives not only won the twentieth century handily but enjoyed a rout. Now they are winning the culture wars handily while capturing young people for their cause in alarming numbers. And top to bottom, progressives have more money and power than conservatives. Yet still progressives get away with presenting themselves as victims and underdogs fighting some mysterious oppression or nonexistent WASP power structure. It is important to understand the dynamics at play, because any worthwhile concept of justice differentiates between aggression and self-defense.

- **Take responsibility for your own information gathering.**

    At this point it scarcely needs to be said that large media organizations promote government narratives almost without exception. Deep skepticism is the order of the day, but with this comes the responsibility to go beyond easy headlines and social media to become informed on the pressing matters of the day. And always remember it is OK not to have opinions on issues that you lack understanding about.

- **Take responsibility for your own education.**

    Learning and improving is a lifelong endeavor, and it has never been easier, thanks to digital platforms. Relentless reading is one of the keys to your personal and professional development. You can choose to constantly improve and expand your knowledge using the principles of kaizen, as personified by Robert Luddy.

- **Application and activism beat debate and theory.**

    Whether we like it or not, most Americans are not interested in political history or economic theory. They are interested in the what—primarily the material quality of their lives—more than the how or the why. And we won't counter the activist progressive project with books and philosophy alone. Now is the time to get active in civil society, to make the case for applied theory, and to approach politics at the most local levels. A single voice can reach outsized audiences with the right digital platforms and the right message. And entrepreneurship may be the single best form of activism against state propaganda, demonstrating the win-win alternative to politics on a daily basis.

So how do we even begin to depoliticize America? This is a fundamental question if we hope to improve conditions. All people of goodwill have an obligation to fight the escalation of politics and reduce the likelihood of outright political violence (as we're seeing this week in Atlanta). Yet as stated many times before, we won't vote our way out of this and we should not expect help from Washington, DC. The incentives for politicians are all wrong. Division sells. In fact, division makes the very politicians promoting it appear more necessary than ever to a fearful and gullible electorate. So we should turn our backs on DC, work to ignore mainstream media and captured institutions, and build out parallel structures wherever possible. We have new rules of engagement, but they conjure up an old one from economist Herb Stein: "If something cannot go on forever, it will stop." Better to realize this ahead of time.

Speeches

35

The Imposers
and the Imposed Upon

I 'd like to talk to you this afternoon about two classes of Americans, and it may not be the two classes you think of, but nonetheless, there are two distinct classes in America, and we have to break up, and we have to break up sooner rather than later.

A nation that believes in itself and its future, a nation that means to stress the sure feeling that its members are bound to one another not merely by accident of birth but also by the common possession of a culture that is valuable above all to each of them, would necessarily be able to remain unperturbed when it saw individual persons shift to other nations. A people conscious of its own worth would refrain from forcibly detaining those who wanted to move away and from forcibly incorporating into the national community those who were not joining it of their own free will. To let the attractive force of its own culture prove itself in free competition with other peoples—that alone is worthy of a proud nation, that alone would be true national and cultural policy. The means of power and of political rule were in no way necessary for that.

The article is adapted from a talk delivered at the Mises Institute's annual Supporters Summit, Jekyll Island, Georgia, October 9, 2020.

Ludwig von Mises wrote this about a hundred years ago and it rings absolutely as true today as the day he wrote it and it's all about the idea of letting people go if they want to form a different political union or political entity. At the end he mentions true national and cultural policy. And so I would ask all of you today to consider: Is America a nation at this point? I would argue no. Is it even a country? Barely. Or is it, as Ilana Mercer calls it, Walmart with nukes? And that's what America feels like very much today. It feels like we're all living in one big federal subdivision, doesn't it?

Last night I mentioned that about a hundred years ago in the interwar period Mises wrote his great trilogy, three books, remarkable books: *Nation, State, and Economy* first, then *Socialism*, then *Liberalism*, all within a ten-year span. These three remarkable books basically laid out a blueprint for both organizing society in a prosperous and peaceful way and also a warning in *Socialism* about how to destroy it. Turns out it's a lot easier to destroy than build.

Mises lays out his conception of what a liberal nationhood might look like. It's rooted in property, of course, and rigorous self-determination at home, and what this means is that he's always stressing the right of secession, back then, for political, linguistic, ethnic, economic minorities. They always have the right to secede, and of course, coming out of the patchwork of the former Austro-Hungarian Empire and in Europe, he understood what it meant to be a linguistic minority in particular. So, for Mises, any kind of nation, any kind of real nationalism, liberal nationalism, requires laissez-faire at home, of course. It requires free trade with your neighbors, to avoid a tendency toward war and autarchy, and it requires a noninterventionist foreign policy to avoid war and empire.

When we think of these three books, we can only imagine what the West and what America might look like today if these books had been read and absorbed broadly at the time. If Western governments had been even somewhat reasonable, let's say over the past century, consuming, let's say, only 10 or 15 percent of private wealth in taxes, maintaining just somewhat reasonable currencies backed by gold, mostly staying out of education and banking and medicine, and most of all avoiding supernational wars and military entanglements. If governments had just been somewhat reasonable in the West, we might still live in a more gilded era, like Mises once enjoyed in Vienna, but with all the unimaginable benefits of our technology and material advances today.

The truth is that liberalism didn't hold and we have to be honest with ourselves about it. It didn't hold in the West, and it never took root in the full Misesian sense anywhere, at least not for long, and that's why all of us are here today. If the world had listened to Mises even somewhat, if Western states had committed to the prescription of sound money, markets, peace, all of our libertarian anarcho-capitalist theory might have been completely unnecessary. We might be sitting here today just sort of grumbling about potholes and local property taxes and local schools. Instead, we're here talking about the state as an existential threat to civilization. So, two very different scenarios. But again, the world didn't listen to Mises; that's why it got Rothbard and Hoppe, by the way.

One of the great progressive achievements of the last hundred years, which goes almost totally unremarked today, goes to the title of my talk: the degree to which the Imposers, we can call them, have been able to portray themselves as the Imposed Upon. It's absolutely uncanny. We see it in every aspect of American society and every aspect of our politics today. We see it in the presidential election; we see it with the culture wars; we see it in academia in spades; we see it with Antifa in the streets. If we think about just the last hundred years since Mises wrote these three books—the past century in America—progressives of all stripes, of all political parties, I want to add, what have they given us? They've given us two world wars, quagmires in Korea and Vietnam, endless Middle East wars in Iraq, Afghanistan—Yemen maybe is coming soon, Iran, who knows? They imposed these enormous welfare schemes that Amity Shlaes has written so much about in the form of the

New Deal and Great Society programs, which have ruined how many untold lives. They created all these alphabet soup federal agencies and departments to spy on us, tax us infinitely, regulate every aspect of our lives. And they built the military-industrial complex and the state media complex and the state education complex. They legislated violations of basic human property rights, which would absolutely shock our great grandfathers if they were alive, all with the courts nodding along in their acquiescence. And to pay for it all, they gave us central banking—the Federal Reserve System hatched up, schemed right here on this island, in November of 1910. What do they, the Imposers, call this? They call it liberalism. If you oppose it, they call you a reactionary.

To be a libertarian today is to be a reactionary against the state degradations and depredations and impositions of the twentieth century. The political class, either the Imposers themselves or their agents, what has the political class gotten us? Well, they managed to ruin peace, they managed to ruin diplomacy, money, banking, education, medicine, not to mention, along the way, culture, civility, and goodwill. And if you oppose the Imposers and the elites, they call you a populist for it. So, call me a populist.

All of this, of course, flows from the Imposers, from their positive rights worldview which animates them. It animates everything they do and that's why they're able to scream at Rand Paul, for example, for denying them healthcare. Once you accept a positive rights view of the world, then anyone who doesn't go along with your program is taking from you, and this is how they see the world, the Imposers. If the twentieth century represents a triumph of liberalism, I'd hate to see illiberalism.

We all know what the Imposers have in store for us now in the fledgling twenty-first century. And I would add, as an aside, a good way to tell a Beltway person from a Rothbardian is to ask them the simple question of whether they consider the twentieth century in the West a triumph of liberalism or not. I think most Rothbardians would say it was not, and I think most Beltway types would say it was. They consider the twentieth century some sort of victory for liberalism.

So, what that got us, along with all of these other problems is, of course, a huge divide in society. What they've gotten us is an almost unbelievable and epic divide in society between the Imposers and the Imposed Upon. How divided are we and along what kind of lines?

This was a nice little vignette, which took place the other day on Twitter. We have Chris Hayes, from MSNBC, who says, Well, you know with covid, "the most responsible way to deal with all these people"—that sounds like Seinfeld, "those people"—"if we survive this, is some kind of truth and reconciliation commission." Wow, that sounds fun. I suspect many of us in the room would be candidates for that. I don't know if there's boxcars outside. So he represents the progressive Left in America today. And then along comes our friend from the neoconservative Right, the great Bill Kristol, with whom we've all had enough but we always get more. I mean, this guy does not go away. He's like when you take the fish oil capsule at seven in the morning, and then at noon, that's Bill Kristol. So, he says, "How about truth and no reconciliation?"

The degree of open contempt and hatred that these lunatics have for us has in part been exposed by Trump and Trumpism. And to that extent we owe Trump a degree of gratitude for letting us see them for what they truly are. I would ask either one of these gentlemen: If you truly believe, let's say, 40 percent of the United States is beyond redemption, irredeemable, what does that mean? What do you propose doing with them? Does that mean some sort of reeducation camp? Presumably it means that either you separate from them somehow or you vanquish them, and by vanquish, that could be economically, politically, or, in the horrific scenario which we've seen repeated throughout history, even physically.

The divide we have in this country today is not so simple as saying blue and red states or counties, Republicans and Democrats, or liberals and conservatives, or even by class. It's a little more complicated than that. There's a company out there called Survey Monkey, which took in a lot of data after the 2016 election between Hillary Clinton and Donald Trump. There was a big *Washington Post* story using this, and they grouped it in a bunch of very interesting ways. I wonder how many people in this room were aware of some of these divides in American culture.

Sadly, there's a huge divide along racial lines in voting patterns. If only white people had voted in the 2016 election, Trump would have won forty-one states and if only nonwhite people had voted, Hillary Clinton would have won forty-seven states. I view this as basically a testament to the Democrat's ability to sell some kind of sick victimhood and dependency and to the Republican's failure to sell any sense of real ownership or opportunity or capitalism. But nonetheless, that's the divide. It's real.

How about union members? If only union member households—in other words, a household with at least one union member—had voted, Hillary Clinton would have won forty states. And if no union members, Donald Trump would have won thirty-seven.

When we get into religion, things get even more stark. What about households that claim that the inhabitants are either atheists or no particular religion? Hillary Clinton would have won at least forty-six states, if only nonreligious people had voted. How about if households which claim Protestant or Catholic membership would have been the sole voters? Trump would have won forty-five states. Evangelical voters only, Trump would have won forty-seven states. People who attend church weekly, Trump would have won forty-eight states. People who seldom or never attend church or synagogue, Hillary Clinton would have won forty-three states.

It strikes me as we go through some of these numbers that these divides are awfully hard to overcome politically. I'm not sure how you do that. How about unmarried people? Hillary Clinton would have won thirty-nine states if only unmarried people had voted. Trump would have won forty-three states if only married people had voted, another huge quiet cultural and political gap in this country.

You've heard a lot about urban versus rural voters; it's a motif which keeps coming up again and again. For purposes of the Survey Monkey data, an urban county is one with greater than 530 voters per square mile and a rural county is one with fewer than ninety voters per square mile. Again, only urban counties vote, Hillary Clinton wins forty states. Only rural voters vote, Donald Trump wins forty-seven states.

The last stat I'll throw out is gun-owning households. (I know that none of you own firearms, but there are people who do. They lock them up and just shoot deer with them. They don't have Uzis, or modified weapons. . . . And I know there's no weapons in this room today; I feel comfortable with that statement.) If only gun-owning households voted, Donald Trump wins forty-nine states. Guess which one he loses? The only one he loses is Bernie Sanders's Vermont, because I think up there you just have a gun anyway just because you're in Vermont but you vote for Bernie. So, if households with no firearms of any kind were the sole voters in America, Hillary Clinton also wins forty-nine states and guess which one she loses? West Virginia, another anomaly.

The point here is that these kinds of divides and problems cannot be neatly solved by politics, especially national politics, and if you think about them, they don't cleave neatly along geographic lines. This isn't the Mason-Dixon line. These kinds of divides exist in every state, they exist within counties. If you go to California, which we all think of as a deep blue state, then go twenty miles inland. You know what it is? It's Trump flags, it's country music, and it's Mexican rancheros. That's what it is. We don't have the Mason-Dixon line in America in 2020. And more importantly, what we have to understand is: even if you could win some national election, if you could somehow get 51 percent of the voters to vote for a candidate like a Rand Paul, it doesn't really matter, because hearts and minds haven't changed. Politically vanquished people never really go away. This is what we have to understand; this is why we have to break up.

A couple of years ago, Bloomberg did some polling in the former Soviet Union, now Russia. There are millions of Russians, especially elderly Russians, who still absolutely pine for the Soviet days when they knew what their job was, they didn't have to pay for their apartment, etc. Seventy percent of those people have overall a generally beneficial view about Stalin, in 2019. They view him as the great reformer who helped save their country from the Nazis, etc. In other words, despite all the historical examples that the twentieth century provided us, despite the fall and the collapse of the Soviet Union, despite all of the obvious benefits of capitalism, there is still a significant amount of nostalgia for the old system. Politically vanquished people don't just go away. And the Hillary Clinton people thought that the Deplorables were going to do just that. They thought they were dying, they thought they were aging out, and they thought there were fewer of them than there were, and that's what happened in 2016 and that sent the entire country into basically some kind of psychosis, which we're still suffering under today.

I know the concept of decentralization is one that's obvious and clear to all of you. I know secession seems like a tough go, but I want to just throw out to you some happy facts, things that are happening slowly right under our noses, some very decentralist impulses which are at work. Of course, they have been absolutely intensified by the covid issue and by these terrible riots which have been roiling across the United States this summer and now into the fall. As it turns out, all crises happen to be local. What do I mean by that?

One beautiful thing about covid is that it has done further damage to our sort of credulousness when it comes to so-called authorities. Neither the UN nor the World Health Organization nor our own CDC has been able to project any sort of authority whatsoever amongst people. They have been able to drive no consensus. As a result, we've had vastly different approaches to covid across international lines and even within our fifty states, and even within some areas within various cities.

No central authority was able to sort of seize it and boss everyone around and tell everyone what to do. Of course, outlets like the *New York Times* tried to do that, but that's just in the United States. It's been absolutely fascinating to watch how places like Singapore and Hong Kong and Sweden have been relatively open and places like the province in China where it happened were drastically locked down. Some places like San Francisco have been drastically locked down, so there have been different approaches in this decentralized effort. And none of this is because people woke up one day and said ideologically, Wow, maybe we should try a more decentralized approach. No, it's just what naturally happens in crises.

Even the vaunted Schengen Area Agreement in Europe, which allows free travel between the member countries, immediately broke down. All of a sudden, a German is a German again and a Frenchman is a Frenchman, and you can't even drive across. I don't think that Americans can drive or fly into Canada right now, even as we speak, with the liberal—supposedly liberal—Trudeau administration up there.

It turns out that when it comes to a crisis, things really get local very, very quickly. No matter who you are, even if you're Bill Gates and you can buy ten vacation houses and go to New Zealand on your yacht, you have to be somewhere physically; you have to exist in an analog world, and that means you need calories, you need kilowatts of energy and air conditioning coming into your home or your abode, you might need some healthcare or some prescription drugs, and all of this becomes unavoidable in a crisis. You have to be somewhere. Even Jeff Bezos had a bunch of protestors surrounding his house, his swanky house in DC. Now I don't know if he happened to be there at the time, but the point is even Jeff Bezos could conceivably be contained in his home by a mob that you can't escape. This idea that we're now on this sort of new global happy plane is being sorely tested, I think, by covid. I think that the idea of political globalism—the bad kind of globalism—is showing its strain. I think it's cracking very badly.

Let's talk about the great relocation that's happening in America, this incredible movement of people out of cities. What's the charm of a New York, a Manhattan, or a Chicago without the restaurants, and the theaters, and the food, and the museums? High rent, high crime, no fun? We find that a lot of younger people are starting to rethink things. I think this form of de facto secession away from these big cities, which tend to be very, very leftwing in orientation, is a wonderful development to see, because some of that political power that the big cities tend to hold is going to be attenuated. Atlanta tends to control Georgia; Nashville increasingly controls Tennessee. We see this in a lot of states. Las Vegas controls Nevada. But if people start to move away from these big cities, then some of that political power similarly is going to go with them.

This decentralist impulse is really the untold story of the twenty-first century: we see it in companies in the way they organize and manage their teams. Now we see all kinds of teleworking (which I think is a mixed bag, but nonetheless it's happening, one way or another). Look at distribution systems, what used to be the old hub-and-spoke model of getting your products, like the JCPenney catalogue, or how you got a sweater forty years ago. We're now looking at companies like Amazon that have a very decentralized system of spider webs. The distribution of goods and services is becoming radically decentralized.

How do we obtain information? It wasn't that long ago, thirty years or so, you had to go to your local mall and they might have Milton Friedman's *Free to Choose* or John Kenneth Galbraith's *Affluent Society*. They didn't have Rothbard. So, libraries and universities and professors were almost kind of like the new versions of monks. They were the literate ones, and you had to go to them to get information. But that's no longer the case. You have something in your pocket the size of a deck of cards that has basically all of human history on it. That's hugely decentralizing.

What we're seeing right now in the education revolution is just absolutely phenomenal. Even before covid came along we had Khan Academy and all kinds of new platforms springing up. We had the student loan debt crisis. We had parents questioning the value of sending their kids to school for $40,000 a year so that they can get a degree which doesn't get them a job and then when they come home after those four years they hate your guts. It turns out that that's not such a good value proposition.

Money and banking itself is becoming increasingly decentralized. We have all kinds of payment gateways now. We have systems like PayPal, we have bitcoin, and so really it's just that top layer of banking that is happening at major banks.

All of these things are happy facts and we ought to be celebrating and thinking about them when we consider the political landscape.

I'm not so sure that what matters for our immediate future is whether Trump or Biden wins. We all know what Biden is and what he will do. We don't know what the hell Trump is or what he will do. That's what it means to be Trump. But nonetheless, I think some of these impulses which are happening are inexorable. I'm not sure that even a Kamala Harris or a Joe Biden can stop them. We ought to celebrate that.

What's interesting is that the one thing which still seems awfully centralized in our world is the political world. In other words, in all these other areas of life, all these things I've just been mentioning, decentralization is something that's happening naturally, it's happening by market force, it's happening inexorably, and it's happening by free choice of people. But the one area out of our lives where we still accept gross centralization, and all the inefficiencies it brings, is government.

Many things that used to be decided at the city level are now decided at the regional or the state level. Things that used to be

decided at the state level, decided at the federal level—and then
sometimes even at the international level. That's really the political story of the twentieth century, the centralization of politics at
higher and higher levels, which is of course antidemocratic, even
though all of these people are telling us about our sacred democracy. Every level of government that's further removed from you is
attenuated by definition, is less democratic, because your input and
your consent, so-called, is less and less meaningful. But I wonder if
there aren't even some hopeful signs when it comes to politics and
the decentralization of political power.

At an event last fall in Vienna, Austria, Hans-Hermann
Hoppe was on a panel, and one thing that struck me about what
he said was, if you look at the nationalist impulses of the nineteenth and twentieth centuries, the patchwork of former Europe
came together—if you think of Germany as all these principalities
and regions, and Bavaria and Prussia, these areas came together.
He said nationalism in the nineteenth and twentieth century was
mostly a centralizing impulse. That's what nationalism meant.
When it becomes belligerent and spills over its borders, you get
aggressive, you get Nazi Germany. But he said in the twenty-first
century, from his perspective, nationalist movements tend to be
decentralist. In other words, they're moving away from this sort of
global government model which we all thought was going to be our
future in the late twentieth century.

Hoppe says, If we look at things like the Brexit vote, if we look at
what's happening in countries like Poland and Hungary, if we look
at Catalonia—the Catalonian secession movement in Barcelona
in the Catalonian region of Spain—these tend to be breakaway
decentralist secessionist movements. That's the difference between
some of the national movements of today versus yesteryear. And I
think this is coming soon to a city near you in the United States.

This kind of talk is really becoming reality. Ryan McMaken,
who is the editor of mises.org, just wrote an article about how even
the mainstream publications now are talking quite openly and

seriously about secession, and I think that's because on some level, nervously, they still think Trump could win. I think that's what's driving it.

There have been very serious people on both Left and Right, not wild-eyed radicals like me, who have been talking about this for the last several years. Frank Buckley, a law professor at George Mason University—oh, we can't say that anymore, sorry; it's GMU. It turns out George Mason had a slave or two. Buckley wrote a very serious book about what secession might look like just a year ago. And this is a sober conservative guy. Similarly, Angelo Codevilla, who writes for the Claremont Institute, a retired political science professor at Boston University, wrote an article back in 2016 called "The Cold Civil War." You can find it at claremont.org. Again, a very sober, serious conservative, the kind of guy who still uses the lexicon and things like *statecraft*; you know what I mean. And they're talking about this. Similarly, people at places on the Left, at places like the *New Republic* and *The Nation*, are talking about this like never before. Gavin Newsom, governor of California, has applied the term nation-state to his own state.

What happens in the fall, in a month, if somehow, some way Trump manages to win this election—I don't know what that's going to look like. I think we are going to see, first of all, an out-pouring of grief and psychosis and outright violence from a significant portion of the country that we're just not prepared for. But when that subsides, you're going to simply see blue state governors saying, No, we're walking away. The sanctuary-city talk will become more and more pronounced, and I think that'll be a beautiful and helpful thing for this country.

Now, the flip side—and when I say who wins, I should say who's actually installed in January; we don't know anything about these ballots and postal delivery carriers dropping them in sewers or whatever it might be. But whoever wins—if Joe Biden and Kamala Harris are installed—I think what you're going to see is nothing short of a new Reconstruction in America. I think you are going to see outright and open attempts, gleeful attempts in the media class to impose themselves on the red states and punish them. Not only for having the audacity to put Donald Trump in the White House instead of Hillary Clinton—who we all knew was going to win—but more importantly on a more macro level, for coming along and interrupting that arc of history that progressives believe in so deeply: that we're always improving and that we're always getting better, the past is always bad and retrograde. To have that upended by Trump is a sin which they still haven't gotten over.

If Biden and Kamala Harris win, the sales tax deduction for state taxes will be immediately reintroduced so that those blue states can start deducting things again. I think you'll see it in myriad ways. You will see sort of an outpouring, a collective outpouring from the Left that wants to use the state as sort of a laser focus, you know, to bludgeon us, the rest of us. And that, in turn, will cause the red state folks and the red state voters to be thinking very seriously about an exit strategy. I wish I could give you something more hopeful than that, because as I mentioned before, the problem here is that nothing goes along neat geographic lines. But the lines are there nonetheless, and we can't ignore them.

I'll close with this: Tom Woods, our friend who spoke earlier, he reminds us political arrangements exist to serve us, not the other way around. Who the hell said that we have to put up with all of this? Can we change ours without bloodshed? That's the question of the twenty-first century. I think the question of the twentieth century was socialism versus property. I think the question of the twenty-first century is centralized versus decentralized. So, in post-persuasion America, where we seem to live, it's not just a matter of intellectual error. There's more to it than that. It's not just about convincing academics and journalists and politicians that our cause is right and you should agree with us. Because it's also about self-interest and power. They don't see for themselves a path to greater self-interest and a path to greater power in the kind of society which all of us in this room would prefer to live in, and they're not just going to let us have it without some effort on our part. And I hope very strongly that that path does not involve bloodshed.

There is reason for optimism: there is a decentralist impulse that is working its way across the world. It's coming to America, and I think that is where we have to put our hopes and our efforts.

36

Austrian Economics Looks East

Mises surely would be pleased by the thought of this gathering today, to know that his Vienna still has a heartbeat in Europe, even as its politicians and bankers and academics all go in the wrong direction. He certainly would be pleased and amazed to know his work would become available across the world, in many languages, free and instantly online. Most of all he would be thrilled to know his name is better known today, and his work more widely read, than during his lifetime. What more could any intellectual or writer want? This alone is a huge achievement.

Yet while even Mises's harshest critics now acknowledge his influence, they do not read him much or understand him at all. A cursory search of the name "Mises" in the *New York Times* or *Washington Post* produces dozens of mentions in recent years,

---

This article contains excerpts from a presentation given at the Seventieth anniversary of the publication of Human Action, *in Vienna, at the Palais Coburg, November 23, 2019.*

nearly always in the context of some nefarious takeover of government by free market radicals. Who knew Mises was an avatar of neoliberalism, something nobody quite defines but everybody knows is bad? The leftwing *New Republic* even asserts neoliberalism "emerged from the ruins of the Austro-Hungarian Empire in the early twentieth century." And *The Marginal Revolutionaries*, a new book by Professor Janek Wasserman from the University of Alabama, just a few hours from Auburn, claims Mises and his movement "not only transformed economics and social theory, but changed our world."

When the Left creates a caricature of you, you know you have arrived.

For most of the last seventy years, Austrian economics, or at least Austrian economists, always looked West. This is why, since about the middle of the twentieth century, Austrian economics grew and flourished in the US, while it slowly atrophied in Vienna. It is why Janek Wasserman and others use the term "American Austrians," with some derision. The Viennese Austrians all seemed to go West.

Consider young Carl Menger, born in what is now the Polish city of Nowy Sącz. His schooling, in Krakow, Prague, and Vienna, took him westward both geographically and intellectually. His position at the University of Vienna must have felt like a cosmopolitan western outpost to a Galician, and his travels as tutor to Archduke Rudolph von Habsburg took him West, through continental Europe and the British Isles.

Mises of course moved westward throughout his life, from Lemberg to Vienna, then Geneva, and finally New York. Hayek too, from Vienna to the London School of Economics, then to the University of Chicago, and even a stint at the University of Arkansas(!) before retiring to the University of Freiberg in West Germany. Murray Rothbard moved from his beloved New York City (where he had been a protégé at Mises's seminar) to Las Vegas and the University of Nevada somewhat late in life. Even our special guest today, Dr. Hans-Hermann Hoppe, seems to have had a west-ward orientation. From his birthplace in Peine, Lower Saxony, he headed at least a little West to university in Saarbruken, detoured slightly back to the East for graduate studies in Frankfurt, but then moved decisively West to New York, and then to Las Vegas to join Rothbard. Maybe Las Vegas in the 1980s and 90s was the high water mark, the westernmost reach of Mises's Vienna.

Now Dr. Hoppe has moved East, even beyond his native Germany to Istanbul. Maybe this is a metaphor for all of us who consider ourselves "Western." Have we become so accustomed to our conception of the West we fail to fully accept how truly illiberal and intellectually decadent it has become? After all, West always meant "new" and East always meant "old." West meant capitalism and East meant collectivism or mysticism.

But is that still true today? And is the Austrian school of economics ultimately geographic, theoretical, or sociological? In fact it is all three. We should consider whether, at least metaphorically, Austrian economics now finds itself looking back toward the East.

From an American perspective, rooted in our history as Anglo colonies, Vienna is the East. Even Germany is "Eastern" in a very important sense, because most Americans think "Western Civilization" is synonymous with Western Europe—which downplays Germany's influence and virtually ignores the Eastern Bloc and its geographic overlap with the former Habsburg Empire. Our great friend and philosopher David Gordon points out historian Jonathan Clark's book titled *Our Shadowed Present*, which examines the relationship between Britain and Europe. Clark contends, and David agrees, that Cold War intellectuals purposely used "the West" to shift focus away from the central role of Germany in European history.

But today the concept of East and West are metaphoric as much as geographic.

Maybe we need to turn back toward Vienna, toward the Balkans, the Baltics, the former Eastern Bloc, and even toward Asia to find people interested in what makes a free and prosperous society. We cannot ignore how sad, tired, and addled the West has become. We cannot ignore how many in the West simply no longer care about what makes us rich, or even worse imagine wealth will continue to manifest itself all around us regardless of incentives or state depredations. This is why we see the rise of candidates like Elizabeth Warren and growing support for socialism among the young across America and Europe.

Many in the West simply have given up.

The great investor and fan of Austrian economics Jimmy Rogers says that young people seeking their fortune in 1900 moved West to America, while young people seeking their fortune in 2000 moved East to Asia—which is why he raises his children in Singapore. Of course recent events in Hong Kong show the terrible reality of Chinese state authoritarianism, but *the people* of the East in the twenty-first century want to get rich, to build wealth, to enjoy all the material comforts of the West—while the West is reduced to socialist schemes for redistribution of already existing wealth. The West consumes capital created by our grandparents, the East builds capital for their grandchildren.

As an aside, China is perhaps the fastest growing market for interest in Austrian economics. We constantly receive requests for materials from Chinese professors who teach at universities we have never heard of, in cities of five or ten million people which are scarcely known in the West.

Consider these questions about people in the East and people in the West: who saves and invests more of their income? Who buys more gold? (in fact the Chinese, Turks, Russians, Indians). Who seeks meaningful and rigorous education for their children, not hyphenated-studies? Who is clear-eyed about human nature, and who is starry-eyed? Who puts more emphasis on family, or even wants children? Who is building, with long time horizons, and who is merely consuming?

Where does Mises's vision resonate most strongly today?

It has been seventy years since *Human Action*, but one hundred years since *Nation, State, and Economy* and nearly that long since *Liberalism*. In those two relatively short texts Mises almost literally laid out a blueprint for Western governments to enjoy prosperity and peace in the aftermath of the Great War.

Dr. Joe Salerno describes Mises's program as "liberal nationalism," a recognition of nation states but rooted in property and rigorous self-determination at home—even to the point of allowing secession for political, linguistic, or ethnic minorities. Misesian liberal nationalism requires laissez-faire at home, robust free trade with neighbors to avoid the tendency toward autarky, and non-interventionist foreign policy to avoid the tendency toward war and empire.

We can only imagine what the West might look like today if those books had been read and absorbed at the time. If western governments had been even *somewhat* reasonable over the past century: consuming, say, only 10 or 15 percent of private wealth in taxes; maintaining reasonable currencies backed by gold; mostly staying out of education, banking, and medicine; and most of all avoiding supra-national wars and military entanglements, we might still live in a gilded age like pre-war Vienna—but with the unimaginable benefits of today's technology and material advances.

But liberalism didn't hold. It didn't hold in the West, or anywhere else. It never took root in the full Misesian sense anywhere, and never took root anywhere for long. That's why all of us are here today. If the world had listened to Mises, even somewhat—if western states had committed to his prescription of sound money, markets, and peace, libertarian and anarcho-capitalist theory might have been unnecessary. We might merely grumble about the state, instead of seeing it as an existential threat to civilization.

The flaw in the Misesian liberal program was democratic voting, something obvious to us in hindsight but hardly obvious a century ago in a Europe just emerging from monarchy. From Mises's perspective, democracy held the promise of liberation from aristocracy. He saw democracy as the mechanism for peaceful transfers of political power, and while this has proven somewhat true, it certainly has not been uniformly true since the interwar years in which he wrote. Democracy did not prevent Franco or Hitler or Tito, and we need only look at Brexit and Trump to see the limits of democratic consensus when the wrong guy or wrong cause wins. Turns out "we" don't really believe in democracy after all.

But more importantly, we now understand how democratic voting necessarily and inexorably erodes property rights. Politicians and their electorates benefit from high time preference, from living today at the expense of tomorrow—not only through government spending, debt, and borrowing, but also through artificially low interest rates, all courtesy of central bank policies so crazed not even the prescient Mises would recognize them as banking practices today. Voters and the political class in a liberal democracy have all the wrong incentives, and thus any liberal program conducted through mass democratic voting contains the seeds of its own destruction. Property and laissez-faire cannot survive democracy for long.

So while Mises's liberalism provided a profound and underappreciated blueprint for the West, it didn't hold. We have to accept this and grapple with this. Western governments could have chosen to leave people alone, they did not. They could have chosen sound money, they chose political fiat. They could have chosen peace, they chose entanglements. The next time a supposed "classical liberal"— an artificial term, as our friend David Gordon explains—criticizes the excesses of Rothbardian anarcho-capitalist theory, or bemoans breakaway movements like Brexit, or attacks AFD in Germany or Orban in Hungary, or is appalled by Trump and anti-globalist populism—remind them that these developments happened as *reactions* to the failures of bastardized Western liberalism. Elites in the twentieth century failed us, on every front: war and peace, money and banking, medicine, education. And they have the temerity to wonder why populists gain support?

The West didn't listen to Mises, so it got Rothbard and Hoppe!

If liberal democracy has failed to defend property, liberty, and peace in the twentieth and now twenty-first centuries, it is entirely justified to consider what should replace it. Of course the Left offers nothing but its program of statism, egalitarianism, positive rights, and identity politics—all totally illiberal in design and practice. Meanwhile the Right offers only a jumbled mix of constitutionalism, "limited government," and "rule of law," while largely sharing progressive ends but advocating slightly different means. Both share the neoconservative foreign policy of US hegemony and occupation—also known as democratic nation-building.

Therefore it is up to us to create a vision for the present age. It is up to us to reconsider Misesian liberal nationalism for the twenty-first century. Not an easy task, but we have the benefit of hindsight. We know what civilization and society require, and must avoid, because we have the twentieth century to learn from. We also have the work of Rothbard and Hoppe, post-Mises, to guide us and correct us.

What does a twenty-first century Misesian program look like, as supplemented by Rothbard and Hoppe?

- First, it recognizes nation is not necessarily state; the former can coalesce organically while the latter is always artificial;
- It is rooted in property and markets, rejecting the utopian virus of egalitarianism that animates the Left;
- It advocates for smaller, decentralized entities—entities more like Liechtenstein or Switzerland and less like Germany or the US, with democratic mechanisms strictly limited to local councils and local matters;
- It permits breakaway entities for any group or minority;
- Beyond this, it advocates fully private communities along Hoppean lines;
- In particular, it demands private provision of education, medicine, and retirement pensions;

- It rejects central banking in favor of private, competitive money and banking—so no monetary hedonism is possible;

- It is strictly non-interventionist and rejects any standing military; and

- finally, for its own self-preservation, the twenty-first century Misesian model encourages and nurtures the vital intermediary institutions of society, including faith and family, and rejects libertine culture. It thus recognizes human nature, and acknowledges the need for internal governance to reduce the need for external governance. It encourages real culture over pop culture, intellectualism over anti-intellectualism, truth and beauty over mindless pursuits, and real liberal arts education, including history and classical languages, over modern curricula and dumbed-down hyphenated studies.

In conclusion, ladies and gentlemen, our revolution is paleo, not neo. It takes its cues from Vienna, and finds its origins in a better, older, Misesian worldview. It increasingly looks East, not West to the failing and sclerotic thinking of Frankfurt or Brussels or London or New York or Washington, DC. It is localist and decentralist, not globalist. And it places property front and center in the liberal program, as Mises did one hundred years ago.

37

The Biggest Myth

I f there is one overriding economic myth that plagues us today it is the notion that society can do collectively what we cannot do individually: get rich by living today at the expense of tomorrow. It is the doctrine of the political class, professional economists, and central bankers. It is monetary and fiscal hedonism masquerading as technical analysis. And, it leads to fiscal default. It is arguably the biggest untold story of our time, but you won't hear about it from Hillary or Bernie or Donald.

Consuming Today—Paying Tomorrow

Part of the problem lies in the fact that the cumulative impact of bad policies will in most cases be felt only many years down the line. Murray Rothbard pointed out when this is the case voters will support destructive policies. The idea persists that we really can live at someone else's expense. At least for now.

This is what the Fed has been doing with all of its "extraordinary" monetary policy since 2008. But even the Fed admits this comes with big risks for future fiscal solvency. In a November 2010 speech, St. Louis Fed President James Bullard said: "The [FOMC (Federal Open Market Committee)] has often stated its intention to return the Fed balance sheet to normal, pre-crisis levels over time. Once that occurs, the Treasury will be left with just as much debt held by the public as before the Fed took any of these actions."

The problem is that the Fed has yet to figure out how it will return things to "pre-crisis" levels. In other words, the end of the

This article is adapted from a talk delivered at the May 2016 Mises Circle in Seattle, Washington.

Fed's experiment in massive debt and easy money will come "some day." But definitely not today.

I'll leave it to you to decide if extraordinary monetary policy is really the new normal. It's hard to conceive of an event where the Fed would reverse this trend or significantly raise interest rates.

There still appears to be no political will at the Fed or anywhere else to forgo consumption today for the sake of fiscal solvency later.

The Lost Art of Investing in the Future

Looking around this beautiful venue, which often hosts symphonies, we see immediately that it was built by people who wanted to create something lasting—something that would not only survive their lifetimes, but that would provide beauty and lasting enjoyment for future generations.

They broke ground on this building one hundred years ago; none of the individuals who built it are alive today. It served for decades as a Christian Science church.

But in a sense the individuals who built it live on through their work, which surrounds us here: through the art glass Tiffany-style lighting, through the terra cotta on the sides of the building, through the thick masonry designed to produce warm acoustics. They persevered for six years to complete it—and while they could not have foreseen what kind of events or people the building would host a century later, undoubtedly, they knew it was built to last and hoped it would remain standing a long time as Seattle grew up around it.

They built something lasting for an uncertain future.

All healthy societies do this. The notion of being concerned with things beyond one's lifetime is innately human. Humans are hardwired to build societies, and the most ambitious humans have always sought to build lasting monuments and modes of living. That's not possible unless people work toward a future they will not enjoy themselves.

This was especially true for our ancient primitive ancestors, who lived very short and difficult lives. We can imagine how much they wanted to have lasting forms of sustenance: food, water, clothing, shelter—instead of having to produce that sustenance day after day.

In fact, this trait perhaps more than any other is the hallmark of civilization. We can call it many things, but we might just say healthy societies create capital. They consume less than they produce. This capital accumulation creates an upward spiral that increases investment and productivity, making the future richer and brighter. Capital accumulation made it possible for human populations to develop beyond subsistence misery. It made the agricultural, industrial, and digital revolutions possible.

Economists talk about savings in the context of time preference, the preference that people have for current consumption over future consumption. People with high time preferences want everything today, no matter the cost, whether buying with credit or simply enjoying the empty pleasure of idleness over productive activity.

People with low time preferences are the opposite: they'd rather forgo some pleasure or purchase today to build for the future, whether their own or their offspring's. And it's not just about the future of the family or tribe: society benefits across the board, through economic, cultural, and philanthropic development.

Of course, time preference is not only a matter of sociological study, but also a fundamental concept in economics.

In the 1800s the French classical economist Jean-Baptiste Say gave us his law of markets, a law that could be reduced to the proposition that production precedes consumption. We have to produce before we consume, because while humans always have infinite wants—i.e., demand—real-world scarcity means that we first have to produce economic goods before we can consume them. The only other choice is a return to that subsistence life our ancestors escaped thousands of years ago.

Mises posited that from the study of human action itself we could derive the assumption that all other things being equal, individuals prefer to achieve an end sooner rather than later. This is why we'd rather buy our dream house at age forty than at age ninety. We can understand this preference by deductive reasoning. The question is how badly we want that house at forty, and what consuming capital or incurring debt today to buy it might mean for our life at ninety.

Professor Hans Hoppe states that low time preference, the willingness to accumulate goods for an uncertain future, "initiates the process of civilization"—a positive feedback loop in which developing societies accumulate more and more capital, which leads to greater productivity, which leads to longer lifespans and greater concern for the future.

Professor Guido Hülsmann, in his great book *The Ethics of Money Production*, addresses the damaging cultural and moral effects of using monetary policy to encourage high time preference via inflation and cheap credit. By debasing money, the political class and its bankers not only hurt the economy, but also grow government, make wars more likely, and create moral hazards that encourage bad behavior.

The Rise of Monetary and Fiscal Hedonism

It seems self-evident that capital accumulation and low time preferences are healthy, virtuous, and necessary elements of an advanced economy and society. So, we should not be surprised that the two most powerful forces in the modern world—central governments and central banks—work tirelessly to thwart both. And democracy, so-called, is at the heart of their experiment.

As the aforementioned Dr. Hoppe explains, democracy turns the political class into high time preference plunderers: without any vested hereditary interest in the future of a nation, elected politicians have every incentive to consume the nation's current capital via taxes and future capital via debt. Why shouldn't a politician win votes today, by supporting popular spending measures, when the consequences won't be felt until long after he's out of office? Buy now, pay later is an inherent feature of any democratic political system.

But the moral hazards created by such a system in America are enormous, and we're not just talking about those living on food stamps and welfare because it's only marginally worse than working a low-paying job.

We're talking about huge middle-class constituencies for entitlement programs like Social Security and Medicare. Why buy a Hyundai and vacation in Florida when you can buy a Mercedes and vacation in Europe? How many economic decisions are subtly influenced by the knowledge that at least a portion of one's retirement costs will be borne by others?

As for the Fed, we could spend all weekend studying how it distorts prices across the board, rigs equity and housing markets, misallocates resources and alters the structure of production, fools entrepreneurs, and punishes savers.

As Guido Hülsmann describes, monetary debasement brings about cultural debasement and ultimately personal debasement. It's not a new concept, but rather a problem that existed in ancient and feudal times just as it does today. It infects every aspect of our society: not just our financial lives, but civil society and our personal relationships as well. Cheap credit, the drug pushed by central bankers, makes us prefer the saccharine pleasures of consumption to the lasting satisfaction of productive achievement. It makes us buy houses that are too big, cars that are too elaborate, and college educations that are too expensive.

It makes us worse people!

In sum, we might say that Congress and the Fed are co-conspirators in a plot to have us live for today instead of building for tomorrow.

It's not hyperbole to say that the political and banking classes have become enemies of civilization. They've sold us a mix of fiscal hedonism and monetary hedonism that threatens to upend the arc of human history.

Our Biggest Challenge Lies in Changing Our Mindset

Remember, our economic future is unwritten. The US economy has very serious structural problems, particularly with respect to debt, the dollar, and entitlements.

But our biggest challenge is mindset. There is no reason on paper that America cannot be a great nation.

Despite all the problems with American schools, we still have one of the most educated workforces in the world. We have abundant and sparsely populated land. In fact, we have more arable land than any other nation—about 17 percent of all US acreage can be farmed. We have 500 million acres of timber. We have two huge coastlines, with access to both eastern and Western markets. And we have huge amounts of cheap energy in the form of oil and natural gas.

Our problems are of our own making, primarily caused by lousy voters, high time preferences, and economic hedonism. It's been a great party, ladies and gentlemen. Good luck electing someone who's serious about the hangover.

38

The Realistic Market
for Private Governance

At this conference and others like it, dealing with alternative legal and monetary structures, I've noticed in recent years a strong bias in favor of action over argument, for building over persuading, for practice over theory. This is laudable and understandable for all of us frustrated by statism and all its terrible offspring: war, bad money, division, along with economic, social, and cultural degradation. We understandably want out, and not one hundred years from now but within our lifetimes.

I saw a response to a tweet promoting this gathering to this effect: you have some great thinkers and theorists scheduled to speak, but what you really need is urban planners! Or, we might think, architects and engineers. This is certainly a fair point! But I must confess to representing the theorists today, and Rothbardians in particular.

In my defense, the theory underpinning any new model for private governance or free cities is as important as the blueprints for a building. Carpenters have a saying, "Measure twice and cut once." Another version of this is found in the Zen koan "Slow down to speed up." Maybe this is a good time to rethink our approach to what private governance could mean, and how better to align this movement with current political, economic, and cultural realities.

This article is adapted from remarks delivered at the Free Private Cities "Liberty in Our Lifetime" Conference in Prague on October 22, 2022.

Remember, "parallel" implies peaceful coexistence with existing political structures. It is nonthreatening and voluntary.

To promote the idea of private governance, we should understand it fully ourselves. We should make sure our vision comports with human nature, which is another way of saying it aligns with the marketplace. As entrepreneurs, we should take the world as it is rather than how we wish it were. Otherwise, we risk creating a product that nobody is buying.

And as an aside, speaking of creating, let's not forget the earliest and most enduring form of private governance is the family! Maybe the fastest way to build your own "parallel structure" is to start having kids. We heard a lot yesterday about living as a digital nomad, seeking multiple passports, and seasteading, but we should not forget that the whole point of building better governance structures is so humans can live better. This requires new humans!

I also suggest an appeal to the better angels among the many nationalist and breakaway movements happening across the world. These are real, they hunger for independence, and we should not ignore them. And of course we should sell community: clean and safe streets, nice parks, good schools, and competent local services from competent local providers. I mean the basic building blocks of a nice community. A good place to raise a family, as the saying goes. The market for start-up or private communities is not only expats or perpetual travelers or bitcoin aficionados, but also soccer moms and religious people and retirees.

We can use the term "private" in more than one sense: the first is personal, relating to private matters in our personal lives, matters which are not public. And we use it as a bright-line distinction between state and civil society, between government action and private action—though, as we've seen, that distinction is increasingly blurred by what Robert Higgs calls "participatory fascism." But when discussing private cities or regions or services or governance, we use "private" as a synonym for "commercial," like any private business. In this sense, we simply mean "not governmental."

But beyond that the possible models are wide open, so we should focus on consumer sovereignty just as the seller of any new product should.

The marketplace—capital and entrepreneurship, as opposed to politics—is the way forward.

I. The Dystopian Vision

When we consider the market for new parallel private structures, we should take a moment to play devil's advocate and consider the typical strawman arguments presented by people who reflexively abhor the notion of private government. These are the people who go on and on about our "sacred democracy" but cannot conceive of the truly democratizing elements of the marketplace, what Mises called a "daily plebiscite." It's uncanny: people have no objection whatsoever to private governance when it comes to vast companies like Google or the British National Trust (the biggest private landowner in the UK) or the ecclesiastical hierarchy of the Roman Catholic Church or the management of Real Madrid football club. But suggest privatizing police or trash pickup in their town of thirty thousand, and they overwhelmingly object. Why?

In large part, "privatization" has become a boogieman for progressives, who treat the concept as a sinister plot for big corporations to run our lives. This is the mentality we must overcome.

In 1992, the sci-fi writer Neal Stephenson published a really enjoyable and groundbreaking book titled *Snow Crash*, which essentially presents a cheeky anarcho-capitalist future—fully privatized, but very messy. The reader senses Stephenson is one of us, but also a bit of a provocateur and contrarian.

Snow Crash takes place in the old territory of California, over which both the US federal government and the state government lost control following a terrible economic crisis (so, unlike our models, the new "startup" territories were born of necessity, not choice).

Government still controls minor aspects of this new world, but authority is mostly now ceded to a complex patchwork of private sovereign agencies, franchises, and mercenaries—some of whom received their training from and work for the now privatized CIA (after a merger with the Library of Congress).

Mafia gangs have achieved the status of quasi-private governments, and rule a network of semiautonomous corporate neighborhoods ("burbclaves"). These regions are linked by privatized roads and protected by de facto mercenaries. Major intersections in Los Angeles now fall under the control of defense contractors and private security (following gunfire battles to determine who would win control of them).

So the new private territories were not born without violence, and the old "Won't warlords take over?" critique of privatization is always lurking behind the story. The protagonist, Hiro, is a delivery driver for Cosa Nostra Pizza, a gang run by Uncle Enzo. But the warlords are at least efficient: when Hiro is late with a delivery, he gets an ominous call from Don Enzo himself implying that the next time he fails the thirty-minute guarantee will be the last time.

Only in the metaverse (a term credited to Stephenson) does Hiro have more status, as a successful denizen of the upper echelons of society unavailable to him in the meat space of his real life delivering pizzas. But even here he is no happier; in the virtual world, every last space is commercialized, monetized, and motivated only by rank status or money. It is a caricature of anarcho-capitalism which ignores the full spectrum of human experience beyond commerce. Stephenson's metaverse is a hellscape, every human interaction is mercenary and transactional and ugly. This is clearly not the way to sell private governance!

II. Rothbard's Vision

What if the parallel communities we seek to build already exist in some form and our task is to identify and coalesce around those existing "nations within nations"? Surely this would be a leap forward.

Natural communities exist everywhere; they may not be libertarian in outlook, but neither are many private entities which don't aggress against anyone. The idea is not only to start up such communities, but also to recognize them. Religious groups like the Amish and the Mennonites in America; ethnic, cultural, and linguistic identifications like the Catalans in Spain or the Welsh in the United Kingdom; corporations; fraternal associations—even country clubs and gated housing developments—all form natural communities which may well increasingly seek to unyoke from their centralized and failing political rulers. They may be socialist or capitalist, right wing or woke, provincial or cosmopolitan, provided they have no desire or incentive to aggress against other private communities.

To sell parallel structures, we should identify them in nascent form here and now.

Murray Rothbard's article "Nations by Consent," written just before he died, in 1994, is an excellent guidepost here:

The "nation," of course, is not the same thing as the state, a difference that earlier libertarians and classical liberals such as Ludwig von Mises and Albert Jay Nock understood full well. Contemporary libertarians often assume, mistakenly, that individuals are bound to each other only by the nexus of market exchange. They forget that everyone is necessarily born into a family, a language, and a culture.

Every person is born into one or several overlapping communities, usually including an ethnic group, with specific values, cultures, religious beliefs, and traditions. He is generally born into a "country." He is always born into a specific historical context of time and place, meaning neighborhood and land area.

Rothbard provides several key takeaways which can benefit the marketing of private governance:

- Nation is not state. Nation stands between individual and state.

- Contractual consent and the right to exit distinguish truly private "nations" from a government or state.

- A true "free private city" does not originate with conquest or decades/centuries of disputed titles, but rather with a fresh start, clear title, and a win-win market approach to services and membership ("citizenship").

- Total privatization "solves" nationality problems, *even while some land areas remain in the governmental sphere.*

- Decentralization and localism "solve" problems of access for enclaves and landlocked areas.

- Voting and citizenship are inferior to consent, contract, and ownership in a true private community.

Rothbard's conception of a nation is very different than a "state," although we have been led to believe the two are synonymous. By identifying existing nations—organic and not contrived, like so many national borders—we dramatically increase the market opportunities for selling private governance to dissatisfied constituencies.

III. Common Law: No Vision Required!

While we identify existing nations and intentional communities, we similarly can identify existing mechanisms for ordering, structuring, and enforcing contractual societies. We don't necessarily need dramatic new constitutions or complex legal structures. Common law, evolved over centuries of hard human experience, provides a dependable model to navigate conflicts and provide governance guardrails in a private parallel structure. We don't need a grand vision; we need the wisdom of the ages.

Moreover, I think we should be very cautious about imagining what we can design. This is not only the lesson of Hayek, but also the lesson of countless entrepreneurs finding their way in the marketplace every day.

Remember, law is about conflict. It is about resolving, hopefully minimizing, violence and property disputes in society—which is precisely why politics is self-defeating, even if you accept its premises. Private societies seek to promote human flourishing in win-win ways, versus the zero-sum political outcomes and deeply harmful state legal systems. But we should remember that a key measure of whether a society is just and flourishing is how it handles the inevitable conflicts and frictions that occur under any kind of system.

But we need the market for this! In Adam Smith's time—despite the *de jure* government monopoly on courts—a Scottish or English peasant had more choice of law than we do today! Parties could use local, manorial, county, ecclesiastical, merchant, chancery (equitable relief versus money damages), and common law venues. Why do we have fewer choices of law in the West today?

In *For a New Liberty*, Rothbard points out how the history of a changing and evolving law can be enormously useful to find just rules: "Since we have a body of common law principles to draw on, however, the task of reason in correcting and amending the common law would be far easier than trying to construct a body of systematic legal principles *de novo* out of the thin air."

Bruno Leoni, the midcentury Italian philosopher and legal theorist, makes the best case for how to have law without legislation—and without legislatures—in his 1961 classic *Freedom and the Law.*

In Anglo-Saxon common law, "law" did not mean what we think today: endless enactments by a legislature or executive. "Law" was not enacted but found or discovered; it was a body of customary rules that had, like languages or fashions, grown up spontaneously and purely voluntarily among the people. These spontaneous rules constituted "the law"; and it was the work of experts in the law to determine what the law was and how the law would apply to the numerous cases in dispute that perpetually arise.

A common law model of governance and dispute resolution solves so many of the thorny questions of how to order a private society:

- Five-hundred-plus years of real-world "models."
- Principles are easier than specifics.
- Emphasis on discovery of law mirrors the entrepreneurial market process, akin to the Kirznerian entrepreneurial discovery process.
- Choice of law is provided by the market.
- Adjudication of disputes by contract, known to both parties prior, reduces those disputes.
- Judge-made law reflects the most hyperlocal culture, lifestyle, geography, and economy—and therefore fashions the most just results.
- Judge-made law is more temporal, individualized, flexible, and proportional.

In closing, let me recommend three additional texts to get us thinking in the right direction. First, Titus Gebel's *Free Private Cities* is quite literally the handbook for this burgeoning movement. Edward Stringham's *Private Governance* is the single best book I've seen on the history and technical aspects of creating economic and social order through private mechanisms. Finally, Prince Hans-Adam II of Liechtenstein's wonderful *The State in the Third Millennium* provides an excellent and erudite argument for transforming states into private service providers as the next stage in human development.

A new and better world is possible through the understanding of private governance, nations within nations, and common law mechanisms for dealing with human conflict. How we market and sell this world is worth understanding, just as any entrepreneurial venture needs both a vision and the hard details.

39

Four Ways to Build a Better Society

The topic of our symposium this morning is "What Must Be Done," which originally was the title of a talk given by Dr. Hans-Hermann Hoppe at a Mises Institute conference in 1997. Hoppe posed his title as a declarative, but it's also the question we all wrestle with as libertarians in a world so dominated by the state and its apologists.

And it's a question we hear time and time again at the Mises Institute: What can we do to fight back against government? We all understand the problem, but what is the solution? What can we do in the current environment to help build a more sane and libertarian world? And how can we find some measure of freedom in our lives today, to live more freely in our lifetimes?

Four Common Strategies

When libertarians talk about what must be done, the discussion tends to revolve around four common strategy options. None of them are mutually exclusive necessarily and there can be plenty of overlap between them.

1. The Political Option

The first, we'll call the political option, or to borrow a tired phrase, "working within the system."

This article is adapted from a talk delivered at the Phoenix Mises Circle, November 2015.

The argument goes something like this: government, and the political process that surrounds it, are inevitable in the real world. Therefore libertarians must not stand idly on the sidelines while politicians inexorably steal our freedoms. Instead we must organize and become active politically, under the banner of a third party vehicle like the Libertarian Party or by working within the Republican Party, because whether we want to involve ourselves with politics or not, politics certainly involves itself with us.

Political action can be viewed as a form of self-defense. This approach usually has a national focus—such as running a presidential candidate—though it contemplates political action at the state and local level as well. It appeals to libertarians in a hurry, so to speak. Ultimately, at least in theory, the political option attempts to mimic and reverse the incrementalism that has been so successful for the political Left over the past century.

Let me say that the political option, at least in terms of national politics, strikes me as the least attractive alternative among those available to us today.

The amount of time, energy, and human capital that have been invested trying to win political and legislative battles is staggering, but what do we have to show for it? The twentieth century represents the total triumph of Left progressivism in the political sphere: central banking, income taxes, the New Deal, and Great Society entitlement schemes were all enormous political victories that changed the landscape forever. Everything has become politicized: from what bathroom transgender people should use to whether online fantasy football should be allowed. Progressives frame every question as "What should government do?"

So we need to understand the political option within the context of the progressive triumph.

2. Strategic Withdrawal

A second approach libertarians often consider might be loosely termed strategic withdrawal. You may have heard of the "Benedict option" being discussed by Catholics unhappy with the direction of the Church and the broader culture. Ayn Rand fans talk about "going Galt," in reference to the strike by the productive class that takes place in *Atlas Shrugged*.

This approach involves separating, withdrawing, or segregating in some way from the larger society and political landscape. It asserts that the current environment is largely hopeless for libertarians politically and culturally, and therefore attempting to play the game where the rules are so heavily slanted in favor of the state is foolish.

It's better to retreat, at least for now, and build a life outside the state's parameters to the extent possible. In this sense, the withdrawal option is tactically appealing: like certain martial arts, it attempts to deflect and redirect a greater force, rather than face it head on.

A strategic withdrawal can take many forms across a range of alternatives, from absolute separation to quite subtle lifestyle changes. In some cases this strategy can mean actually physically uprooting where one lives and works. We have examples like the Free State Project in New Hampshire or Liberland in Europe, along with various seasteading proposals and attempts to create libertarian homesteads in Central and South America.

But withdrawal can take other forms. Some libertarians choose to live off the grid, both literally and metaphorically. The prepper movement represents a form of strategic self-sufficiency, as does simply choosing to move to a rural or remote area.

Withdrawing from the American way of endless consumption and debt—"living small"—offers another form of strategic retreat, and often allows libertarians not only to lead happier lives, but also minimize or avoid the state's regulatory and tax clutches.

Of course, homeschooling represents one of the greatest examples of libertarian strategic withdrawal in the modern age, enabling millions of kids and parents to escape the state education complex.

And withdrawal can be as simple as abandoning state media or unplugging from the digital white noise that surrounds us.

Finally, expatriation—voting with one's feet—is a time-honored historical strategy for removing oneself from a tyrannical state. This happens domestically in the US, with people fleeing high tax states, as well as across borders. I'm sure many people in this room have at least considered leaving the US, and increasing numbers of Americans are not only doing just that, but renouncing their citizenship as well. Who could judge a young person today who looks around and decides to leave the US for greener, or freer, pastures?

3. Hearts and Minds

A third tactic that libertarians often advocate is what we might call "winning hearts and minds." This approach is multi-pronged, involving education, academia, traditional and social media, religion, books and articles, literature, and even pop culture. Hearts and minds is why we hold conferences like this. The hearts and minds strategy is all about education, persuasion, and marketing, at every level. And it's the approach through which I think the Mises Institute has made the most headway.

A hearts and minds strategy argues that no change can occur unless and until a significant portion of a given population shrugs off its bad ideas and embraces sensible ideas, particularly in the areas of politics, economics, and social theory. Politics is a lagging indicator, and it follows downstream from culture. We should focus on the underlying disease, not the symptoms. Just as Left progressives have captured the institutions of the West—academia, news media, government, churches, Hollywood, publishing, social media—libertarians ought to focus our efforts on reclaiming these institutions for liberty and a brighter future. So it makes sense to launch liberty-minded people into the streams of academia, business, media, and religion. This is how we strike the root of, or at least chip away at, the mindset that supports the state.

Clearly a wholesale attack on these institutions is a daunting task. It's a long game. But the argument goes like this: until we win hearts and minds, it scarcely matters whom we elect, what bill gets passed, or how we arrange our personal and professional lives. The same statist mentality will surface time and time again to work against us.

Surely the state's education racket offers the ripest target for this approach. As public schools deteriorate into mindless PC zones, and as universities continue to produce heavily indebted graduates with uncertain job prospects, it becomes increasingly obvious to the public that the whole model is unsustainable.

That's why we have an opportunity like never before to appeal directly to the intelligent lay audience, and bring Austrian economics and libertarian theory to the masses at very little cost. The digital revolution has been the great leveler, and we should use it to its full advantage in changing as many hearts and minds as possible.

But this strategy is not for the faint of heart, and it doesn't promise a quick fix. It's a strategy for sober people with long time horizons.

4. Resistance

Of course another strategy often discussed among libertarians involves simple resistance to the state, whether open or covert. This tactic contemplates actions like civil disobedience, tax protests, evading or ignoring regulations, and engaging in agorism and black markets.

It also contemplates the use of technological advances to advance freedom. "Third way" libertarian technologists promote this approach, citing advances like encryption, cybercurrencies, and platforms like Uber—all of which when first developed existed in a sort of grey area as regards their legality.

Agorism was the preferred approach of the late libertarian theorist Sam Konkin, who encouraged people to bypass the state by devoting their economic lives to black-market or gray-market activities, thus avoiding taxation and regulation and helping to shrink the beast. Konkin called it "counter-economics."

Agorism and its variants was critiqued by Murray Rothbard, who found Konkin's antipathy to wage labor and "white markets" as anti-market: after all, what does agorism offer the vast majority of wage workers? And who will provide "legitimate" goods and services like automobiles and steel? Rothbard saw agorists as "neglecting the overwhelming bulk of economic life to concentrate on marginalia."

And let's be frank: the notion of living an agorist's life in the shadows, without, for example, having a driver's license or owning real estate, might not hold mass appeal.

As for applying new technology to bypass the state, I'm all for it. Any innovation that makes it harder for the state to govern us, as a practical matter, is something to be celebrated. But we should guard against false hope: the same technology which serves to facilitate privacy or title transfers or stealth movement of money or people can be exploited by the state's spying apparatus. And no innovation can change the fundamental questions of whether and how human affairs should be organized by the state.

Hoppe's Revolution

So these four basic approaches—politics, withdrawal, "hearts and minds," and resistance—provide us with a framework to consider, in an unfree world, what must be done.

These questions bring us back to Professor Hoppe and his aforementioned speech. I encourage you to read it, it's a fascinating topic and his treatment of it is razor-sharp.

Keep in mind that when Hoppe delivered his talk in 1997, the digital revolution was still in its infancy. Social media and mobile devices did not exist. Several precipitating events—the introduction of the euro, the September 11 attacks, the wars in Iraq and Afghanistan, the Crash of 2008, Greenspan and Bernanke's monetary hyperdrive, the rise of Obama, and the full contagion of PC in the West—had not yet occurred.

Each of these events intensified the growth and scale of centralized government power. But even in what now seems like the carefree year of 1997, Hoppe's explicit focus was the fundamental fight against any and all centralized political power.

The Problem of Centralization

And, in fact, decentralization is a linchpin that connects each of the four tactical approaches mentioned earlier. If there is one principle, and only one principle, that libertarians ought to apply when considering strategy, it is this: radical decentralization of state power must be our relentless goal.

The twentieth century, the Progressive century, witnessed the unprecedented centralization of political and economic power in the hands of the political class. We see this in Washington, DC, in Brussels, at the UN, at the Fed, at the European Central Bank. Our overriding goal therefore must be the reversal of this terrible trend to create a critical mass of "implicitly seceded territories."

Hoppe prescribes a bottom up strategy that identifies natural elites not found among the political class, its court intellectuals, or its state-connected allies. These elites are simply accomplished, upstanding local citizens. These natural elites form the counterbalance to the parasitic centralizers, and serve as the vanguard of the bottom up revolution.

Hoppe posits three strategic keys for this revolution:

- First, protection, defense, and justice must be de-monopolized. These are the very areas—policing, courts, armies—where libertarians often falter in their advocacy of a truly private society. But here we must be steadfast: if these functions remain under the sole power of a central state monopoly, no progress toward liberty is possible. We can't trust the state with guns, lawyers, and jails.

- Second, political decentralization must be ruthlessly pursued, and here Hoppe makes the case that voting on local matters can be morally justified on grounds of self-defense.
- Third, democracy as a concept must be attacked and ridiculed whenever possible. Private property forms the basis for a free society, while majority rule—i.e., the system that permits the theft of private property—forms the antithesis of a free society.

Conclusion

Let me conclude with a quote from Rod Dreher, writing in *The American Conservative* about the Benedict option I mentioned earlier:

> Rome's collapse meant staggering loss. People forgot how to read, how to farm, how to govern themselves, how to build houses, how to trade, and even what it had once meant to be a human being.

Has the world fallen so far into reflexive statism that we have forgotten how to be free? Are we living, like Dreher says, on the edge of a new dark age? Or is a revolution, a radically decentralized Hoppean "bottom up" revolution brewing? Is the pushback we see all around the world—against central states and their cobbled together borders, against political elites, against the UN and the IMF, against the euro, against taxpayer bailouts, against cronyism, against PC, against manufactured migration, and against drug laws, a last gasp? Or the sign of worldwide movement toward political decentralization?

Finally, let us remember that every society worth having, every advanced liberal society, was built by people with long time horizons. Horizons beyond their own lives. And generally those societies were built under very difficult circumstances and conditions of material hardship far beyond what we're likely to face. So let's appeal to our better natures and turn "What Must be Done" from a question into a declaration.

40

Our National Psychosis

What a week for our sacred democracy. Wow! You know, it's so sacred that just a few thousand votes in a few states here and there could have turned it from sacred into profane, couldn't it? Real easy. But no, as long as it goes a certain way, it shows the wisdom of the crowd.

We're generally told that there are three particular benefits to democracy and one of those benefits is a peaceful transfer of political power. So, that's increasingly being questioned, but Mises wrote about this way back in the 1920s. He said this is why we need democracy. He wrote about it again in the 1940s in *Human Action*. He said this allows us to change from one government to another without violence. That's largely been true in the twentieth century, and in the seventy-odd years since he wrote that, that's largely been true.

But two of the other reasons that we're told to revere democracy, I think, are not true, and one of them is that it creates a compromise, some sort of down-the-middle policy, so that the Far Left doesn't get everything it wants, the Far Right doesn't get everything it wants, but somewhere down the middle there's a happy compromise, we all get a little bit of what we want. And of course we see that's not true at all. The whole country's at each other's throats, and what we really have is a sort of bureaucratic and oligarchic overclass and just a bunch of average, regular people like us who

---

This article is adapted from a talk delivered at the Mises Institute's Ron Paul Symposium, November 7, 2020, in Angleton Texas.

are unhappy with the results of democracy, so I don't see any great compromises coming from it. And then, of course, probably the worst excuse for democracy is that it represents some sort of consent of the governed. So, in a country of 330 million people that becomes entirely meaningless, and I think we all get that.

So, I hope many of you I don't know have read Hans-Hermann Hoppe's *Democracy: The God That Failed*—came out in 2001. If you haven't had a chance to read it, I wish you would. Unfortunately, we don't own the rights to that book, or there'd be a $6 paperback of it, but nonetheless, well worth purchasing, well worth reading. There's a PDF online which may or may not be pirated. Not by us; that's the market, baby. So, if you have a chance to look at that book, every chapter reads very well as a standalone chapter. I encourage it. There's a great chapter in there disabusing you of conservatism and all these other things. But the introduction to that book is all about what Hoppe sees as the turning point of World War I, when we went from what we might call the Old Right, which was a real liberalism rooted in property and self-determination, into mass democracy.

And so World War I, Hoppe says, is what changed everything, and it's where we decided that all the benefits of Enlightenment rationalism and the Industrial Revolution would start to fray because we would turn them over into democracy. And one thing he points out is that prior to Woodrow Wilson—you remember a year ago we were talking about Edward Bernays, who was Woodrow Wilson's propagandist who came up with the phrase "Make the world safe for democracy"—prior to Wilson's war and World War I, most wars were actually territorial. They were about turf. And so World War I, Hoppe tells us, was the first truly ideological war in human history, and that's the result of mass democracy and wanting to impose democracy on other countries, our way of life on other people. So, not coincidentally, Hoppe points out, there were actually far more civilian casualties from starvation and disease than soldier casualties on battlefields in World War I. I wonder how many people know that. And he says, This is not a surprise; this is what happens when you have total wars as opposed to regional or territorial wars. So, also because of ideology, the ideology of democracy, there couldn't be any compromise with the Germans. There could only be total surrender, humiliation, punishment, reparations, and we all know what came a few decades later.

So, Hoppe's book is about the results of mass democracy; it's all about results. So, we think of the marketplace as producing goods and services. Governments produce bads, Hoppe says. They produce bad things; they take from us and they make things worse. So, what do we get from democracy in terms of results? Well we get bad politicians, we get bad voters with high time preferences, we get bad policy, we get war, taxes, regulations, surveillance, cultural degradation—the whole nine yards. But the other thing we get in terms of bads which the state produces in a democratic system is this centralization of state power. Hoppe describes we had thousands upon thousands of city-states and principalities and territories which used to make up Europe, and now today they've turned it into these managerial superstates, like we think of the modern Germany, for instance. And in the United States they turned fifty states (you know, we used to say "these United States"—well, we didn't, but our grandparents used to say "these United States") into basically what are glorified federal counties—shabby glorified federal counties, I might say. And it also put about 330 million people with wildly diverse interests under the boot of just a few thousand people in Washington, DC, and sometimes it's even fewer than that. Sometimes it's just five or seven Supreme Court justices.

So, we think about democracy producing bad results. But what Hoppe's book doesn't talk about, and what is so fascinating to me, especially this week, is, What about process? We think about the results of democracy, what about the process? It turns out the process is lousy too. You know, it produces another kind of bads, which is it takes the form, as we see this week and as we certainly saw in 2016, of a national psychosis, this sort of emotional breakdown of people who are emotionally invested in government and politics and the winner of these elections. And so, this kind of division which we're living under is actually another bad result of democracy, but from the process side.

So, we have this election result still in limbo. I think that Biden is going to prevail, however you want to call that prevailing, but we have maybe 100 million or more Americans whose entire psychological well-being over the next couple weeks is bound up in this process over which they have no control. You know, a few tens of thousands of people in a few swing states will determine two completely different narratives for the next few years. It'll be like, Well, our sacred democracy: the Americans were too smart to be fooled again by this strange orange reality-show conman and they wisely chose Joe Biden. Or it'll be, America is this fascist reprobate state. Just a few tens of thousands of votes are going to make the difference in that narrative.

That doesn't make any sense to me. So, the process doesn't work; the process itself is dysfunctional, and millions of Americans like us, they just don't accept the process as legitimate anymore, any part of it, from the vote counting to the recounts, to the campaign spending and the PACs and the dark money groups, to the voter registrations, the mail-in ballots, the deadlines, some of these dubious electronic systems. I was thinking, Press the button and behind it it's like that game, Operation, where the clown's nose lights up and it doesn't go anywhere. I don't know. You press a little button, who knows where it actually goes, right? It might just be a bare wire back there. And so, people are also not going to accept the recounts and legal challenges—the whole process. And if you think about it, it would actually be hard to design.

If some sadist wanted to design a process every four years that would produce more bads than our current system, I don't know how you'd do it. Division, hatred, distrust, waste, and yet all of it at the end of the day settles nothing. It doesn't produce some sort of lasting compromise or sense of finality to it. The next four years are going to just be one side saying "not my president" all over again. So, the process does do one thing, though, for the state. It hides the bad results. The process becomes the thing, so we're so preoccupied with politics and these votes, we forget about what we ought to be thinking about—the overseas wars, the debt, the devaluation, the surveillance—all the result side of democratic voting.

So, the question becomes, What do we do? That's always the question, that's always the frustration. That's what people ask me over and over and over, what should we do, where do we go? First of all, you have to start with this: everybody in this room has an advantage when it comes to this national psychosis. Everybody in this room has some natural antibodies, I think, to this whole thing. We've already recovered, we're already immune. We understand and recognize what millions of Americans are just starting to understand, namely that it's not just that mass democracy doesn't work, but that it can't work. So, we don't have any illusions. That's our benefit, that's our bonus. We have a head start, so to speak, on this national psychosis, and I really think that's a form of power which we all ought to employ in our personal lives and in our emotional well-being.

A couple of weeks ago, my wife happened upon an essay from 1978 by Vaclav Havel, the Czech dissident leader who was also the first president of the Czech Republic after the fall in 1989, and this essay is called "The Power of the Powerless." It was new to me. My friend Pete Quiñones told me last night that it's actually been circulating in the blogosphere for several years. It's really a fascinating essay, about eighty pages. And so, he's writing this in the '70s when the former Czechoslovakia is still under Soviet domination but not as much Soviet domination as the USSR itself, perhaps. So, I'm reading this essay (and Vaclav Havel was also a literary guy and a poet, so he's a tremendous writer, and you guys should all find this, "The Power of the Powerless," easy to find), and I'm struck by the fact that the parallels between the Eastern Bloc situation he's describing (the former Soviet Bloc) and the atmosphere in the US

today are so striking. And I don't mean to imply that we face anything close to the hardships that they did, but it's striking. It's still
striking, and it's ominous. It is happening here, and we can feel it;
I think we can feel it. Not everything can be verbalized and intel-
lectualized. Sometimes it's just a feeling.

So, the good news is that he's writing this as a dissident in 1978
and not too much later in 1993 there was actually a happy outcome
in the creation of the first Czech republic. So, sometimes when
things look particularly dark, maybe you got to keep on moving forward and something good is going to happen if you do so. So, Havel
talks about how the Czechs didn't live under what we think of as a
form of actual physical dictatorship. It was sort of a soft totalitari-
anism. In other words, he says, Well, it took the form of this almost
hypnotic secularized religion where the metaphysical and existential realities of the world, they succumb to ideology. And that's what
we think of when we think of the Soviet Union. We think of people
who tried to just command human energy into something new, to
create a new man and also to ignore, for example, the laws of economics—that this could be willed, that this could be done by fiat
or by legislative action. And so, when we think of communism, we
think it ignores certain underlying metaphysical realities and realities of human nature. That was one of the big criticisms of Soviet
communism. So, he says, Well, you know, this is happening here,
but he talks about how people would just sort of purposely lie to
themselves and their friends and family to remain in good standing
in both society and with the party in Czechoslovakia.

And again, the analogy today: I'm sure you've seen this going
around, that $2 + 2 = 5$. Does $2 + 2 = 4$? Well, it depends because
mathematics, like everything else, is not some hard science or
some branch of logic where we just simply describe a reality which
already exists and which is underlying and we're trying to grapple
and figure it out. No, no, no. $2 + 2$ might equal 5, depending on
your outlook, depending on your identity and the circumstances,
and maybe the color of your skin or your religion, or the country

you come from. And of course, this is a recipe for disaster. This is a recipe for eliminating any basis of social cooperation amongst us, for having markets, for having prosperity, and of course it results in just somebody having to have the power to enforce $2 + 2 = 5$.

Ideology enforced by the state becomes the only animating force in society. So, Havel gives an interesting example. He demonstrates this $2 + 2 = 5$ mentality by talking about how in Czechoslovakia shopkeepers would dutifully put up the little sign that says Workers of the World Unite. They would just sort of dutifully do this. Like how back in the day people used to put up pictures of the presidents in their living rooms, and if you travel to foreign countries, oftentimes people still do that: in Latin America; in Turkey, you'll see pictures of Erdogan and sometimes you'll see pictures of Ataturk on the walls. So people revere these figures. So he said, Nobody actually believed this, "workers of the world unite." The grocer didn't do this because he means it, it was just an act of rote conformity on his part, it was a signal. It's a signal of acquiescence, and since all the other shops do it, you do it too. This is what it meant to be a greengrocer in Czechoslovakia in 1978. And we see this in America today. We see the same kind of signaling, the same kind of acquiescence of things like masks or some of these goofy signs, All Lives Matter or Black Lives Matter or Back the Blue. These are signals, and people put them up in their yard. There's that one that says This House Believes X, Y, and Z, and it's this sort of hectoring thing which is supposed to prove what a great person you are in that house. So, we have the same thing happening in America today.

Most people in this room, though, are prepared to be dissidents today. Most people in this room are not willing to just go along with this stuff, and most people in this room already consider themselves the real resistance, not the fake kind where you have all the support of the political parties and the mainstream media and academia and Hollywood and corporate America. That's not a resistance. So, we're already past any of these illusions about democracy or politics or constitutionalism. I would argue that we've reached the point where loving our country requires us to identify and begin to separate the various nations which are within it. I think there's nothing more important today.

So, if you get an opportunity to read Hoppe's book, I think you will find it enlightening. I think you will identify a lot of the problems which he identifies, and I think you will come away with a better understanding of really what a radical experiment mass democracy really is. It's not what we imagined it to be. There's no sort of 51:49 electorate which gives anything legitimacy, because oftentimes votes are won with fewer than 51 percent. Bill Clinton became president because of Ross Perot, with less than 51 percent of the electorate. Even the Reagan revolution in 1984, where he won every state, forty-nine states, except for, I guess, Mondale's Minnesota and the District of Columbia—forty-nine-state route, something like 60:40 in the raw numbers, and yet what we think of as an absolute landslide, one of the biggest victories in electoral history in the United States for president, something like 24 percent of all Americans voted, cast an affirmative ballot for him. So, if you begin to look at the numbers a little differently, you begin to question all of this, and you begin to wonder where it came from, and you begin to hope that people can start to think again a little bit more about having fifty states. In other words, what happened last Tuesday, there were fifty state elections. There wasn't one national election, there were fifty state elections. Yes, people were voting on who's going to hold a national office known as the president, but it wasn't a national election. Those are two different things.

So, I want to leave you with this great quote from Havel. He says, "Ideology is a specious way of relating to the world. It offers human beings the illusion of an identity." How many libertarians get their identity from goofy libertarianism? "It offers human beings the illusion of an identity, of dignity and of morality while making it easier to part with them." Told you this guy's a poet. "It is a veil behind which human beings can hide their own fallen existence, their trivialization and their adaptation to the status quo." I think that's just an absolutely phenomenal way to put things, because I really believe that liberty, in the political sense, is not an ideology which you impose on other people; it's the absence of ideology. It's what happens when you leave people alone, when civil society and marketplaces are allowed to function and flourish. It doesn't need to be imposed on anyone—it's the state which is the imposer—and of course it's the natural condition of social cooperation. Mises almost called his book *Human Action*, his magnum opus, Social Cooperation. He says it's the only way you can organize society peacefully. But we have no choice, all of us here today, but to recognize that millions of Americans, millions upon millions of Americans—maybe a majority of Americans—simply don't see the world the way we do. That's a fact. So, the goal of this national psychosis, which they produce and impose on us every four years, is of course demoralization, more than anything. Don't let that happen.

41

We Need Truth and Beauty

The architect Frank Lloyd Wright played an important role in the design of this beautiful desert resort. I'm sure I'm not the only person here tonight who was introduced to his work through reading Ayn Rand. His touches are plainly visible in the stonework, wooden touches, and organic approach to melding the buildings with the landscape.

This article is adapted from remarks made at the Mises Institute's Supporters Summit in Phoenix, Arizona on October 9, 2022.

His style appeals to my personal aesthetic tastes and evokes something both intellectual and emotional.

Perhaps there is a lesson here about how we win, or at least how we advance. We need something more than intellectual appeal.

I suggest we have not thought enough or talked enough about beauty in our Austrian circles. Because truth and beauty are inescapably linked. Austrian economics is a beautiful logical deductive system, a way of looking at the world just as Frank Lloyd Wright had his way of looking at the world.

Consider this quote from Joe Salerno, in his great article on the sociology of the Austrian school: "The essence of Austrian economics may be defined, then, as the structure of economic theorems that is arrived at through the process of praxeological deduction, that is, through logical deduction from the reality-based action axiom." This is quite a definition.

Austrian economics is, in other words, an edifice: a body of knowledge every bit as rooted in tangible reality as architecture. But architects consider beauty far more than economists!

Both Mises and his protégé Murray Rothbard wrote quite a lot about method, about the search for truth in economic science. But both had had precious little to say about the connection between beauty and truth, or about aesthetic sensibilities generally. In fact, a look through the indices of their biggest works shows very few references to art, architecture, or beauty more generally. We do know Mises was an aesthetic subjectivist, which we glimpse both in *The Anti-capitalistic Mentality* and this quote from *Theory and History*: "Only stilted pedants can conceive the idea that there are absolute norms to tell what is beautiful and what is not."

Maybe Mises and Rothbard did not contemplate beauty too much because it was all around them, both in prewar Vienna and midcentury Manhattan: wonderful architecture, music, literature, theater were all just part of life.

We know Austrian economics is fundamentally true; in fact truth is its most important and fundamental responsibility. Yet we cannot afford to ignore the corollary to truth, namely beauty. Without beauty, divorced of any higher human longings, economics devolves from a beautiful theoretical edifice into a bastard cousin of accounting and finance, a business discipline. Or even worse, it becomes nothing more than an intellectual veneer for so-called public policy, which is really just a sanitized euphemism for politics.

Is economics really bloodless, or does it have a soul? Can it serve beauty and truth?

Progressives abandoned beauty a long time ago, in fact they promote and advance ugliness as a matter of principle—while attacking even the idea of truth. Some conservatives at least give lip service to the importance of beauty; I'm speaking of the Roger Scrutons and Douglas Murrays and Trad Catholics. They at least see it as worthy of consideration. But the Heritages and Claremonts and *National Reviews* are too busy defining themselves as: Not progressive. They are mired in policy and can't seem to explain markets and capital and ownership in human terms which resonate. And even the best conservatives (our friends Paul Gottfried and those at Chronicles magazine are exceptions) tend to be mired in faulty economics and delusions of statecraft. They don't have truth.

The writer Steve Sailer recently showed a collection of US city hall buildings constructed before and after 1945, which he identifies as dividing year in architecture. "Before then," Sailer says, "Westerners tried, in many different styles, to make buildings look beautiful. After 1945, they felt like they didn't deserve beautiful buildings."

Of course the older city halls, especially those from the 1800s, evoked European classical and neoclassical architecture. Those built in the 1960s and '70s tended to be brutalist monstrosities of concrete and glass—deliberately ugly, we can only assume, and plainly dehumanizing.

Why in the world are economists not noticing this? Austrians understand fiat money, but what about fiat architecture, fiat food,

302 A Strange Liberty

fiat art, fiat culture, fiat everything? Economics does not somehow stand separate and apart from the cultural ramifications of our disastrous economic policies. It is here to help us make sense of the ugliness growing around us, and not just in politics.

Beauty without Truth?

There is no doubt: The hunger for beauty in the West today is real. We are starved for it.

I'm sure many of you watched the events surrounding Queen Elizabeth's death and funeral. There was plenty of distinctly English pomp & circumstance and marching—one thing the old empire still does well! They could sure use some of that precision over at the National Health Service.

But what pulled us in was the sheer spectacle of it all. We witnessed reverence, even veneration, for tradition, country, for a figurehead, for a hereditary monarch!

We saw beautiful buildings, robed clergy conducting religious ceremonies in majestic cathedrals (though they brought in plenty of vaguely nondenominational speakers at the funeral, along with a cameo by the dreadful Liz Truss), and open religiosity in 2022. Not to mention plenty of men in military dress, order, precision, and appeals to continuity. Everything progressives hate!

And yet it was all somehow hollow. It felt more like an end than a beginning. Nobody is excited for the prospects of "King Charles III," who of course is a woke crazed environmentalist who literally praised the Great Reset in a speech to the World Economic Forum. His sons are cut from the same cloth, and due to tabloid and social media we know all their personal foibles and see them in a very different light than the departed Elizabeth. They are unserious people.

It all felt like beauty without truth or substance, like an empty pageant or a museum display. And it was made worse by the clownish Biden stumbling around and the nauseating BBC commentary.

But there was something there, a hunger for seriousness and substance and meaning. Whether the Queen and the faltering monarchy provided this is dubious, and whether Charles and Co. can is even more dubious. Yet millions of people were out on the streets of London and millions around the world watched on television. I suggest they were looking for beauty.

Modern elites are not up to the task. They cannot satisfy this hunger because they are ugly at their core. But here is the good news: at no point in modern history, at least in the West, have they been less impressive and more vulnerable. They are deeply unserious people: the Blairs and the Borises, the Klaus Schwabs, the Zuckerbergs and Bezos, the Pelosis and Squads and Bidens and Bushes and Clintons and Cheneys; the sociology professors and the pop stars and moronic "influencers" and useless Twitter pundits.

Our elites don't care about truth and beauty. They possess neither, they demonstrate neither, nor see neither as worthwhile. They care about power, status, and money.

But we can replace them, and we must.

We Need New Elites

Every society needs elites; the question is always whether they are natural or imposed, whether they earned their wealth and position in society or captured it through state connections. But we must expect this. Rule by elites, at least to an extent, is indeed inevitable. Every society, across time and across place, manifests this. Democracy doesn't solve or change it, but merely transfers status away from merit and natural authority toward politics and cronyism.

Political and economic liberty is about the freedom and prosperity average people enjoy in any society. This should be our focus. In the poorest and most corrupt countries, elites fatten their own Swiss bank accounts while parasitically draining citizens of their meager resources. In the wealthiest and least corrupt countries, elites act far more benevolently (I submit Prince Hans-Adam II of Liechtenstein as a benevolent example). Most countries across the West today lie somewhere in the middle.

How do we identify "good" elites, wise leaders who will act and guide the world in benevolent ways? Leaders who care about civilization, property, prosperity, peace, justice, fairness, conservation, and charity?

We start by turning our backs on politics, media, academia, and popular culture and recognizing the real-world examples around us. Then simply look around you. In our family, work, social circles, and local communities are the men and women who can replace our very unnatural overlords. Men and women who understand inequality and human differences as the inescapable starting point for human society. Or as Mises said, we need "collaboration of the more talented, more able, and more industrious with the less talented, less able, and less industrious," which "results in benefits for both."

Progressives of all political stripes oppose the idea of natural elites not because of their claimed egalitarianism or democratic impulses or dislike of hierarchies: *they oppose the idea because it contemplates a hierarchy not established by them, a hierarchy where they are not at the top.* A natural elite also means that intelligence, ability, attractiveness, charisma, wisdom, discretion, and quiet confidence—all very unequally distributed in nature—become the characteristics of those holding greater influence in society.

We have a responsibility to be the actual "adults in the room." We desperately need to desanctify the current crop and replace them with much better and nobler people.

It Is Up to Us

None of this is easy. And it comes with a heavy price, to be paid by all of us.

Most of us want to focus on our families, our personal lives, our business or professional lives. We want to take care of our own.

We don't see ourselves as leaders, certainly not as radicals or revolutionaries. We are not wired for constant agitation and, or else we would be progressives. And we certainly don't want to live political lives.

Richard Hanania, a name some of you might know, did some research and published an interesting article in 2021 titled "Why Is Everything Liberal?" By which he meant: How did progressive come to control all of our institutions? And in his view, it all comes down to cardinal preferences: The Left cares more, and wants it more. They are far more willing to engage politically, to donate, to agitate, to choose college majors and seek jobs in academia or media or NGOs or HR departments for influence rather than building businesses for money.

In this sense our natural modesty, our live and let live attitude, our inclination to tend to our own, does us no favors.

In 2003 Lew Rockwell gave a talk at the Mises Institute titled "The Path to Victory." I know some of you were in that room. He argued against quietism, against retreat, against accelerationism, against attempting to capture lost institutions like academia and Congress and mainstream media. He argued instead for robust adherence to truth, to education, to using every available platform, and to recognizing that influence can be indirect and far off temporally. Success, he said, can take many forms and change can happen very suddenly.

Understand this: our personal happiness or self-actualization is not the focus here. Action is not ease or contentment, in fact it happens because of what Mises termed "felt uneasiness." Contentment, as opposed to happiness, comes from serving others—as our own Bob Luddy so eloquently explains in his writing about entrepreneurship.

Mises has this zesty quote about happiness near the beginning of *Human Action*, and I'll apologize in advance to any Buddhists in the audience:

> Some philosophies advise men to seek as the ultimate end of conduct the complete renunciation of any action. They look upon life as an absolute evil full of pain, suffering, and anguish, and apodictically deny that any purposeful human effort can render it tolerable. Happiness can be attained only by complete extinction of consciousness, volition, and life. The only way toward bliss and salvation is to become perfectly passive, indifferent, and inert like the plants. The sovereign good is the abandonment of thinking and acting.
>
> Such is the essence of the teachings of various Indian philosophies, especially of Buddhism, and of Schopenhauer.
>
> The subject matter of praxeology is human action. It deals with acting man, not with man transformed into a plant and reduced to a merely vegetative existence.

So we need volition, what Mises like to call our natural "élan vital," or life force. Let us not be vegetative!

Conclusion

There is a dangerous hubris, a conceit, in imagining we live in particularly dangerous or troubled times, or times of intense and unprecedented rapid change. Relatively speaking, I'm not sure we do.

Consider the lifetime of Ludwig von Mises, who died nearly fifty years ago, in October 1973. Remarkably, in a roundabout way, he is the reason we are all together tonight.

In his time, coming from a village in what is Ukraine today, he was able to live and work in prewar Vienna—one of the most beautiful places and times in western history. It was a high point for intellectualism, for architecture, for classical music, a crossroads for productive and dazzling thinkers. Beauty was all around him.

But Mises also saw tremendous ugliness. He saw his beloved Vienna fall to the barbarism of Weimar and hyperinflation. He saw two incredibly destructive World Wars ravage Europe. He saw Leninism and Stalinism; Nazism and Italian fascism, Wilsonianism and FDR's New Deal, and the development of nuclear weapons. He was forced to flee war twice. He saw socialism and Keynesianism take over academic economics as "scientific." His saw his own career interrupted, as he had no choice but to leave for America and a very uncertain future—while learning a new language in his fifties.

Along the way he saw the world go from outdoor plumbing and kerosene lamps to widespread electricity. He saw newspapers yield to radio and television. He saw the world go from horse and buggy to automobiles, from the earliest propeller planes to jets to space travel and satellites. He saw communication go from telegrams to radio to television to the earliest internet. He truly lived through enough changes for ten lifetimes.

So we can hardly claim to live in more perilous or rapidly changing times than Mises!

To conclude:

We win by serving truth, but also beauty. We cannot separate the two or have one without the other.

We win by placing economics squarely at the vital center of understanding all human social cooperation, a discipline that helps us understand the beauty of that cooperation and the ugliness of state power.

We win with a focus on the long term, not the short run.

We win by building better elites and better institutions.

We win by going out unapologetically and forcefully into the world.

Did you see the British SAS soldiers at the aforementioned Queen's funeral? Their motto is: Who Dares Wins. The future belongs to confident people. Let that be us.

42

The End of Monetary Hedonism

D oes cheap money and credit make us richer? Does more money and credit create more stuff, or better stuff? Do they make us happier and more productive? Or do these twin forces actually distort the economy, misallocate resources, and degrade us as people?

These are fundamental questions in an age of monetary hedonism. It is time we began to ask and answer them. Millions of people across the West increasingly recognize the limits of monetary policy, understanding that more money and credit in society do not magically create more goods and services. Production precedes consumption. Capital accumulation is made possible only through profit, which is generated by higher productivity, thanks to earlier capital investment. At the heart of all of it is hard work and human ingenuity. We don't get rich by legislative edict.

How we lost sight of these simple truths is complex. But we can begin to understand it by listening to someone smarter! The great financial writer James Grant probably knows more about interest rates than anyone on the planet. So we should pay attention when he suggests America's four-decade experiment in rates that only go down, down, and down appears to be over.

> The striking thing about the bond market and interest rates is that they tend to rise and fall in generation-length intervals. No other financial security that I know

---

This article originally appeared in the fall 2022 issue of Bitcoin *magazine.*

of exhibits that same characteristic. But interest rates have done that going back to the Civil War period, when they fell persistently from 1865 to 1900. They then rose from 1900 to 1920, fell from 1920 or so to 1946, and then rose from 1946 to 1981—and did they ever rise in the last five or 10 years of that 35-year period. Then they fell again from 1981 to 2019–20.

So each of these cycles was very long-lived. This current one has been, let's say, 40 years. That's one-and-a-half successful Wall Street careers. You could be working in this business for a long time and never have seen a bear market in bonds. And I think that that muscle memory has deadened the perception of financial forces that would conspire to lead to higher rates.

—James Grant, speaking to the *Octavian Report*

Do the brilliant young Ivy League quants working at central banks and investment houses really understand this history? Why should they? The baseline cost of capital has been less than 3 percent throughout their careers. Cheap credit and rising stock markets are all they know. Lots of projects make sense when funded with debt rather than equity; or as we might say, with other people's money. And when those projects go public, the numbers go up!

Until they don't.

One fears our under-forty financiers really have little understanding of the basic function of interest rates, a function Mises explained so clearly more than one hundred years ago. Interest rates should act as "prices," as Mr. Grant states, or more precisely, as exchange ratios. They bring together borrowers and savers, thus performing a critical function of capital markets and allocating resources to their best and highest uses.

Yet, in 2022, interest rates are widely viewed as *policy tools*. They are economic controls, determined and tinkered with by technocratic central bankers when the economy overheats or chills. We expect central banks to "set" interest rates, an impossibility in the long run but also a perverse goal in a supposedly free economy.

310 A Strange Liberty

What other prices do we want centrally planned? Food, energy, housing? Should the Fed direct how many cars GM produces in 2022, the price of a bushel of wheat, or the hourly wage for an Amazon warehouse employee? Is this the Soviet Union?

Of course not. But those who view money as a political creation are once again prone to fundamental errors. *They don't understand money qua money.* They certainly cannot imagine a world without "monetary policy," which is plainly a form of central planning.

Austrian economists like Carl Menger and Ludwig von Mises illustrated how money can arise on the market as simply the most tradeable commodity, with the most desired features of "moneyness." We don't need state treasuries or public banks to issue it. And we should care about the quality of money, much as we care about the quality of the goods and services we exchanged for it.

But in fiat land, that quality goes down, down, and down. Everything politics touches gets worse; why would we expect money to be an exception?

This four-decade experiment in price fixing of interest rates, described as cyclical by Mr. Grant, not surprisingly corresponds with a dramatic rise in the US M1 money supply. In January 1982, the Fed's "narrow money" was less than $450 billion. In January 2022, it was more than $20 trillion—roughly forty-four times bigger!

We can call this monetary hedonism: a combination of low rates and ever-growing money supply designed to create an illusion of real wealth. Monetary hedonism is an arrangement which encourages our whole society to live beyond its means, using monetary policy rather than direct tax-and-spend policy. It directly benefits both the Beltway and the banking classes, who enjoy an exorbitant political privilege due to their proximity to newly created cheap money. After all, Congress can service $30 trillion+ of debt with interest payments of less than $400 billion—thanks to a weighted average interest rate of only about 1.6 percent on that debt. And it's awfully nice for spendy politicians to know the Fed stands ready to create an instant market for Treasurys owned by commercial banks.

To be sure, cheap money and low rates benefit all of us in a shortsighted sense. They make the cost of doing business lower and enable corporations to carry more (tax-deductible) debt. They make house payments and mortgages more affordable. They make college and cars and dinners and vacations purchased on credit cheaper. They make it easy and fun to spend.

Yet there is always a price to be paid for unearned profligacy. The hangover follows the party. We all sense it. A reckoning is coming for the inflationary US dollar. That reckoning will come for entitlements, for congressional spending, for deranged US foreign policy, and for Treasury holders.

But this *economic* reckoning is not the full story. We must also consider the incalculable but rarely considered *social and cultural costs.*

What happens to society when spending is encouraged and saving is for chumps?

Our grandparents understood the power of compound interest rates. They could save 10 percent of their income at, say, 10 percent interest rates, and their nest egg doubled roughly every seven years. They could get ahead simply, if not easily, through sheer thrift. They could follow the most human of compulsions, the deep-rooted desire to put money away for a rainy day. They could leave something for future generations. Even when consumer inflation approached 10 percent in the 1970s and '80s, they could get 14 percent on a simple CD or money market account!

Compare their experience to that of a hapless young person today, attempting to save up a 20 percent down payment on a modest $300,000 house. In 2022, with inflation at least 6 points above simple savings rates, this seems like a pipe dream.

This is the perversity of our times: with inflation rates higher than savings rates, the overwhelming incentive is to spend and borrow rather than produce and save.

Bitcoiners already understand the problem. The simple economic concept of time preference explains so much: some people are more than willing to forego consumption today to reap a larger reward later—even if that "later" is beyond their lifetimes. Time preference is the only way to make sense of interest rates and their critical function in society; interest rates reflect the relative preferences of borrowers and savers. Manipulation of interest rates by central banks severs this critical mechanism, allowing bubbles to occur in the form of new credit without new saving.

Without interest rates determined by time preference, society's signals become mixed up. We all understand, axiomatically, why humans prefer something today (certain) over something in the future (uncertain). We may die unexpectedly, our financial positions could change radically due to unforeseen events, or external conditions could influence our desires. We all understand borrowing money to buy a dream home at age forty instead of paying cash at age ninety. We all understand why lenders, given the uncertainty and forbearance that goes with lending, want to be paid interest for their risk.

It is a matter of time.

Everything we do in this corporeal world has a temporal element. When governments or central banks interfere with money and interest rates, they distort the vital information provided by real people's relative time preferences.

Hans Hoppe, in his infamous *Democracy: The God That Failed*, goes further—describing time preference as the *essential* civilizing or decivilizing element in society.

> The saver-investor initiates a "process of civilization." In generating a tendency toward a fall in the rate of time preference, he—and everyone directly or indirectly connected to him through a network of exchanges—matures from childhood to adulthood and from barbarism to civilization.

When lots of people save and invest, across society, we call it capital accumulation. And as Hoppe posits, this is not just economic—it is cultural and civilizational. Thrifty people like our grandparents, generation after generation, bequeathed to us an almost unimaginable world of affordable food, water, habitation, transportation, communication, medicine, and material goods of every kind. They did this out of love and sacrifice, but they also did it because the monetary system rewarded saving.

Today, the opposite is true. Monetary policy across the West is an agent of decivilization. It upends the natural, innate human impulse to save for a rainy day and leave our children better off. It encourages consumption over production, profligacy over thrift, and political promises today that will be paid for by savers and taxpayers tomorrow. Monetary policy degrades and deforms the economy, but ultimately its corrosive effects impact the broader culture.

In short, it makes us worse people.

Does bitcoin fix this? Maybe. In the eyes of many maxis (or "bitcoin realists," per Cory Klippsten), certainly. But time is running short. We face a toxic mix of high–time preference junkie politicians and central bankers who are only too willing to provide the fix. We are depleting capital and borrowing against the future. We consistently display high time preference, both as individuals and as a society. This cannot end well for our children and grandchildren.

It is past time for all of us to demand better money, not better monetary "policy." It is time for money to comport with human nature and reward the saving impulse. It is time for us to reconsider our bequest to future generations and make their lives better and more prosperous than ours.

Monetary hedonism, in the form of low interest rates, is coming to an end. The hangover will not be pretty. Readers would be well served to prepare themselves and act accordingly. Politicians and bankers are unlikely to do this for us.

Tributes

43

The Man the World Still Needs: Murray Rothbard

We hear a lot about young people turning to socialism. Ashton is not one of them. She worked for a Texas congressman not named Ron Paul when I met her. You'd be shocked at how many young fans Murray Rothbard and the Mises Institute have in DC. There are more of them out there than you think, on Capitol Hill and agencies and think tanks.

They would come to our meetings in Ron's office with these sheepish looks on their faces, and say "I work for senator so and so," or the department of such and such, blah, but I'm a libertarian!" And they read Rothbard, they love the Mises Institute. I think Murray would be thrilled to hear this.

Those of you who joined us in Asheville last September, it's been a long year. Now I know you all called it, and knew Trump was going to win. But it's such a shame we didn't have Murray Rothbard around to give us his perspective on Clinton vs. Trump.

This is an excerpt from the opening speech given at the Mises Institute's Thirty-fifth Anniversary gala in New York City, October 6, 2017.

Imagine Murray on deplorables and missing emails and Russia Gate and California secession and "not my President." And imagine Murray giving the stick, and sometimes the carrot, in response to the daily Trump show. *That* I would pay to read. Did you hear this statistic recently, that only a quarter of Americans can name all three branches of government? Great, isn't it? I immediately thought Murray would say we shouldn't let them get away with this "separation of powers" nonsense anyway.

But I'd like to talk about Murray Rothbard's legacy.

As I mentioned, Dr. Paul's office was a frequent gathering spot for libertarians in DC. We held a series of great lectures for staff, including one with the great Dr. Walter Williams. At the time he lived on a farm in Valley Forge, Pennsylvania, and drove to northern Virginia during the week to teach at GMU. It was a long drive back, and he got home late. His wife would worry about him driving in the dark. So he liked to joke that he wanted enough life insurance to take care of his family if something ever happened, but not so much that his wife would secretly, deep down, start to think about all the things she might do with the proceeds.

Obviously he was joking, but his point was nobody is indispensable or so important the world can't live without them. The best we can hope for is to leave some legacy for the future, and he pointed out how great men and women leave a legacy through their work.

This is true for Murray Rothbard, even though he died much too young. What we're left with is Murray's work, which is to say *a lot*. We're left with a lot.

This is his sixty-two-page bibliography, spanning from 1949 to his death in 1995. Thirty full-length books, 100 book chapters, 1,000 scholarly and popular articles. Imagine if he had lived another ten or twenty years!

Professor Guido Hülsmann, who is here tonight, says it's impossible to read everything Rothbard wrote.

Rothbard's critics sometimes dismiss his non-academic work, and his willingness to write for lay audiences on philosophy and ethics and political theory and all kinds of areas beyond economics. We can only ask them how many academics are more widely read than ever twenty years after they're gone? How many have 500-page manuscripts lying around to be published as "new" books twenty years after they die? Who today remembers Arthur Burns, former chairman of the Fed and Columbia professor, who tried to block Murray's dissertation on the Panic of 1819? Whose legacy endures?

Millions of people around the world read and know Rothbard because he didn't limit himself to academic journals. Yet there is a recurring theme in his life: if only he had tempered himself a bit, downplayed his more radical views on war and foreign policy, anarchism, banking, and especially politics, he could have secured a comfortable tenured position at a major university. He certainly had the intelligence and the resume for it, with multiple degrees from Columbia and an incredible publishing ethic.

It's hard not to see the parallels between Murray's career and Ludwig von Mises's career, although they were two very different men. But both were treated shabbily by academia despite having written major treatises, both were seen as intransigent even by their ideological compatriots, and neither ever made much money. Their reward lies in their legacies.

Many of you know there was an effort to downplay the work of Mises for strategic reasons. Dr. Joe Salerno recalls this shift beginning in the late 1970s, in libertarian circles. Joe was present for some of those conversations. This was not a conspiracy or an attempt to hurt Mises personally, but a tactical decision—made not by his intellectual enemies but by his fellow travelers.

His intransigence was a problem. His memoirs were a problem. More palatable voices who could win over the mainstream were needed. And so a tacit decision was made to promote in particular the work of Friedrich Hayek, Milton Friedman, and James

Buchanan—all of course good and brilliant men with brilliant careers. Hayek and Friedman already had the cachet of a Nobel prize; Buchanan would win one in 1986. But arguably none of the three approached the depth and breadth of Mises or wrote anything on the level of *Human Action*.

But despite all of this, despite everything Mises faced, his work was too important to be ignored. His work broke through and spoke for itself. His legacy today is secure. Even his worst critics now admit he was among the most influential economists and thinkers of the twentieth century. He earned his status. Many people in this room, along with Murray Rothbard and Lew Rockwell, played a role in securing Mises's legacy, in making sure he held his rightful place in the history of economics.

If we judge Mises's influence by how vocal and highly placed his critics are, then his legacy remains intact. We know this because every six months or so the *New York Times*, the *Washington Post*, Paul Krugman, etc., produce an article lamenting how libertarians have taken over everything. And they always mention Mises in these articles. That's as good an indicator as any that you've made it.

These same outlets frequently attack Hayek, Friedman, and Buchanan as well—in fact the latter recently was the particular target of a very dishonest and shameful book written as a political hit job.

So maybe there's a lesson there. Maybe intransigence is not such a vice. Maybe even small compromises will never win favor from those with a political axe to grind, those who will never support good economics or liberty. Maybe Austro-libertarian thinkers should just focus on the truth. Rothbard took this lesson to heart, and did not hesitate to challenge even his great mentors, much less the academic orthodoxy.

But for all of his output, and all of his brilliance, his legacy is still very much in question. Murray's place in history, as an economist and a thinker, is not secure. Like Mises, Rothbard continues to face headwinds even after his death. Many libertarians consider his work too radical, too focused on anarcho-capitalism, or insufficiently devoted to egalitarianism. They don't like his insistence on a natural rights justification for laissez faire, or his ironclad anti-war views. Some economists don't like his forays into political theory, despite Hayek having done so. Some don't like his strategic overtures to both the Left and Right in different periods of his life.

But we do.

This doesn't mean his work can't be refuted or criticized or expanded upon. Certainly everyone here disagrees with Murray about *something*, because he wrote about *everything*. We need not lionize him. But he deserves to have his legacy made secure, to take his rightful place in the ranks of great twentieth century economists and political theorists, as the rightful heir to the Austrian tradition.

We should care about Murray's legacy not out of spite for his detractors, not because we want to prove he was "right," and not even out of a sense of justice for a man who contributed so much.

The world, especially young people who don't know his work, needs Murray.

- We still need his unbelievably trenchant analysis of politics and culture. Go back and read his *Rothbard-Rockwell Report* articles from the early 1990s on Rwanda, or Kosovo, or the Clintons, or PC, or politics ruining sports—every word holds up today;

- Economists, especially economics students, desperately need Rothbard and *Man, Economy, and State* as the bridge back to *Human Action* and the Austrian tradition—as they suffer through 800 level math classes and learn to force data into predictive models that don't work;

- Libertarians still need Rothbard for his uncompromising ethical case for laissez-faire, to prevent libertarianism from sliding into a hybrid ideology of "low-tax liberalism" that sells out principle but still doesn't win;

- We still need Murray to show us that progressives, far from being the champions of the poor and marginalized, represent nothing more than an unholy alliance of state interests and court intellectuals; and to remind us that conservatives are nothing more than a jobs and war program, who consolidate the gains of the Left; and

- We need his wit, wisdom, spirit, and bravery—all of which are in short supply today.

The world needs Murray because he still matters. And it's up to all of us to secure his legacy as one of the twentieth century's great economists and thinkers.

The world has Mises. It still needs Rothbard.

44

What Would Mises Think about the West Today?

Those of us who read and enjoy Mises, and he wrote so much about so many things, might well wonder what he would have to say about the state of America and the West in 2019. After all, he was a sociologist and philosopher and political theorist as well as an economist. Surely we could use his perspective today, and so much of what he wrote was prescient and still relevant.

Of course it is always dangerous to imagine what any departed intellectual or thinker would think about today's world and today's events, and this is certainly true of Mises too. We all love to do this,

This is an excerpt from a talk at the Mises Institute's Supporters Summit, October 2019, in Los Angeles.

though. We all want to use Mises to make our points about topic X, Y, or Z today, to confirm our own biases or bolster our arguments—and why not? I'm always mystified by facile objections to "appeal to authority"—I recognize Mises may in fact be wrong, and you, Mr. Arguer on Facebook, may in fact be right. But I doubt it.

Two problems present themselves. First, we know how difficult it is to compare eras in sports. How do we measure Babe Ruth and Mickey Mantle against Barry Bonds or Mike Trout? Mises was a man of Old Europe, born before the Great War and the fall of the Habsburgs. Even the world of New York in 1973 when he died is a long way from Woke America 2019.

Second, if we think of scholars like artists or musicians, how do we weigh their work as a whole? Do we accord more weight to his later work, representing a more developed worldview? Or do we approach his work like a rock band, where *The Theory of Money and Credit* was his promising freshman album and *Human Action* was his best and biggest seller? What were his greatest hits?

It's a very fraught question, considering his bibliography consists of nearly twenty full length books, hundreds of articles and monographs, and millions of words written over nearly six decades. It's daunting to draw simple conclusions from such a varied body of work because people change over time. And of course while brilliant and prolific thinkers should be read as authorities, as Mises certainly was regarding socialism, no mortal has the dispositive last word on any issue or topic.

But of course we should apply Mises's counsel to the world today. After all, what's the point of learning from him? He's someone you can spend a lifetime reading and learning from, someone whose work never feels dated or irrelevant. He is someone we still have to grapple with.

So we do wonder what Mises might think about all kinds of things, like the Nobel prize his protégé Hayek won just after Mises's death. Or about Austria today, a shadow of its late nineteenth century glory. Or the collapse of the Soviet Union and the

Eastern Bloc. Or about the European project, especially the euro-zone, the creation of the ECB, and the euro itself, and the political state of Europe today. About European immigration and the Schengen Agreement. About negative interest rates and QE and crazed central bank policies in the decades since his death. About business cycle busts in 1987 and 2000 and 2008. About gold and cryptocurrency. About Trump and the current crop of Democrats, and Brexit and Merkel and Mario Draghi. About democracy as a mechanism for peaceful transfers of political power. About renewed calls for socialism in the West. About the state of Austrian school economics. And we might especially wonder about what Mises would think about the current state of the liberal project he laid out one hundred years ago.

Mises the Neoliberal?

Is Misesian liberalism in retreat across the West, or has it triumphed? I suspect he would be shocked to discover he is now viewed as a central figure of today's dominant ideology of neoliberalism, which we are assured has taken over everything. It's an ersatz form of liberalism, certainly, that nobody has a precise definition for. But we might take a stab at it:

Neoliberalism is loosely the basic program of late twentieth century Western governments (social democracy, public education, civil rights, entitlements, welfare, feminism, LGBT rights, and a degree of global governance by supra-national organizations), coupled with at least grudging respect for the role of markets in improving human life. This vision, of course, includes Western interventionism (military, diplomatic, and economic) in all world affairs, led always by the US. Neoliberals are left-liberals who accept the role of markets and the need for economic development as part of the larger liberal program, coupled with unwavering belief in neoconservative foreign policy. Think U2's Bono, or Hillary Clinton.

In other words, neoliberalism is a mixed bag. Property—what Mises considered the distillation of the entire liberal program—

certainly is not the animating force in the neoliberal world. But let us not gloss over the tepid acknowledgement by neoliberals that markets work. This was in no way established in the first half of the twentieth century, when Western academics told us socialism was scientific and inevitable. This alone is a huge achievement—and who in the twentieth century did more to make the case for markets than Mises?

Even a cursory search of the *New York Times* and *Washington Post*—someone would have to show him how to Google this—reveals his name mentioned in dozens and dozens of articles just since 2015. These mentions usually come in the context of how economists took over politics, and thus public policy is completely captured by free-market radicals who got their crazy ideas from Mises. Just this year, a University of Alabama history professor published a book titled *The Marginal Revolutionaries: How Austrian Economists Fought the War of Ideas* which is a leftwing homage to the continuing influence of the Austrian school among the (supposedly) anti-socialist upper echelons of business and government—with Mises as its leader.

Mises, as much as Hayek, is now one of the Left's favorite avatars for market liberalism. His name is far better known today, and his work far more widely read today, than it ever was during his lifetime. What more could any intellectual hope for? And most of the big names in economics who dominated the twentieth century, men like Arthur Burns who enjoyed comfortable positions at Columbia and later chaired the Fed, are footnotes today. Mises's name and legacy, by contrast, have been elevated. Even his worst critics now see him not only as a giant not only of economics, but a hugely influential figure in Western capitalism. This was not the case when he died in 1973.

The Health of Austrian Economics

Mises's posthumous renaissance reflects an upswing in the broader fortunes of Austrian economics generally. It's easy to look at the central bankers of the world and think economics is hopelessly lost, but this would miss a very strong subcurrent in the profession.

A few years ago professor Walter Block had an email exchange with the late Dr. Gary Becker, the Nobel Prize winner at the University of Chicago. Block, a former student of Becker, lamented the treatment of Austrian scholars in certain academic journals. In response, Becker argued that much of what is good and groundbreaking in Austrian theory already has been incorporated into mainstream economics.

Becker reminded Block that Austrians already made huge advancements by explaining the impossibility of socialist calculation, presenting a theory of entrepreneurship, and pioneering the role of time in capital and interest theory. All of this came from such a famous economist who viewed the Austrian school from an impartial and somewhat skeptical vantage point. Becker did not mention, though he hardly needed to, how the earthquake known as the Marginal Revolution was in good part Mengerian. The point is that we often underestimate the impact Austrians have had on both economics and society. It's baked into the modern cake, so to speak, so we take it for granted.

Imagine Mises's reaction to having virtually every important Austrian treatise, book, paper, and article available free and instantly online, often translated into multiple languages. Imagine his reaction to the number of Austrian and Austrian-friendly professors teaching in economics departments and business schools across the world. And imagine his reaction to organizations like the Mises Institute dedicated to advancing his work. Certainly the Austrian school is in far better shape today than he could have imagined, even with the degradation of academia.

That's not to say he would think very highly of economics generally today. He might wonder why people like Thomas Piketty, Paul Krugman, Binyamin Appelbaum, and Noah Smith at Bloomberg are viewed as economists at all, given their lack of substantive work. He would lament the hyper-specialization of economists, none of whom are faintly equipped to write treatises. He certainly would be dismayed by the abandonment of theoretical work for mathematical and statistical modeling, and the conflation of trendy disciplines like behavioral economics with real academic work.

Central Banks and Money

What about monetary economics? I suspect he would be amazed by the sheer force of central bank money creation in the 1980s, 1990s, 2000s, and 2010s. He didn't live to see Paul Volcker's Fed Funds Rate of 20 percent, and he undoubtedly would view today's near-zero and negative central banks rates as un-economic forms of monetary alchemy, a central bankers' version of animal spirits. Undoubtedly, he would see figures like Greenspan, Bernanke, and Draghi as untethered radicals who made things up as they went along. He would not see programs like quantitative easing as banking at all, but purely as political machinations.

Ours would not be a rational central bank world to Mises, who perhaps never foresaw how long fiat currencies could operate as political money—if powerful enough governments back them up. I also suspect he would see the business cycle theory he helped develop has not been further developed by economists who recognize its broad brush strokes as correct but lacking in detail. Yes, inflation is a monetary phenomenon, and yes central banks create cycles of malinvestment, boom, and bust—but understanding the timing and duration is where I think Mises would want Austrians to focus today.

Academia and Socialism

But beyond economics and banking he might be appalled to see how universities in general have become what he termed "nurseries of socialism" even more today than in his time. Because today socialists don't organize in union halls or loading docks, they organize in university sociology departments. The working class failed them, so today they've turned to woke intersectional academics as the vanguard. The animating spirit of Bernie Sanders and Elizabeth Warren and Antifa lives on campus, and I think Mises would deplore this very much. I think he would especially shake his head at the rising amount of support for socialism among young people, nearly one hundred years after he wrote the definitive case against it, and against the backdrop of the twentieth century's collectivist failures. Surely it would be hard for someone who believed so strongly in using arguments instead of bullets to see the West today backsliding politically toward collectivism and bloodshed.

Immigration and Nationalism

Regarding immigration and the aforementioned Schengen Agreement, Mises might well wonder what the fuss is all about. Lew Rockwell points out how in Mises's young life a businessman could take a train from Vienna to London and disembark without ever showing or needing a passport. But of course early 1900s Austria was a very different time and place, before two world wars with all their dislocations, mass immigration into and across Europe, and centralized bureaucratic welfare states.

We can say with certainty he worried about the idea of polyglot countries and the plight of ethnic or linguistic minorities. That is precisely why both *Liberalism* and *Nation, State, and Economy* were radically decentralist in their approach, making the case for a liberal nationalism rooted in property, self-determination, and laissez-faire at home; peaceful nonintervention abroad, and free flowing, international trade to deter the bellicose expansionism of autarky.

Our world today is not exactly full of Misesian liberal states; obviously, the opposite is true. And, in fact, Mises was concerned about migration into illiberal states, where recent arrivals seek to change existing institutions for the worse. But don't take my word for it: Professor Ben Powell of Texas Tech University, himself a vocal advocate for completely open borders, recently wrote a paper titled "Solving the Misesian Migration Conundrum."

Quoting Powell:

The problem, for Mises, lies in the fact that states, in his time and ours, are not liberal. They are interventionist. Once states interfere with economic activity, some people are able to use the state to secure economic gains for themselves at the expense of others living under that same government. Once different nations are living under the same government, they come into conflict with each or, as Mises put it, "Migrations thus bring members of some nations into the territories of other nations. That gives rise to particularly characteristic conflicts between people."

However, the institutions of freedom are not exogenously given. Among other factors, they depend on the ideology, political beliefs, and culture of the population controlling the state. Immigrants often migrate from origin countries with dysfunctional institutional environments that lack economic freedom. If the immigrants' own belief system, was, in part, responsible for that dysfunctional system, and they bring those beliefs with them to the destination country in too great of numbers, too rapidly, to assimilate to the beliefs in the destination country, they could erode the very institutions responsible for the high productivity that attracted them in the first place. Thus, immigration itself could, in principle, turn a relatively free destination country, where Mises wouldn't see immigrants as a problem, into a more interventionist state where immigration does create the problems Mises fears.

So while Mises certainly understood migration restrictions just as surely as he understood trade restrictions, it's an outright mistake and not just an oversimplification to insist he would unequivocally support open borders in Europe today.

Conclusion

There is so much more to say about what Mises would tell us today. Most of all I know he would be thrilled by this event happening today, in his honor. Of course, he knew Lew Rockwell from their Arlington House days, but he never imagined a Mises Institute. He never imagined a university in the American South would become a haven for studying his work and the broader Austrian school. He never imagined a digital world which would make much of his writing, his life's work, available online to anyone around the world, almost instantaneously and free of charge. And as mentioned, he never imagined his work would be more widely read, that he would be more famous, after his death.

Yes, liberalism—the good and true version, has unraveled. It didn't hold. We shouldn't lie about this, or pretend it hasn't happened. The West is politically illiberal today, and getting worse. But that does not counsel despair. Whether we are gaining or losing ground, whether we are winning or losing, is a matter of perspective. Mises sometimes succumbed to pessimism, as evidenced by his memoirs. Anyone who lived through the Great War, who had to flee authoritarianism twice, can be excused for this. We don't have that excuse. We have the full body of Mises's work to read and enjoy, to guide us in our thoughts and actions today. And we should share his sense of élan vital, what he called the "ineradicable craving" that compels us to seek happiness, minimize discontent, and spend our lives "*purposively* struggling against the forces adverse to [us]."

What would Mises think of this gathering today, in this room? I think he would be thrilled to know, seventy-five years after speaking here, that an audience of people still find his ideas captivating and worth considering.

45

A Word of Thanks, Lew

Many mises.org readers know that Lew Rockwell, founder of the Mises Institute and quiet benefactor to countless individuals in libertarian circles over the decades, continues to recover from a recent back injury. While the episode has not quelled his enthusiasm for liberty, recovery is no picnic.

Apparently medicine remains in the Dark Ages when it comes to backs, especially lower backs. Some treatments are sketchy and unreliable, cortisone injections provide only fleeting benefit, pain management is fraught with nausea and other nasty side effects, and surgical options portend Armageddon. All that said, Lew is in great hands with innovators at Emory University (yes, xenophobes, we have wonderful doctors down South) and feeling much better. A procedure performed earlier this week appears to have yielded tremendous benefit, and we expect Lew back at 100 percent very soon.

My point in writing this is twofold: first, to update friends and supporters of the Institute on Lew's progress, and second to remind all of us of the tremendous debt of gratitude we owe him.

Let me risk Lew's wrath by sharing a few personal details about him.

Few people know that his much older brother was killed as a young pilot during World War II—by friendly fire. The family never fully recovered, of course, and the event instilled a deep antiwar sentiment in Lew as a boy even though he could not fully grasp the depth of the tragedy and his parents' grief. And while he grew

---

This article originally appeared December 14, 2017, on mises.org.

up as a Taft and later a Goldwater conservative, Lew soured on the GOP during the Nixon era and dismissed it as a hopeless and even malevolent force.

Lew and Mardi Rockwell are adoptive parents to a wonderful special needs daughter, who came into the world lacking the devoted parental care she would need. It was Ron Paul who brought her to Lew's attention, and with his medical partner, facilitated everything.

I'm always puzzled when Lew is attacked as a "right winger," especially by libertarians. This is a charge made by those who insist on attaching a left-cultural component onto political libertarianism, and thus find Lew's commitment to his Catholic faith and the natural rights tradition suspicious if not disqualifying. But political liberty is about state power, not extra-libertarian cultural preferences. Lew's America would allow any and all voluntary social arrangements; that he would not endorse all of them is beside the point.

As mentioned above, his antiwar bona fides are beyond reproach. He opposed the vicious war on Vietnam, and was, and remains, among the earliest and most effective voices against the (latest round of) US wars in the Middle East. While conservatives, progressives, and many libertarians spent 2003 and 2004 merely debating the parameters of Uncle Sam's domination in Iraq and Afghanistan, LewRockwell.com was busy decrying empire altogether. The silence from those who clamor endlessly about "brown people," by contrast, was deafening.

For his troubles, he was labeled an "unpatriotic conservative" by none other than the deplorably un-self-aware David Frum, writing in the addled pages of *National Review*. At least Lew was in good company, as our great friend Justin Raimondo was attacked in the article as well. Lew never accepted either the stated aims of these invasions nor the pyramid of corpses they wrought. He has been consistently friendly toward the cause of self-determination in the Islamic world, always seeking to understand and ameliorate conflicts between religions and civilizations through his advocacy of peaceful trade and diplomacy (see, e.g., this terrific conversation about Islam and capitalism).

We need not delve into decades of Lew's written work to dispense with the right-wing charge, as his seminal article "The Reality of Red State Fascism" does the job in one neat package. It is hard to imagine Code Pink or *Salon* issuing a more damning indictment of the Bush II era—and in fact they could not, because they lacked Lew's ability to capably diagnose modern conservatism.

More than anything, we owe Lew gratitude for having the foresight to create the Mises Institute in 1982. It was his relationships with people like Margit von Mises, Murray Rothbard, Henry Hazlitt, Ron Paul, and Leonard Read that finally convinced him to give up a far more lucrative think-tank career and undertake the thankless task of building a radical new organization.

Without a salary, without a building, and without wealthy benefactors, Lew set about using his typewriter and kitchen table to put Austrian economics back on the map. Remember that while Rothbard's *Man, Economy, and State* and the famous South Royalton conference both helped resuscitate the flagging Austrian school in the 1960s and 70s, the landscape for Austro-libertarian thought remained extremely challenging. The creation of the Mises Institute provided a sorely-needed beacon of hope and visibility. Henry Hazlitt especially appreciated Lew's "giving Murray a platform."

In the thirty-five years since, many thousands of individuals, students, and scholars from every walk of life have benefited from the organization Lew created. It put Austrian economics online and made its foundational texts available free to all. He created undergraduate and graduate programs that helped launch hundreds of careers.

Quietly, always working behind the scenes, Lew helped (and continues to help) countless Austrian and libertarian scholars with paid jobs, stipends, speaking fees, scholarships, tuition assistance, research fellowships, book publishing, office space, library access, letters of recommendation, and travel expenses. In sum, he provided much-needed help for libertarian intellectuals to grow and make a name for themselves.

It's no exaggeration to say many of those individuals would not have succeeded without the help of Lew and the Mises Institute. Lew's beneficiaries work at organizations across the libertarian spectrum, including many well-known people at:

American Institute for Economic Research

Campaign for Liberty

Cato Institute

George Mason University

Grove City College

Hillsdale College

Independent Institute

Institute for Humane Studies

Libertas Institute

Loyola University New Orleans

Mercatus Center

Mises Brasil

Mises Canada

Mises Deutschland

Mises UK

Mont Pelerin Society

Nevada Policy Research Institute

Property and Freedom Society

Ron Paul Institute

Society for the Development of Austrian Economics

Students for Liberty

University of Angers

Universidad Francisco Marroquín

Universidad Rey Juan Carlos

Young Americans for Liberty

As Dr. Gary North points out, Lew has proven unique in his ability to raise money and build a viable libertarian organization without compromising on principle or watering down the message. He deserves appreciation for helping to right the Austro-libertarian ship, for creating an intellectual space to consider anarcho-capitalism, and for resisting the siren song of "public policy" and deep-pocketed donors with agendas. He provided an intellectual home for Rothbard and Hoppe, Salerno and Gordon, Raico and Hülsmann, de Soto and Klein, Herbener and Thornton, Woods and Murphy, and many more, plus thousands of lay readers of mises.org just like you. We all owe him a debt of gratitude.

46

Ron Paul Remains Unstoppable

When Dr. Ron Paul suffered a health scare during his live *Liberty Report* show last Friday, I was perhaps less worried than most. His remarkable vitality, vigor, and energy are well known to those around him, along with his penchant for exercise, clean living, and light eating. Having known him thirty years, I simply had no recollection of him ever being sick or out of commission. This is a man who had never missed a day of work or an event, at least in my memory. In my mind he was simply always there, a fixed feature of life. So my immediate reaction was to think he would be fine.

As it turns out, he is fine. Even unstoppable.

In Dr. Paul's congressional office during the early 2000s, his mostly Generation X staff joked about how Ron would bury us someday despite being several decades older. Now that we're in our fifties, the joke hits a bit closer to home! But we were all familiar with his relentless nature. His pace was legendary: waking early, printing articles to read, gathering newspapers, putting together his busy schedule for the day, and preparing for votes.

It was always tough to keep up with him, literally, legging around Capitol Hill to hearings, media hits, or finalizing details for one of his infamous "special order" speeches at the end of the congressional day. Ron bid for our office in the Cannon House building primarily for its proximity to the Capitol building itself, so he'd spend the least amount of time "commuting." When he needed

---

This article originally appeared September 29, 2020, on mises.org.

knee replacements there was no question about doing both the same day, over the congressional Christmas break. Always true to form, he was up and about almost immediately and eschewed even over-the-counter pain medication.

He was always moving, and absolutely hated to wait. His years as a busy obstetrician, with babies arriving at all hours of the night in far-flung rural Texas hospitals, certainly served him well when it came to the less serious job of Congress—with its late night votes and sudden schedule changes. Unlike medicine, however, the work of Congress is defined by motion rather than action. And unlike many of his colleagues, when the votes ended Ron headed back to his nondescript condo in Alexandria. There were no DC steakhouse dinners with lobbyists, no Capitol Hill bars and nightlife, and certainly none of the fleshy graft which ensnared so many pols over the years.

Dr. Paul's energy spills over into his life at home, where he is always busy walking, biking, swimming, tending to his prized tomatoes, and hosting a steady stream of family and guests. His "retirement" from Congress at the end of 2012 finds him producing five live *Liberty Report* episodes every week with his cohost, Daniel McAdams, along with writing, public speaking, and media appearances. But he is much happier without the dreadful weekly slog back and forth to Bush Intercontinental Airport on the far side of Houston, along with the infuriating kabuki theater known as TSA. His family life is no doubt much improved.

Speaking of family, Ron and his wife, Carol (née Wells), stand atop a pyramid of children (five, with three MDs), nineteen grandchildren, and ten (for now) great-grandchildren. The Pauls have been married sixty-three years; their children have been married 167 years combined! Family, more than anything he has done in medicine or politics, will be Dr. Paul's lasting legacy.

But there were a lot of nights and weekends away from that family over the years, starting all the way back in the 1970s. So a bit of history is in order. Today happens to be the birthday of Ludwig von Mises, who played a brief but important role in the

Ron Paul story. Nixon cut off gold convertibility by foreign central banks in 1971, and the alarmed young obstetrician began reading everything he could on money and inflation—including Mises. A year later, Dr. Paul managed to get away from his busy medical practice for a day to hear the great man speak at the nearby University of Houston. That talk, titled "Why Socialism Always Fails" (listen here!), made a deep impression on Ron. He knew he had to do something.

That "something" took form in his decision to run for Congress in 1974. And in a very real sense Dr. Paul is the only Misesian ever to serve in Congress.

His first stint in the US House only deepened his concerns about the monetary system, and in 1984 he took the gambit of giving up his seat to run against Phil Gramm for US Senate. Gramm prevailed, but Ron returned home to his medical practice determined to remain active. He became involved in the precious metals community, began building contacts, and ultimately became the Libertarian Party candidate for president in 1988.

Those involved with that presidential campaign, including Lew Rockwell and the late Kent Snyder, can tell you it was no luxurious affair. With no internet, mobile phones, email, or social media, campaign events were hit or miss. Local newsletters and bulletin boards were the only source of information, and media appearances were distinctly "earned" in those days. Often a supporter in a beat-up car was the only campaign contact in any city, hopefully there to meet Ron after another cheap Southwest flight. Small groups of twenty or thirty people would gather at someone's home or a local diner, hear Ron speak, and pass the hat for travel funds. It was a shoestring of a campaign, and hardly energizing or optimistic. But Ron persevered, knowing his efforts would bear fruit someday.[1]

---

[1] Perversely, some libertarians of various stripes would turn on Dr. Paul later in his career. The Libertarian Party itself is today hostile to the Ron Paul revolution; its members seek to drive his influence and memory from party ranks.

So the "famous" Ron Paul of 2012—who spoke to five thousand students at Berkeley, raised $30 million, and appeared in CNN debates—first spent years away from his family and his medical practice building up his reputation.

His return to the House of Representatives in the 1990s was both helped and hindered by his identification as a libertarian. His extensive contacts and earlier time in Congress gave him a fundraising base and name recognition, but also earned him the ire of the GOP. Upon informing Republican leaders of his intention to run for Congress again, and suggesting he could win the south Texas seat from a sitting Democrat, the party swung into action against him. His by then well-known antiwar and anti-Fed views alarmed them, and his departure from the party in 1988 angered them. So Newt Gingrich, the powerful speaker of the House, convinced that Democrat (Greg Laughlin) to switch parties by promising him a seat on the powerful Ways and Means Committee.

Dr. Paul thus found himself in a primary race against the sitting congressman he intended to face in the general election. But Ron knew the district, and campaigned effectively against the outsiders trying to dictate who would hold the seat—especially Newt Gingrich, who blundered by flying to Texas for a Laughlin event. Meanwhile, then governor George W. Bush and his chief of staff Karl Rove were working behind the scenes to help Laughlin as well, but to no avail. When Ron won the primary, they called him over to the statehouse in Austin to offer both their surprise and their congratulations.

During Paul's 2008 presidential campaign, DC-based *Reason* magazine published a bizarre article based on a smear job from a discredited neoconservative hostile to Paul's noninterventionist foreign policy views. This article attempted to portray the doctor as "racist" based on decades-old newletters which contained untoward statements about blacks in Los Angeles following the Rodney King riots—despite members of *Reason*'s staff knowing Paul personally as anything but a racist. Other DC organizations like the Cato Institute also pursued this puzzling line of inquiry.

His Democratic opponent in the general election, a trial lawyer named Charles "Lefty" Morris, attempted to paint Ron's position on the drug war as irresponsible and crazy. But Ron's campaign responded with an ad showing the mild-mannered doctor in his medical coat, the down-to-earth trusted physician who had delivered thousands of babies across the congressional district. His personal reputation for sobriety, as a family man deeply involved in his community, blunted the political hits—which is of course an important lesson in itself.

But even winning the general election in 1996 did not endear the GOP to Dr. Paul. Congressional leaders took the almost unprecedented step of disregarding his earlier time in Congress for purposes of seniority. Undaunted, Ron requested and received a seat on the Banking Committee, considered a boring backwater. Little did they know the Enron scandal and the Arthur Andersen collapse a few years later would make the newly christened "Financial Services" Committee one of the most powerful and sought after. (Why? Remember the Sarbanes-Oxley Act regulating public companies, and all the lobbying surrounding it? Imagine the post-congressional career riches!) And little did they know that the Greenspan-Bernanke economy would implode about a decade later, making monetary policy a hot issue and presenting Dr. Paul with numerous chances to grill both men at committee hearings.

Ultimately, he was awarded his delayed but rightful chairmanship of an important monetary policy subcommittee in 2010. Not surprisingly, Ron immediately turned the opportunity into a teachable moment—inviting Austrian economists as witnesses and luncheon speakers, and creating a truly intellectual atmosphere for interested members and staffers who had started to question the status quo.

It was a brief but glorious time, when Mises finally had a voice in Congress.

Dr. Paul's other committee, Foreign Affairs, dovetailed perfectly with his warnings about monetary policy. Ron was able to make the connection between central banking and war finance, and also press Congress for a full-fledged declaration of war before invading Iraq in 2003. Here he built the foundation for a crossover antiwar coalition, and gave his most impassioned arguments against war, the ultimate form of expansionary state power. It was here he opposed American quagmires in the Middle East, setting the stage for his 2008 and 2012 campaigns. And it was in the Foreign Affairs Committee that he cemented his reputation as the greatest peace advocate in Congress for decades.

Despite his troubles with congressional leaders, Dr. Paul had many personal friends in Congress. He was well-liked and respected. His great friend, the late Walter Jones, stands out as someone who took Ron's antiwar message to heart and changed his position. Jones's district contained the huge Army base Ft. Bragg, and in part due to Ron's influence, he came out strongly against the war in Iraq. He attended many military funerals and comforted many spouses, in some part thanks to the humility he saw in Ron. The great Jimmy Duncan of Tennessee also was a close friend, talking to Ron about reading antiwar.com articles by "Justin Ray-mon-duh" in his distinct Southern drawl. Spencer Bachus of Alabama, chair of the Financial Services Committee during the crash of '07, told the entire House Republican caucus that "Ron Paul was right" in his predictions of housing and equity bubbles. Barney Frank of Massachusetts was always cordial and ready to collaborate, as was the great peace advocate Dennis Kucinich of Ohio.

The outpouring of love and affection shown to Dr. Paul last week after his incident shows the degree to which his revolution lives on. Ideas matter, but they are worthless without good people to advance and personify them. Dr. Paul is loved because he is genuine, a quality in short supply today. A quality which cannot be bought, borrowed, summoned, or faked. It's a quality our dangerously politicized country needs, in spades.

Ron Paul seems unstoppable, but of course no one is. He gave us, and continues to give us, a genuine alternative vision for a non-political world.

But who will take his place?

Made in United States
North Haven, CT
27 April 2023

35948987R00192